Within the Veil

Pamela Newkirk

WITHIN
THE VEIL

BLACK JOURNALISTS,

WHITE MEDIA

New York University Press

New York and London

NEW YORK UNIVERSITY PRESS
New York and London

Library of Congress Cataloging-in-Publication Data
Newkirk, Pamela.
Within the veil : Black journalists, white media / Pamela Newkirk.
p.   cm.
ISBN 0-8147-5799-5 (alk. paper)
1. Afro-Americans in the newspaper industry. 2. Afro-American
journalists—Biography. 3. Afro-Americans—Press coverage.   I. Title.
PN4882.5 .N49 2000
070'.89'96073—dc21   00-008897

New York University Press books are printed on acid-free paper,
and their binding materials are chosen for strength and durability.

Manufactured in the United States of America

10 9 8 7 6 5 4 3 2 1

To my parents and guideposts,
Gloria Spencer Newkirk and Louis Harding Newkirk

my husband and anchor, Michael Nairne

my wings and inspiration,
Marjani, Mykel, and Stacey Pamela

and my sister, Dorothy Moran,
whose continual encouragement has been
a lifelong motivational force

With love and appreciation

CONTENTS

All illustrations appear as a group following p. 98.

Derrick Bell

The print media is in what many view as a death struggle with the more dramatic communication forums of television and now the Internet. The casualties include literally hundreds of papers and consolidation of many that remain. At present, a handful of publishing magnates control the great majority of newspapers and news magazines. Profit rather than professionalism has become priority number one. News is defined by its entertainment value. Scandal that titillates trumps substantive news. Stories about crime that frighten are favored over stories that inform. To this end, coverage is often full-blown where the victim is white and the perpetrator black or Hispanic. Similar crimes where neither victim nor assailant is white are often ignored. Features on celebrities, no matter how tawdry, once the metier of the tabloids, now receive prominent attention in the most sober dailies. Revelations about even the most intimate matters are rationalized under "the people's right to know."

Journalistic conscience has gone the way of serious content. Editors not only permit but insist on favorable coverage of major advertisers, a policy rendered more effectively by loosening the traditional barrier between editorial and advertising departments. Editorial positions are not cabined with the editorial pages. The publisher's political views influence how stories are written and what stories even find their way into print. If this criticism appears excessive, it is because the media maintains a self-righteous stance of integrity based mainly on denial. This posturing is regularly punctured by small, little-read publications like *Extra*, the *Nation*, and the *Progressive*. Even without the facts available in these journals, the public is not fooled, regularly rating newspapers as deserving little more trust than that afforded used-car salesmen.

Given the media's commitment to commercialism, pity the poor journalist drawn to the profession by the desire to get at the truth in the story and to report all the facts both fully and objectively. Even given the necessity of compromise as a prerequisite to orderly life in a civilized society, the way of the journalist trying to do his or her job and maintain a measure of integrity must be tough. And if that journalist is a person of color, the task becomes a continuing challenge of truly awesome proportions. How can persons long excluded from the profession because of color barriers overcome the continuing suspicions of incompetence and disloyalty that burden the careers of those permitted to enter the media's mainly white ranks?

In *Within the Veil*, Professor Pamela Newkirk responds to this question with a richly textured account of truths about minority status in journalism. Relying on careful research and her years of journalistic experience, Newkirk's work reflects an understanding about the difficulties of her profession that are heightened by a racial perspective that is much needed and not much available in today's news outlets. Her careful review of the last three decades of black inroads in mainstream journalism reflects advances far more grudging and far less permanent than many of us would have predicted after the 1968 Kerner Commission's hard-hitting criticism of the media's all-white make-up.

The plight of minority journalists, of course, can serve as a metaphor for all black professionals. Our predicament goes beyond our token status in most mainly white enterprises, a status in which we are rewarded most when we challenge least the paucity of our numbers or the difficulty of getting the assignments that can lead to promotion. Even being taken seriously requires major effort when our views differ from those who by reason of their majority status presume to know best. James Baldwin, the definitive chronicler on this subject put it well in "The Evidence of Things Not Seen." [p. 44]

It is a very grave matter to be forced to imitate a people for whom you know—which is the price of your performance and survival—you do not exist. It is hard to imitate a people whose existence appears, mainly, to be made tolerable by their bottomless gratitude that they are not, thank heaven, you.

We know that our struggle for standing in what is often an alien atmosphere does not prevent pointing to our presence as sufficient justification for inaction in adding to our numbers. Given the pressures for cultural conformity, it is nothing short of a miracle that so few of us resist the very real temptation to get ahead by mimicking the conservative shibboleths that so comfort those who do not much care whether we really believe it when we disparage our own.

That our very presence in jobs barred to us in earlier times becomes support for the position that racism is at an end is not the only—and is far from the most dangerous—threat the success of some blacks poses for real racial progress or even bare racial survival. Robert L. Allen in his 1969 book, *Black Awakening in Capitalist America*, reminds us that the growing gap in income and status between those blacks who are making it and those who are not, tracks developments in colonial countries where the colonizing countries maintained their control by establishing class divisions within the ranks of the colonized.

Allen views black America as a domestic colony of white America. Colonial rule, Allen claims, is predicated upon "an alliance between the occupying power and indigenous forces of conservatism and tradition." Allen finds aspects of this policy in American slavery where divisions were created between field hands and house hands. "Uncle Tom," is the term used to describe the collaborator torn, with conflicting loyalties, between his people and the foreign rulers.

Developments in the three decades since Allen's book was published, including the gains made by some blacks and the lessening of discrimination that led to those gains, serves as a support for, rather than a response to, Allen's domestic colonialism thesis. He points out an analogy to the transformation of once-colonized nations into neocolonial nations after gaining their "independence." Allen explains, "Under neocolonialism an emerging country is granted formal political independence but in fact it remains a victim of an indirect and subtle form of domination by political, economic, social or military means."

While his book was written prior to the affirmative action era, Allen would argue that such policies serve to coopt a portion of the black middle-class who, without their privileged positions, might provide leadership to rebellious activity by the black masses, now locked in poverty-stricken areas from which their potential leaders have been permitted to escape. Separated from their benighted brethren by social class and economic status, the black middle-class are often objects of deep suspicion rather than role models for those locked in poverty-based despair. Journalists are particularly vulnerable, working as they do quite literally for "the man."

Writer-journalist Jill Nelson, articulated well the complexity of this undertaking in her book *Volunteer Slavery*. There she describes how difficult it is to maintain one's ethical bearings as she completes a day-long series of interviews at a major white newspaper that was considering her as a reporter:

> I've been doing the standard Negro balancing act when it comes to dealing with white folks, which involves sufficiently blurring the edges of my being so that white folks don't feel intimidated and simultaneously holding on to my integrity. There is a thin line between Uncle Tomming and Mau-Mauing. To step over that line can mean disaster. On one side lies employment and self-hatred, on the other, the equally dubious honor of unemployment with integrity. In the middle lies something like employment with honor, although, I'm not sure exactly how that works.

The universality of the journalist experience frames questions which cannot be ignored. Are African Americans locked into a permanently racist society and can developments in that society be leading towards a return to the overt subordination of the "separate-but-equal" era? Certainly, there is little in Pamela Newkirk's book that enables the hope that journalists of color will be given the chance to document the danger or suggest routes away from a repetition of the past. Note, for example, her review of the patterns of excluding people of color from coverage of the O.J. Simpson trial. The assumption that blacks could not be objective while whites could, is a patently racist rationale that could—and is—leading to a resegregation of journalism.

Much will depend on the willingness of those in the business, however marginally, to insist that in this post-integration age, we must have interpreters who bring racial experience to their skills and commitment. The end of the "we shall overcome" era has taken from us: the rhetoric of rights, the eloquence of equality, and the fluency of faith that by working twice as hard, we could gain—at the least—half as much. Someone must tell that story with courage and consistency. Pamela Newkirk's *Within the Veil* provides a book-length exemplar of the interpretive writing we must have on a daily basis.

Can it happen? The outlook is not encouraging. We should not forget, however, that the biblical prophets spoke and too often the people did not understand and thus ignored what they heard. We are more fortunate. There are, if not prophets, commentators in our midst capable of reporting our contemporary danger. Some of them have the integrity and courage to communicate their messages in ways that make us accept the truth about our condition with all its pain and all its potential glory.

ACKNOWLEDGMENTS

The support of so many people was vital to the successful completion of this project. I would like especially to acknowledge Denise Stinson for guiding me through the proposal and seeing early on what others could not; Marie Brown for her cheerleading and soothing counsel; my colleagues Derrick Bell, David Dent, Felicia Lee, DeWayne Wickham, and the late Edwin Diamond for their wisdom, criticism, and reassuring praise during the difficult days; Karen Alexander for child care, heavy doses of encouragement, and a steady ear; my dad for his generous advance during an unpaid leave; the library staff of the Schomburg Center for Research in Black Culture; the Media Studies Center, especially Marlene Sanders and Debbie Rogers, whose extraordinary research assistance saved the day; Niko Pfund, for his admirable patience and soft touch as an editor; *The Nation* for providing an invaluable sounding board for many of the ideas advanced in this book; Stacey Patton for her profound insights during a critical phase of the project; Brooke Kroeger for the use of her lovely writer's cottage; Regina Hall for her contagious enthusiasm; the many journalists who gave their time and compelling stories; and, most especially, my family, especially my husband and daughters, without whose sacrifice and support this endeavor would not have been possible.

PREFACE

Since my first by-line in the high school newspaper I have been enthralled with journalism because of the opportunity it gave me to effect change and increase understanding. Many of the people I most admired throughout my formative years were crusading reporters in the print and broadcast news media, and landing my first newspaper job at a small afternoon paper in Albany, New York, was the realization of a dream that was years in the making.

As a daily journalist at four different news organizations I was, on occasion deeply satisfied with the extent to which I could shed light on compelling issues affecting the communities I covered. But when it came to writing about African Americans, I often encountered difficulty filling out the puzzle that is race in this country because my editors resisted perspectives that were foreign to the white cultural mainstream. They found it easier to exclude or malign *alien* viewpoints than to attempt to understand ideas that did not mesh with their own.

My experience is echoed daily by black journalists around the country who say their stories and ideas are often viewed with suspicion and alarm, seen as a threat rather than part of the answer to racial accord. So cautious must African American journalists be about confronting antiquated attitudes about blacks—so tense are discussions of race in the newsroom—that many become, in time, too battle-weary to try. This is the experience of both the fresh-faced neophytes who are only now entering the profession and of successful veterans like Bryant Gumbel and Charlayne Hunter Gault.

It is not that African Americans cannot attain success in the industry. But it is precisely because of the prominence and high pay accorded a handful of highly visible African American journalists that a discussion of racial misinterpretation, mistrust and apprehension is so difficult to engage. Our failure to effectively communicate across the racial divide in the very media we entrust to advance communication is confounding and, at the dawn of a new century, wholly unacceptable. The news media are perfectly positioned to improve race relations. But first, we must learn each other's language, come to appreciate our different vantage points and be prepared to shed our denial, animosity and deceit.

I have, without a doubt, fulfilled my childhood fantasy to work in the news industry. I was assigned to South Africa to cover the dismantling of apartheid, and have had the opportunity to witness firsthand numerous historic events in the life of this nation from Capitol Hill, New York's state capital, and the streets of New York City. I have written and continue to write for some of the country's leading publications, and, from the hallowed halls of academia, enjoy a modicum of success that some might assume would preclude my writing a critical book about the news media, or about race. But my criticism stems both from a deep and abiding respect for an institution that has the greatest potential to stir our best impulses, as well as deepening our disappointment with its unfulfilled promise.

Many African Americans of my generation were drawn to the news media after witnessing its imposing impact on the civil rights movement and, later, Watergate. It should, by now, go without saying that the media's role in moving us to action and shaping our perceptions is profound, as is their potential for changing those perceptions. Even as public regard for the media ebbs, rises, and ebbs again, journalism remains, at its height, a noble profession. But too many African Americans have found their contributions undervalued or outright ignored, as news organizations time after time miss the opportunity to bridge the racial chasm that threatens to engulf us. Blacks are still, at the dawn of the twenty-first century, still viewed as secondary people, a steady diet of slights fueling resentment in them that lurks barely beneath the surface. Meanwhile whites, unable to see what they don't experience, continue to cling to some of the most damning views of black people, as the mass media routinely highlight the exceptions in black life—criminality, celebrity, and buffoonery—offering them as the norm. In an increasingly sensationalized media climate, the prospect for the news media to offer even more damaging images of blacks increases.

At the close of the twentieth-century there was a resurgence of demeaning images of black people in the mass media. Television shows such as "The Diary of Desmond Pfeiffer"—which took a comedic look at a butler in the Lincoln White House—rivaled the worst nineteenth-century portrayals of blacks while testing the depths to which the callous disregard of their plight can sink. The major networks found themselves under fire for the dearth of black characters in their shows. Of twenty-six new comedy or drama series set for the 1999 fall line-up, none featured characters of color in lead roles.

I focus on the plight of black journalists even as Latinos and other groups have begun to tip the racial scale because the story of African Americans in the American media is a unique and historic one spanning two centuries which warrants an independent inquiry. Indeed, other groups, particularly Native Americans, Latinos, and Asians are similarly aggrieved and their plight deserves closer investigation, which, I hope this volume will inspire. That said, many of the issues I raise apply to all so-called racial minorities even as I examine race in the newsroom through the experiences of African Americans. The battle for racial parity in the news media, and in society, encompasses all races. We have yet, as a nation, to reconcile some of the most painful racial injuries of the past, and, it appears we must do so if we are to reach a new plateau in our discourse.

The difficulty in writing this book is that the media is not a monolith, and neither are the members of the racial groups within it. Blacks and whites cannot be cast as predictable stick figures, especially because some of the giants of progress toward media diversity have been white, whereas some of the worst offenders of journalistic privileges and foes of diversity have been black. To that extent, I will make no attempt to cast blacks as heroes and whites as villains. That said, this book is about the uphill battle to diversify the mainstream media, an endeavor that began in the mid-1800s when general circulation newspapers first employed the services of black journalists. That story, then, will necessarily be told largely from the standpoint of African Americans, their views buttressed by an analysis of newsroom events, industry patterns, and statistics, historical documents and other available data that bear on the subject.

The newsroom is the prism through which I explore race relations in the three decades after the National Advisory Commission on Civil Disorders highlighted the media's exclusionary hiring practices and stereotypical coverage of and indifference to African American people. I will examine why many of the issues raised by that panel are still relevant, and why it matters that we come to grips with them. None of what follows is a personal attack on "the media" or the men and women who toil in it. Ideas, rather than personalities, are the issue.

As I write, it appears that race in the media is the story of a glass both half full and half empty. In the early days of 1999, a group of prominent African Americans, frustrated by the slow progress towards diversity of thought in the mainstream press, was still seeking financial support to start a national black newspaper that would be staffed by some of the most accomplished black journalists in the country. They see *Our World News* as the answer to the inadequate news coverage of blacks. And as I write, black journalists by the dozens are bailing out of some of the top news organizations in the country, unable to reconcile their intimate knowledge of black America with the disjointed picture offered up by major news media. The leadership of the National Association of Black Journalists has continually voiced its frustration and disillusionment with the snail's pace of change. In my New York University classroom, students conducting a photographic content analysis of six major publications found African Americans disproportionately represented as sports figures and entertainers, Asians largely viewed as foreigners, and Latinos and Native Americans hardly portrayed at all. For example, in *Time* magazine, 37.5 percent of African Americans featured during the period studied in 1999 were sports figures, compared to 3 percent of whites.

But there have also been encouraging signs of progress. Mark Whitaker became editor of *Newsweek*, the first African American to edit a mainstream newsmagazine. Both Whitaker's ascension and the critique of news coverage validly depict race in the modern news media, but are only fragments of the complex puzzle.

Any discussion of race is difficult, in part because of our clashing racial perceptions, and largely as a result of restrictions that have been placed on the debate. This book is an attempt to set up new parameters for a constructive and meaningful dialogue on race in the news media. Because many of our arguments in the public realm lack context and clarity, sending us around in circles without resolution, the ground rules for the debate must be radically altered. Political affiliations and labels of persuasion such as liberal, conservative, and moderate are continually erected as ideological markers even though, on issues of race, these classifications have lost all meaning. We have entered an era when so-called liberals claim that racism is the figment of black people's imaginations, while some so-called conservatives offer some of the most creative solutions to the racial quagmire. Neither must we allow sound ideas to go unexplored simply because they are presented by people considered controversial. To get where we must, the debate must encompass the best ideas from all ideological domains—as long as the arguments are sound, the intentions pure. Valid and constructive solutions, whether they come from sinners or saints, radicals or traditionalists, academics or lay people, will be given equal weight in the interest of resolution.

Also, in much of the current discourse on race, the history of slavery and discrimination have been deemed off-limits by those who would rather pretend the past has little relation to the present. Here, no such time constraints exist. For the sake of clarity, all gag orders must be lifted.

African Americans, too, must be challenged when their impulse to blame racism drowns out constructive ways to view their racial dilemma. In this book, I will challenge both extremes through a presentation of anecdotal and empirical evidence and historical context, and through the obliteration of the kind of pretense, crudeness and denial that has paralyzed much of our discourse. So, in addition to identifying the steadily evolving symptoms of our problems, I will attempt to root out the underlying cancer in our racial realm. This book is my endeavor to rekindle a candid and sober dialogue on race in the news media begun by the National Commission on Civil Disorders in 1968. Let the dialogue begin.

Significant Dates in the History of African American Journalists

1827   *Freedom's Journal*, the nation's first black newspaper, is launched in New York City by the Reverend Samuel Cornish and John Russwurm.

1833   The *New York Sun*, the first successful Penny Press newspaper, ushers in mass media in the United States. The publisher, Benjamin Day, is pro-slavery.

1847   Willis Hodges, an African American, and Thomas van Rensselaer publish *The Ram's Head* after *New York Sun* editors tell Hodges that the *Sun* does not shine for black people.

Frederick Douglass begins publishing *The North Star* in Rochester, New York.

1864   The *New Orleans Tribune*, printed in both English and French, becomes the first black daily newspaper in the United States.

Thomas Morris Chester becomes the first black correspondent for a major daily newspaper when he is hired as a Civil War correspondent for the *Philadelphia Press*.

1889   Henry O. Flipper, the first black to graduate from the U.S. Military Academy at West Point, becomes the first black editor of a white-owned newspaper, the Arizona *Sunday Herald*.

Political cartoonist Henry J. Lewis, whose work had already been featured in *Harper's Weekly,* joins the staff of the *Indianapolis Freeman.*

1890   The U.S. Census records 310 black journalists in the United States.

1892   Ida B. Wells flees Memphis after the office where she published *Free Speech* is destroyed because of her crusade against the lynching of black men.

1900   Booker T. Washington, the nation's most prominent African American, secretly subsidizes several black newspapers and promotes accommodation to Jim Crow.

1901   William Monroe Trotter, a black Harvard graduate, begins publishing the *Guardian,* which challenges Washington's accommodationist stance. He edits the paper until his death in 1934.

1902   Lester Walton is hired to cover general news and sports for the *St. Louis Globe-Democrat,* a mainstream daily, and, in 1906, *The Star Sayings,* which became the *St. Louis Star.*

1905   Robert S. Abbott founds the *Chicago Defender,* which, by 1915, has a weekly circulation of 230,000.

1910   W. E. B. DuBois becomes editor of *The Crisis,* the NAACP magazine, which for more than two decades was a leading black journal.

1922   Lester Walton is commissioned to write a series of articles for the *New York World,* which soon after hires him as a staff reporter. He later joins the *New York Herald Tribune* staff.

1936   Ted Poston becomes a staff reporter at the *New York Post.*

1941   Earl Brown, a contributing writer to *Time* magazine and editor of the *Amsterdam News,* is hired as a staff writer at *Life* magazine.

1943   The National Newspaper Publishers Association, a group comprised of black newspaper publishers, is founded, with John Sengstacke as its first president.

1944   Harry S. McAlpin becomes the first black admitted to White House press conferences as a White House correspondent for the National Negro Press Association and the Atlanta *Daily World*.

1945   John H. Johnson launches Johnson Publishing, which becomes the most successful black publishing enterprise in the world with the success of *Jet, Ebony*, and *Black World*.

The black press reaches its zenith, with circulation at the *Chicago Defender*, 257,000; the *Pittsburgh Courier*, 202,000; and the *Baltimore Afro-American*, 137,000.

1947   The Negro Newspaper Publishers Association and individual black news correspondents are accredited to the Congressional Press Galleries and the State Department.

1949   WERD in Atlanta becomes the first black-owned commercial radio station in the United States.

1950   Marvel Jackson Cooke becomes the first full-time black woman reporter for a mainstream daily, the *Daily Compass*.

1955   The NAACP files a lawsuit against Mississippi station WLBT-TV, charging that it deliberately cut off a network program in which Thurgood Marshall appeared by flashing a screen that said "Sorry, Cable Trouble."

1958   Louis Emanuel Lomax becomes the first black television newscaster, for WNTA-TV in New York City.

1962   Mal Goode becomes the first black network television correspondent when he is hired by ABC-TV and covers the Cuban missile crisis. He becomes the first black member of the National Association of Radio and Television News Directors in 1971.

1965   First court ruling to revoke WLBT-TV's license after a lawsuit by the United Church of Christ on behalf of Jackson,

Mississippi's African American community, whom the church contended was not being fairly represented.

1968   The National Advisory Commission on Civil Disorders, impaneled by President Johnson in 1967, condemns the news media for racial bias in hiring and coverage.

The Federal Communications Commission begins regulating broadcast industry employment practices, and announces that stations that deliberately discriminate will lose their licenses.

1969   The Court of Appeals orders the FCC to revoke WLBT-TV's license stemming from the United Church of Christ's lawsuit on behalf of the African American community of Jackson, Mississippi, which the church contended was not being fairly represented. The station's license is revoked on December 3.

1971   Melba Tolliver of WABC-TV in New York is suspended for appearing on air with an Afro hairdo.

1972   William Dilday is hired as station manager at NBC affiliate WLBT, becoming the first African American to run a television station.

1975   The National Association of Black Journalists is founded, with fourty-four members. The first president is Chuck Stone of the *Philadelphia Daily News.*

WGPR-TV (Channel 62) in Detroit becomes the first commercially licensed black-owned television station in the U.S.

1976   A black reporter in Macon, Georgia, is banned from covering a speech because of the club's restrictions against blacks.

1978   Max Robinson becomes the first network television anchor when he is hired by ABC-TV.

Charlayne Hunter Gault becomes the first black woman to anchor a national television newscast, *The MacNeil/Lehrer Report.*

The American Society of Newspaper Editors pledges to have newsrooms that reflect the proportion of minorities by the year 2000. At the time, African Americans held 2 percent of the 43,000 newsroom jobs, and were roughly 10 percent of the nation's population.

1980 Robert L. Johnson launches Black Entertainment Television in Washington, D.C., the first black-owned national cable television network.

1981 Janet Cooke of the *Washington Post* wins a Pulitzer Prize, but is asked to return it when it's discovered that her article, "Jimmy's World," was a fabrication.

Dorothy Reed is suspended for a week from her job as a television reporter at KGO-TV in San Francisco for appearing on air with her hair in corn-rows.

1983 Robert Maynard becomes the first African American to own a major mainstream metropolitan newspaper when he becomes editor and publisher of the *Oakland Tribune*.

1986 In its annual "State of America" report, the National Urban League says the newspaper industry "remains largely segregated, especially in positions where decisions are made on what news to cover and on what play and space to give the news." It reported that 97 percent of news executives were white.

1987 Four black journalists at the *Daily News* in New York win a discrimination lawsuit against their employer, which marks the first time a major news organization is successfully challenged for discrimination in court. They are awarded $3.1 million in damages.

1990 The National Association of Black Journalists' membership reaches 1,800.

1993 Bob Herbert becomes the first African American columnist at the *New York Times*.

1994　"Unity 94," the first joint convention of the National Association of Black Journalists, and the associations of Asian American, Hispanic and Native American journalists, is held in Atlanta.

1995　The National Association of Black Journalists' report, "Muted Voices," says black journalists are "strangling with pain" over issues of promotion and assignments.

1996　William Kennard is appointed chairman of the Federal Communications Commission, the first African American to hold the post.

1998　Mark Whitaker becomes editor of *Newsweek* magazine, becoming the first African American to edit a major news weekly magazine.

　　　　The U.S. Court of Appeals for the District of Columbia rules that the FCC's thirty-year-old Equal Employment Opportunity rules are unconstitutional.

　　　　The American Society of Newspaper Editors scales back its year 2000 goal to have newsrooms that reflect the proportion of the population, calling the goal out of reach. In 1998, minorities were nearly 30 percent of the population, but held 11.4 percent of newsroom jobs. The new goal was at least 20 percent by the year 2010.

1999　Minorities comprise 11.55 percent of the newspaper work force and 20 percent of the broadcasting work force. Blacks hold 5.3 percent of newspaper and 10 percent of broadcasting jobs. Forty-two percent of U.S. newspapers employ no minorities.

ONE

Within the Veil

Within the Veil

Leaving, then, the white world, I have stepped within the Veil,
raising it that you may view faintly its deeper recesses—the
meaning of its religion, the passion of its human sorrow, and
the struggle of its greater souls.

—W. E. B. Du Bois, 1903

In 1994, *Time* magazine correspondent Sylvester Monroe proposed a story on Nation of Islam Minister Louis Farrakhan, whose appeal, he argued, was far more complex than the media had portrayed. Monroe noted Farrakhan's popularity among blacks across class and ideological lines, drawn to his passionate brew of rage and pride and his prescription for economic self-sufficiency, discipline, and family values. But despite the controversy that Farrakhan's racial rhetoric often provoked, Monroe noted that none of the national news magazines had ever provided for readers an in-depth profile that pierced the surface of his racially charged sound bites.

However, Monroe, who hoped to infuse the story with his intimate grasp of black America, did not anticipate how difficult it would be to filter so unconventional and controversial a black figure as Farrakhan through the prism of white interest that is the mainstream news media. Nor did he predict the emotional white backlash within *Time* as word spread that Farrakhan would appear on the cover.

"People in the bureaus were demanding to know why we were putting him on the cover," recalled Monroe, who had earned journalistic acclaim for "Brothers," his moving portrait of the black men he had grown up with in a Chicago housing project that was first a *Newsweek* magazine cover story, and later a book. "They said he doesn't deserve this kind of attention. A researcher came to me and said, 'This is shameful.' I later heard she was in tears. My response was, 'We're journalists here. What we think of him should have nothing to do with it. We put Adolph Hitler and Khomeini on the cover.' It was the most disingenuous argument for not doing a story that I had ever heard."[1]

For many of Monroe's white colleagues, a cover story on Farrakhan was an affront. Since Farrakhan's role in the black community was, to whites, largely inconsequential, they could not fathom raising his stature merely on the basis of the aspect of him they cared about: his virulent racial views. It is one thing to present a one-dimensional sketch to remind people he was anti-Semitic, but quite another to suggest his importance and complexity by dedicating a cover story to him.

This argument is similar to the one made by critics of the media's intense coverage that same year of *The Bell Curve*, a book by the late Richard J. Herrnstein and Charles Murray that theorized that blacks were genetically inferior to whites. All three major news weeklies and the *New York Times Magazine* seriously entertained the notion of black inferiority by devoting cover stories to a question that their coverage left unanswered. The preposterous idea that race—a loose social construct, which, in our society, is determined less by genes than by appearance—has the ability to determine intelligence was hardly explored.

Scientists and anthropologists have long maintained that race is not a biologically valid scientific concept. The American Association of Physical Anthropologists has declared that pure races do not exist, and maybe never had. How the theory in *The Bell Curve* could be seriously considered in spite of centuries of interracial mixing underscored the predisposition of many whites—including those in the media—to at least consider innate black inferiority as a way of explaining, or even justifying, the plight of blacks.

Rather than explore what the immense public interest in the best-selling book suggested about our society's view of blacks, many in the news media framed the notion of black intellectual inferiority as a legitimate debate, even while scientists such as Luigi Luca Cavalli-Sforza, a Stanford University geneticist, dismissed race as a "useless" biological and genetic concept.[2]

The media continues to perpetuate a debate on black inferiority, perhaps because it mirrors the dominant culture's own view of the status of blacks in the racial hierarchy. Some theorize that the primary means by which whites have sustained and legitimated their domination is by communicating the dominant white ideology on the assumptions of black inferiority (and white superiority) through the mass media.[3] Some blame the continuing debate on the scientific community's silence.

Still, the media did, in some instances, raise doubts about the credibility of the data and the conservative agenda of the *Bell Curve* authors, who used their purported findings to argue against affirmative action and for the end of welfare in order to reduce the births of low-IQ babies. Near the end of *Newsweek*'s 2,600-word feature story, it noted the contradictions in the work and quoted a Yale psychologist who dismissed some of the scholarship as "pathetic." *Newsweek* nonetheless devoted another 2,800 words to a defense of the authors' premise. Written by Geoffrey Cowley, it concluded this way: "It's also clear that whatever mental ability is made of—dense neural circuitry, highly charged synapses or sheer brain mass—we didn't all get equal shares."[4] A 867-word rebuttal from Ellis Cose, a black journalist, argued that the advancement of these theories undermine black achievement by fueling self-doubt. Readers were then left to decide if blacks belonged, as many had already suspected, to an inferior race.

Black supremacists who theorize black genetic superiority have all been dismissed in the media as racist crackpots. In New York, City University's professor of history Leonard Jeffries has built a following behind his sun-people, ice-people theory, arguing that blacks, the African-derived sun people, are innately good, and whites, products of cold European climates, are by nature cold and ruthless. Supporters of his theory believe it helps explain slavery, the colonization of Africa, the near extinction of Native Americans, and other atrocities against people of color by whites worldwide. Frances Cress Welsing, a Washington, D.C.–based psychologist, maintains that white supremacy stems from the genetic inferiority of whites and their concomitant fear of racial obliteration. But neither Jeffries nor Welsing have found a neutral forum for their black supremacist ideas in the mainstream media, even though their theories are no less credible than the one offered by Herrnstein and Murray.

Jeffries was widely vilified in New York newspapers for linking Jews to the slave trade.[5] Many papers published the transcripts of a speech in which he made his highly publicized remarks, and ran a series of editorials calling for his ouster. In March 1992, Jeffries was removed as chair of the Black Studies department at City College of New York, a position he had held for two decades. The rap group Public Enemy was assailed in 1990 for promoting the Cress Theory—Welsing's fifteen-page hypothesis on white supremacy—in the album *Fear of a Black Planet.*[6] But the media's tolerance for white extremism is not accorded equally to blacks who hold similar radical views on race. While Jeffries and Farrakhan captured prominent headlines, the revelation in 1999 that Senate Majority Leader Trent Lott was associated with the Council of Conservative Citizens, a white supremacist group, received scant attention. When an executive board member of the group said that Lott was an honorary member. The *New York Times* ran a story on page A9, and many papers ignored the story altogether. *Time's* coverage of Farrakhan illuminates the kind of intolerance shown by whites in the media of black extremism that served to undermine Monroe's attempt to present Farrakhan objectively.

Monroe's uphill and emotional battle to bring an objective portrait of Farrakhan to the public illustrates the challenges that blacks who began integrating America's newsrooms in the 1960s still face in their attempts to present the complexities of black life in the mainstream media. More than thirty years after the National Commission on Civil Disorders chastised the news media for reporting news "from the standpoint of a white man's world," and for reporting on blacks "as if they don't read the newspapers, marry, die and attend PTA meetings," the news continues to be firmly rooted in white ideology, which fosters a racial hierarchy that places blacks, and other minorities, below whites. This dominant view persists in spite of the growing non-white population and the infusion of thousands of journalists of color in America's newsrooms, followed, in recent years, by the industry's much trumpeted embrace of diversity. As late as 1997, members of the American Society of Newspaper Editors reaffirmed their commitment to more culturally and racially diverse newsrooms despite attacks on affirmative action and their newsroom diversity efforts.

But progress has been glacial. In 1968, blacks accounted for roughly one percent of newsroom jobs. Near the close of the century, blacks comprise five percent of the newspaper and 10 percent of the television-news workforce.[7] Nationally, in 1999, people of color held 11.5 percent of newspaper jobs—representing about one-third of their proportion of the population—and 21 percent of broadcasting jobs, with the percentages significantly higher in urban markets. Still, nearly 45 percent of the nation's daily newspapers remain lily white.

Behind the obvious, albeit small, numerical gains, a wide and deep racial and cultural chasm still divides blacks and whites in the newsroom. Despite their heightened visibility, African American journalists and their minority counterparts, woefully underrepresented in the industry and in news management, are far from integrated into the newsroom culture, largely because of status quo assumptions about race. While black journalists occasionally succeed in conveying the richness and complexity of black life, they are often left, as was Monroe, restricted by the narrow scope of the media, which tends primarily to exploit those fragments of African American life that have meaning for, and resonate with, whites. For while the media has allowed the complexion of its newsrooms to better reflect society, the target audience of the major media has changed little. News continues to be constructed for a primarily white audience.

As such, Farrakhan is primarily covered by the media in proportion to the controversial comments he makes about whites, particularly Jews. As Monroe tried to take readers behind Farrakhan's disturbing rhetoric to explain *why* his message resonates across a large swath of black America, his editors were intent on focusing on remarks they deemed anti-Semitic and racist, which Monroe agreed could not be ignored. But he said centering a story around them distorted the reason for his wide appeal across black America.

Nonetheless, the measured, unemotional tone that defined *The Bell Curve* coverage was replaced with white-hot emotionalism by whites in *Time's* Farrakhan cover story. Monroe's attempt to present a balanced, unfiltered portrait was overshadowed by intemperate headlines and captions that conveyed unequivocal abhorrence for Farrakhan and his views. The first cover dummy bore an image of Farrakhan with the headline "Ministry of Hate." Monroe urged Steve Kemp, the national-affairs editor, to tone it down, saying it failed to capture Farrakhan's appeal to many African Americans, who would take umbrage at the characterization.

However, Kemp appeared concerned about the magazine appearing too soft on Farrakhan. The magazine sought to distance itself from views the top editors found repulsive. Their concern for delineating the subject's views from their own, however, did not extend to the less emotional *Bell Curve* coverage. Monroe insisted he could not live with the cover line, and after a tense standoff they compromised on "Ministry of Rage." Monroe had little energy left by the time he learned what the subhead would be: "Louis Farrakhan Spews Racist Venom at Jews and all of White America."

The publisher's letter in the news magazine's October 24, 1994, issue went further, explaining why *Time* was profiling Farrakhan. On the page appeared a photograph of Monroe interviewing Farrakhan, with the caption, "Vile views, moral conundrums: Correspondent Monroe interviewing Farrakhan last week at the black leader's home in Chicago." The *Time* caption under the photograph of *Bell Curve* co-author Charles Murray was more tempered. Said *Time:* "Breaking a taboo or propagating racism?" The caption under Murray's photograph in *Newsweek* read: "Embroiled in controversy, Murray poses placidly at his Maryland home."

In the *Bell Curve* stories, on the other hand, the headlines were as dispassionate as the captions. "For Whom the Bell Curves," was the tepid headline on the *Time* story. *Newsweek* was even more equivocal: "The Battle Over IQ and Destiny: A Hard Look at a Controversial Book on Race, Class, and Success. Is it Destiny?"

Monroe did manage to present the highlights of his six-hour interview in a question-and-answer format. "I really didn't care what he said," said Monroe. "I just didn't want us to paraphrase. For one of the first times in a magazine with the stature of *Time*, I wanted to let his voice come through. Don't just dismiss him by saying he's anti-Semitic. He's much more complex than that."

While Monroe's portrait went far in presenting a side of the leader many had never seen—including Farrakhan's role in ridding dangerous housing projects of crime and fear and reforming scores of drug addicts and criminals—his attempt at neutrality failed, undermined by his editors' overt intolerance for Farrakhan. That is not to suggest that whites, or blacks for that matter, in or outside of the media do not have ample reason to take exception to some of the racial views espoused by Farrakhan. Rather, it is to underscore how utterly subjective the awarding of neutrality and objectivity is in the news media, and how prominently race factors into that decision. Because so few blacks and other people of color are at the helm of major news organizations, much of the news coverage reflects the views of people who are typically white and male. Monroe, and other black journalists, then, are forced to compromise their own sense of fairness to satisfy the journalistic standards of news editors whose own objectivity is clouded by their own subconscious assumptions about race.

This failure by the media to explore fully the complexity of black life not only limits the understanding by whites of black culture, but crucially defies the ideals of balanced journalism that require a fair exploration of ideas that transcend the journalist's own experiences and belief system. While black reporters, like other members of the black middle class, must gain an intimate knowledge of cultures other than their own, few whites are required to grasp the intricacies of black culture, since their very survival does not depend on such an understanding. As such, many white journalists fail to suspend their prejudices long enough to fairly or accurately portray people unlike themselves. In some ways, they operate at a disadvantage. Because their superiors often share the same ideology that colors their stories, white journalists are not as sensitive as Monroe and other black journalists must be to words or sentiments that can be viewed as racially biased.

The measured way in which the media explored *The Bell Curve* theory is as offensive to blacks as an equivocal portrait of Farrakhan's views on race, Judaism, and Jews would have been to whites. On matters of respect and notions of human equality, some things are, or should be, beyond debate. So rather than argue for emotion-laden reporting on *The Bell Curve* to rival the conventional coverage of Farrakhan, or for equivocal reporting on Farrakhan that seriously examined whether his blatantly anti-Semitic remarks had merit, it would be more instructive for the media to treat both in a way in which the ideas are contextualized less by white tolerance or intolerance, and more by reason. In any context, Farrakhan's sweeping portrayal of Jews as ruthless merchants has the hurtful and ugly ring of unbridled bigotry. But his views are no less vile than the race-inferiority theories that are cloaked under a veil of pseudoscience which debase our shared humanity.

Just as *The Bell Curve* is more important for what it says about the slow evolution of this nation's racial attitudes, Farrakhan is newsworthy because of the resonance of his larger message in so much of black America. But this message—particularly his appeal to black pride and self-sufficiency and the way in which he has tapped into black pain—was clouded in the *Time* profile by the fixation on his inflammatory words, which were neither new nor illuminating. Many white readers don't care to go behind the rhetoric to learn why many blacks are drawn to Farrakhan, believing instead that blacks should throw out the baby with the bathwater. Only a sober analysis of Farrakhan and his appeal across class and educational levels can guide readers over the chasm of hysteria and fear that further polarizes us all.

Such a portrait would not further legitimize Farrakhan, nor would it validate claims by some blacks that blacks and other minorities cannot be racist because they are not in positions of power. But whether Farrakhan is simply a racist demagogue, and why that matters, should be a function of clear-headed reporting and not of emotionally charged packaging that closes, rather than opens, avenues of understanding. The issue is less Farrakhan than it is the desperate quest by African Americans for self-reflection and improvement. A drowning man will grab hold of anything to keep him afloat. He won't take time to decide if he likes the construction, the color, or the maker of the raft. Farrakhan's widening reach was partly a reaction to the increasing alienation of African Americans as a conservative tide swept through the nation's capital and local governments, a tide that was reflected by and in the media. But Monroe was unable to clearly convey this dynamic to his readers because of his editors' decision to focus almost exclusively on the inflammatory rhetoric that represents a minute fraction of Farrakhan's speeches rather than on the larger message that more accurately explains his appeal. Instead of offering light where there was heat, *Time* editors, despite Monroe's best efforts, chose to turn up the heat. In the process, they further removed white America from an understanding of black Americans, and all of us further away from a rational dialogue across color lines.

In post-civil-rights America, the pervasive racial caste system in the news is neither acknowledged nor reckoned with on a grand scale, as it had been three decades ago by the authors of the Kerner Commission Report. Black reporters, readers, and viewers, like other racial minorities, continue to be secondary players in a game that marginalizes their interests and culture. Even the many journalists who seek to be fair and objective in their reporting on people of color are, in time, conditioned to write stories that, first and foremost, conform to the ideals and attitudes of white America.

This practice does not always grow out of a news organization's economic interests, since the ideology on which news judgment is based is not simply reflected by the national media but is in evidence at news organizations in markets like Washington, D.C., where whites are a minority. Even in a city as racially diverse as New York, the news industry continues to place greater emphasis on the interests and actions of whites while marginalizing those of all others. A mind-set already unacceptable in pre-civil rights America, when an expectation of racial equality in American institutions was just beginning to take root, reeks of stubborn hypocrisy and deceit in a multicultural, post-civil-rights era.

The failure by so many in the media to grapple with the pervasive racial and cultural bias in the news media has served to deepen the bitter and widespread cynicism by blacks that few whites ever take the time to comprehend. Like an alcoholic who refuses to acknowledge his chemical dependence, too many whites in journalism live in a constant state of denial about the ways in which they perpetuate the notion of a racial hierarchy—indeed, the assumption of white supremacy—and how that denial, perhaps more than any other single factor, contributes to racial animosity and mistrust.

White journalists would have to imagine seeing the world through a colored lens, where news was first filtered through the interests of people of color. To do this, they could simply read, as their primary source of news, a newspaper like the *Amsterdam News* in New York, which similarly minimalizes white people, considering them only when their actions have consequences for African Americans. Thus, crimes against whites, for example, no matter how heinous, would pale against similarly heinous crimes against African Americans. Similarly, the legislative achievements of white lawmakers would have little appeal unless they had a direct impact on the communities with a sizable African American population. Also, only those writers, artists, and thinkers who captured the imagination of African Americans would be featured. Unless they had crossover—that is, appeal also for black people—the newspaper would render them unimportant. To compound the insult, this African American–centered paper would be the primary source of news in a city like Des Moines, where blacks comprise a minority of the population.

Far from being an objective process, news judgment is an outgrowth of the experiences, attitudes, interests, and perceptions of those at the helm of a news organization, beginning with the owner. As has been noted, the prevailing news judgment filters down from the top, reflecting, for the most part, the values and interests of editors who are almost always white and male. That is not to say that those perceptions cannot be influenced by people with different news values, but, as in the case with Monroe at *Time*, the challenge to alter those perceptions rests squarely on the shoulders of those whose interests, values, and perceptions conflict with those in power. Black journalists, then, are often confronted with the option of moving with or against newsroom currents.

To succeed, black journalists must continually devise strategies to present the world of black people in a way that white people can or care to process them. Stories they propose on black people must conform to the interests, desires, and tastes of a white audience. Those who buck the system and go beyond preconceived notions of black life—as Monroe tried to do with his Farrakhan profile—are often perceived as renegades and typically become outcasts in their news organizations. Sociologist Herbert Breed's 1955 study on the socialization process in the newsroom illustrated the system of reward and punishment in the news industry. Editors do not explicitly tell reporters what news has value and what doesn't, but they foster the socialization process by a system of rewards and punishments. In the newsroom, this system can translate into prominent play—or story positioning—coveted assignments and, as in any organization, raises and bonuses.

Respondents to Breed's survey said they learned newsroom policy by "osmosis" rather than through explicit instruction.[8] In "Deciding What's News," sociologist Herbert Gans picked up on Breed's theme, saying the values in the news "are rarely explicit and must be found between the lines—in what actors and activities are reported or ignored, and in how they are described."[9] Gans added: "[T]he news reflects a white male social order, although it sides with blacks and women who try to enter it and succeed. Nevertheless, its conception of both racial integration and sexual equality is basically assimilatory; the news prefers women and blacks who move into the existing social order to separatists who want to order it."[10] In most newsrooms, the socialization process is thus dictated by white male cultural norms and values, which results in media that seem to operate in concert. It is not coincidental, then, that in a two-tabloid city like New York, the news judgment of the newspapers is often the same, reflecting the interests of people with similar tastes, interests, and backgrounds. Conversely, it is not a judgment shared by editors at the *Amsterdam News*, a black weekly whose front-page stories are often ignored by the mainstream papers.

There were, in the 1990s, several noteworthy attempts by mainstream news organizations to counter the white-centered thrust of the news media. One of the most extraordinary undertakings was a seven-month series in 1993 by the *Times-Picayune* in New Orleans, "Together Apart: The Myth of Race," which brazenly tackled racism in society and in the news media. In a departure from much of the news coverage on race, the *Times-Picayune* uncovered unfair practices in its own newsroom and in its reporting offered the kind of historical context and current-day relevance sorely lacking in discussions of race. One front-page segment confronted slavery and its lasting legacy. The bold series sent the newsroom and the city into a frenzy to the point where editors had to call in facilitators to help the staff through raw and tearful encounters across the racial divide.

One of the most exceptional articles traced the trajectory of racial attitudes at the paper: its support of slavery and poll taxes which kept blacks from voting; the paper's reference to blacks as "besotted barbarians"in the 1880s; its support of segregated schools and hotels in the 1950s and 1960s, when it also labeled Dr. Martin Luther King Jr. a "trouble-maker"; and the hiring of its first black reporter, in the 1970s. The article also revealed that until August 12, 1990, the paper had run accounts of black and white debutantes on segregated pages: white debutantes were featured in the Sunday paper, their photographs accompanied by brief profiles, while the black debutantes were pictured over several days during the week without profiles.

"That separate-but-unequal debutante policy is but one part of a long history during which the *Times-Picayune* and its predecessors demonstrated racial hostility, racial intolerance and racial insensitivity," said the article. "For most of its years, historians and journalists said, the newspaper has been a powerful force in New Orleans, shaping and reflecting racial attitudes and the character of the city. And for the greater part of its years, the newspaper gave readers an image of black people as intellectually and morally inferior, relegated to a lower social caste than white people and often little more than lazy or criminal. It's that image of black people that many people carry today."[11]

It went further, saying the newspaper's reflection of New Orleans was still "out of focus." It said the vast majority of photographs and stories still feature white people, "white people getting married, white people shopping, white people as advertising models. In a recent month of society pages, for example, 96 percent of the photos were of white people; 85 percent of the brides and grooms were white, and a recent Sunday comics section had 58 white characters and four black characters. There were more animal characters—two dogs, two cats, one tiger, one bird and one penguin—than black characters."

In contrast, African Americans comprised 62 percent of the city's population and 35 percent of the metropolitan area's, according to the 1990 census. At the time, blacks made up 11.9 percent of the *Times-Picayune* staff, according to the American Society of Newspaper Editors's annual survey.

The article disclosed that the paper had set up a support group for black and female journalists to address the hostility and exclusion they felt in the newsroom. The paper had also hired a diversity trainer to help the staff cope with racial intolerance. When one meeting dissolved into bitterness and harsh language, Jim Amoss, the editor, called a meeting in which he told white employees they "had to change their attitudes" toward black co-workers. Amoss also, according to the article, explained "why the newspaper had to change—why it had to do a better job writing for all its readers in the New Orleans area, not just white, male readers."

Stories such as these touched off a firestorm of protest in New Orleans, where many whites believed the paper had gone too far. Six to seven thousand readers, many of them angry whites, called the paper's special hot line. Many of their comments were published on fifty pages over the duration of the series. Hundreds more wrote letters, and five thousand people canceled their subscriptions, although many later returned.[12] Many whites on staff felt persecuted. "It was received with such venom by white people and I guess there were times when it felt like, Jesus, what are we doing, who are we doing this for?" said Mark Lorando, a white team member. "There was such an atmosphere of hostility towards the *Times-Picayune* in general and anyone who worked on the project, even within the newsroom."[13] Lorando added that many white staff members were angered by the diversity workshops, spilling over into animosity toward the project.

Meanwhile, within the newsroom, friendships were wrecked and feelings frayed as the team of reporters working on the series candidly confronted their own racial attitudes with the help of the diversity consultants. For several days, the group stayed in a hotel to discuss journalism and race. Keith Woods, the black city editor who had proposed the series, was among the blacks on the team who insisted that whites come clean about their own racial baggage. All were asked to say if they believed blacks were inferior. Amoss, who was raised in Germany and New Orleans and was Yale educated, said he thought of himself as racially enlightened until the sessions.

"It dawned on me and others the extent to which we too were part of the racial mind-set of our society and not some neutral force hovering over it and writing about it objectively," said Amoss.[14] "It was an extremely painful experience."

In the course of the sessions, Amoss admitted that he, as a child of privilege, never knew the last names of the black nursemaids who helped raise him. "When you kind of accept that as the way it is, and never question it, it's quite a shock to wake up and realize that . . . it's shocking. They [blacks] are not viewed as full people. The whole notion of white privilege is not obvious to most white people until they go through some kind of epiphany. And even after going through the three-day workshops, a large number of white staffers still don't get it."[15]

For the project to work, the newsroom hierarchy had to be completely dismantled. In the framework of the series, Amoss was put on the same level as his reporters as all sought to come to terms with the attitudes that would shape the stories. Amoss recalls that he had been one of the whites who resisted the proposal to examine slavery and the historical aspect of race.

"I was one of the people who rolled my eyes when it was suggested. I thought it was absurd that the structure of slavery persists in today's race relations. I had trouble buying that."[16]

But over the course of the sessions, Amoss came to realize that the process of dehumanization and the institutionalization of inferior and superior concepts still hold sway, and that they are the primary legacy of slavery. Keith Woods insisted that no story go in the paper until an African American editor or reporter had reviewed it. While the mandate caused friction, Amoss conceded that it often resulted in articles with a sharper perspective.

Woods said the project was the most emotionally wrenching experience of his life. Most heartbreaking was that it damaged one of his closest friendships because of a dispute over a story. Woods had gone over the head of his friend, a section editor, in an attempt to kill a story he and other blacks found offensive. His friend, he said, later quit the team. "The edit was crushing," he said of his remarks on her story, which could be viewed by other staff members in the computer. "She was distraught over the tone and public-ness. . . . It had a chilling effect on our relationship." In retrospect, he wonders if the article was worth the broken friendship.

Jim O'Byrne, a white reporter, said members of the staff "damn near came to blows" during racial debates. "You know: 'I hate you, you're the devil.' 'What, I thought we were friends!' 'Well, we are friends but you're the devil.' When you really cut through all the crap, that's what you're dealing with, that kind of mistrust."[17]

Because of the fallout in the community and in the newsroom, many of the team members left the paper within a year. "What had sustained us was our belief that we were doing something profoundly important," said Woods. But at the end of the project, he said, "The motivation to go on was no longer there. . . . It took something out of me that the paper didn't put back." After ten years at the paper, Woods left to work at the Poynter Institute for Media Studies.

The series was nominated for a Pulitzer Prize, but it was not a finalist and ultimately lost to the *Akron Beacon Journal*, which, the same year, had run its own groundbreaking series, "A Question of Color." Less explosively judgmental and more optimistic, the *Beacon Journal* series promoted interracial harmony by facilitating gatherings and activities. As at the *Picayune*, the staff retreated to a room and shed some tears. And like the *Picayune*, the paper—which has a black publisher and white editor—published an article that spotlighted its own coverage of race, assisted by black and white staff focus groups whose perspectives often clashed. While black team members believed that black crime was overplayed, white team members believed black-on-white crime was underplayed. But the series was upbeat and goal oriented and never required whites on the staff to confront their racial attitudes. The focus was on bridge building, with blacks and whites equally responsible for the city's racial harmony. In a city of 500,000, some 22,000 people mailed in coupons pledging to improve race relations, while more than 140 organizations volunteered to do the same.

Amoss, who was on the all-white Pulitzer jury that year, said some jurors privately criticized the *Picayune* series as too historical. Because of the emotional toll the series took on the *Picayune* staff, many were devastated over the loss of the prize to the *Beacon Journal*. Some complained that the *Beacon* series oversimplified the racial problem and glossed over the role of whites in perpetuating it. They rationalized their loss by saying the *Picayune*'s series was too honest and pessimistic about racial issues.

"You don't come to the end of it and go, 'Wow, this is great, there's hope,'" said O'Byrne. "This is really hard stuff. We're not sure how you fix it. We don't have a clue how you fix it. . . . This is 300 years of hard. What the hell do you do?"[18]

The stress and strain the series placed on the paper, especially in light of the vociferous reader reaction, would make a similar effort unlikely in the near future. According to Woods, since the series the paper has, if anything, retreated from such courageous endeavors. "A physical body that has been stressed and strained avoids the things that stress and strain it for a while. We as an organization pulled back and took a breather."[19]

Amoss reported that white staffers underwent the most profound change, and that the series had given them "the vocabulary" to discuss race, the subplot of many news stories. In 1999, for example, the paper aggressively pursued the disclosure that Louisiana's Govenor, Mike Foster, had secretly spent $150,000 during his 1995 campaign to purchase the list of supporters of David Duke, an avowed white supremacist. The paper criticized the governor on its editorial page and demanded that he address black voters about his motivation.

"It was a story that I think we would have covered differently had we not gone through that experience," he said, noting that the paper played it as a major story over several days because of its profound racial implications.[20] He said that the race series also made the staff more aware of the ways in which African Americans are routinely stereotyped and that they are, as a result more conscious about story and photograph selections. "We have a better sense of what it means to portray people in stereotypical ways."

The *Times-Picayune* had, by 1999, won two Pulitzers since the series, but Amoss maintains that "Together Apart" is "the best thing we ever did."

Indeed, the race series stands in stark relief to most daily news coverage, which rarely delves deeply, and contextually, into the abyss of race. To do so would mean that the men and women in the newsroom would also have to confront their own racial views, which whites rarely are required to do, with the result that just one point of view, the white one, is aired unchallenged.

"The fundamental thing that was different about this project was that every other project starts with the point of view that there's a problem, and the problem is black people," said Kristen Gilger, one of the white project editors. "It's like black pathology projects. OK, we're going to go look at the schools: why do black people have low test scores? We're going to go look at the housing projects: why are they living in these kinds of places anyway? . . . They become series about social issues that equal black pathology."[21]

Such discussions of race also require an active voice. Race and racism cannot be treated passively, as if racism is a historic relic and blacks and whites currently operate on the same playing field. But the walk down the path of racial honesty requires the kind of courage and introspection rarely evident in newsrooms today. Instead, editors and news directors go about their work as if race does not infect their operations, or color their products.

Studies by various groups, including the National Association of Black Journalists, News Watch, the University of San Francisco's Center for Integration and Improvement of Journalism, and Project FAIR in New York, consistently substantiate claims of pervasive stereotyping of African Americans and other racial groups by the news media. A 1997 survey by the Roper Center for Public Opinion Research found that African Americans are 13 percent more likely than whites to say bias in reporting is a major problem with the news.[22] African Americans are still routinely portrayed as people who appear—as they do for most whites—on the periphery of society. In many instances, they are societal burdens, routinely superimposed onto the traditional bread-and-potato stories about crime and tax-burdening social programs. In these stories, the overburdened taxpayers are presumed to be non-black. H. Himmelstein suggests that newspapers reflect and perpetuate a myth of the puritan ethic that equates hard work with success, and therefore people who are black and poor are seen as lacking motivation. "Rarely do we get an adequate exploration or analysis of the increased susceptibility of the lower socioeconomic classes to physical danger in the workplace or in inadequate housing, unsafe transportation, or lack of sufficient police portection outside the work environment; or of their desertion by the educational apparatus that teaches them at best how to cope in the technological world; at worst, how to fail. Instead, the success of those who have escaped these conditions through hard work is celebrated, while the basic structure of oppression is ignored."[23]

The message is also conveyed in photographs. A 1995 study of photographs that were taken and edited for four U.S. daily newspapers found "a broad and consistent photographic portrayal bias in favor of white males." The photographs, according to the study, *routinely* showed white males in decision-making positions.[24] Meanwhile, blacks are virtually absent from stories on science, medicine, business, and lifestyles, or from stories that propose solutions to non-race-based problems. A year-long news content analysis of television news, newspapers, and magazines, undertaken by News Watch and released in 1994, concluded that the media's coverage of people of color "is riddled with old stereotypes, offensive terminology, biased reporting and a myopic interpretation of American society. In day to day coverage, minorities often are ignored except for certain categories of stories—notably crime, sports and entertainment." Stories that call for experts on a range of issues, from astronomy to medicine and business, typically feature white subjects. "Women, Men and Media," a study funded by the Freedom Forum that examined nightly network newscasts during the first six months of 1998, found that nine out of ten experts interviewed were white and male.

Thus, the widespread mistrust by blacks of the news media, as documented in the Kerner Commission report, persists. According to the Kerner Report, the white press "repeatedly, if unconsciously, reflects the biases, the paternalism, the indifference of white America." Many blacks believe this is still true today, according to a 1994 USA Today/CNN/ Gallup Poll that found that blacks are twice as likely as Hispanics, Asians, or whites to believe that the media is responsible for worsening race relations. It also found that 62 percent of blacks are angry at least once a week over how the media covers racial issues, and that half of blacks and a third of Hispanics believe their local crime coverage is unfair to them. Black journalists also hold a dim view of the ways in which the media portrays African Americans: only one percent of NABJ members surveyed in 1995 felt that the media did a very good job of covering their racial or ethnic group. Forty-eight percent responded that coverage of African Americans was poor.

The perpetuation of black pathology is occasionally addressed in mainstream publications, as it was in the 1990 Pulitzer Prize–winning series on minorities in the media by *Los Angeles Times* media critic David Shaw. "Only 15 percent of the poor people in the United States are black, but one would not know that from most press coverage. Nor would one know that most violent criminals, drug users, prostitutes, drunks, illiterates, high school dropouts, juvenile delinquents, jobless and poor people in this country are neither black nor Latino, but white. Or that the vast majority of blacks and Latinos are none of the above."[25]

Noted author Ishmael Reed has written extensively and persuasively about the big business of black pathology in newspapers and on network news. Reed has noted that contrary to the impressions made by the news media, two-thirds of teenage mothers are white, two-thirds of welfare recipients are white, and white youth commit most of the crime in this country.

Reed has compared the scapegoating of blacks in the popular imagination to the way in which Jews were blamed for the Black Plague, even in countries with little or no Jewish population. "The only difference between white pathology and black pathology is that white pathology is underreported," said Reed.[26]

The news media, more than any institution, shapes the way African Americans and others are perceived. But instead of extinguishing irrational white fear of blacks, the news media more often fuels it, causing further polarization along racial lines. For example, it focuses on a disproportionate incidence of black-on-white crime, which is not borne out by the national crime statistics compiled annually by the Justice Department's Bureau of Crime Statistics. These figures consistently show that the majority of violent crime is black-on-black or white-on-white. Nonetheless, the media harps on black crime, as it did in 1991 during the Los Angeles riots. Television viewers across the country were inundated with images of a black gang mercilessly beating Reginald Denny, a white truck driver caught up in the maelstrom. Paula Walker was the acting news director of WNBC-TV in New York City, which was broadcasting Los Angeles's KNBC signal by satellite. Walker, at the time a resident of New York's Harlem community, was concerned that the violence would spread to New York, "and if there was going to be a reaction, it would be in my neighborhood—Harlem."[27]

Trying to avoid violence in an already racially tense New York, Walker instructed her New York control room staff not to linger on images of violence any longer than necessary. "I told them you've got to show what's going on but you don't have to show thirty seconds unedited of someone getting hit in the head with a brick twenty five times."

Walker paced from one of the fourteen edit rooms to the next, asking to see any pictures or stories on Denny or the beating of Rodney King by police. She instructed the staff to edit the provocative tapes, and she called Los Angeles, advising reporters there not to publicize the locations where looting was taking place without a police presence. "What I said to reporters is if you live in a neighborhood, are you going to tell people they can loot and there are no police around. Then don't do it in Harlem and don't do it in South Central L.A."[28]

A glaring instance of the media cultivating irrational white fear was in the coverage of the shooting death of Amadou Diallo in New York City. Diallo, an unarmed and innocent African immigrant, was shot at 41 times by four white New York City police officers in 1999. The senselessness of his brutal murder sparked weeks of protests throughout New York City, bringing together people from a range of religious, racial and political affiliations. Some in the media tried to absolve the officers, and minimize the outrage, by suggesting that white police officers are justified in their fear of black men in black communities—even those like Diallo who innocently stand outside their doorways. *New York Times* metropolitan columnist John Tierney argued that the worst form of racism by police was to ignore black-on-black crime. "Whatever mistakes were made by the white members of the street crimes unit who fired at

Amadou Diallo on Feb. 4, they were not guilty of ignoring black on black crime," Tierney wrote. He said protesters should consider who would be hurt by police passivity. "So if the police are searching less aggressively for that serial rapist, who is believed to have struck again on Sunday, the chief victims will probably be black and Hispanic women. And if there were a rise in the number of homicides—which are now finally back down to the level of the early 1960's—the victims would be mainly black and Hispanic men. The police would do just fine if they stopped bothering strangers at night. They'd be much safer watching a Tarzan movie."[29]

Tierney seemed to suggest that blacks must contend either with overly aggressive police who fire indiscriminately at unarmed citizens or have no police protection at all. He does not consider the fact that blacks, like whites, wish for and expect basic respect and humanity in their interactions with police officers. It is hard to imagine such a cavalier response to the execution-style killing of an innocent and unarmed white man, even one who resided in a poor or working-class community.

Black critics of the media, frustrated by explicit bias and stereotyping, are often tempted to dismiss the "white media" as racist, but it is pointless to ascribe conscious racist motivations to the ideology transmitted by the mainstream news media. If we are to tackle the problem, we must first understand what is at work. And if news executives want to fix what ails much of the media and society in terms of race, they must be willing to listen and not deride all criticism of the news media's racial weighting system as black paranoia.

The white cultural bias reflected in the mainstream news media is precisely related to the differing sensitivities and sensibilities of people in accordance with their role as members of a dominant or a subordinate group. These biases grow out of a dominant worldview. Social scientists have defined social relationships between members of the dominant and subordinate groups as those based on common sympathy and understanding, and on communication in which both parties share a common definition of situations. But given the starkly different worldviews of whites and people of color, we are often not able to see eye to eye, particularly on issues related to race.

Given our turbulent racial history and the stubbornly segregated nature of our communities, schools, social clubs, and churches, our perspectives are, perhaps not surprisingly, disparate, filtering down to even the shows we watch on television. The annual analysis of Nielsen Media Research data by BBDO, a New York advertising agency, has revealed that the top-rated shows in black households, which in the 1996–1997 television season was *Living Single*, ranked eighty-fourth in total households. Conversely, the most watched shows in white households, which in 1996/1997 was *ER*, followed by *Seinfeld*, failed to rank in the top twenty most-watched shows in black households. Only four shows made both black and white top 20 lists; two of them were *NFL Monday Night Football*, and the *Monday Night Movie*.[30]

In 1998, TN Media, a New York–based media research group, also showed that fourteen of the twenty most popular shows among African Americans didn't rank among the top one hundred shows watched by whites. The number 1 show among blacks, *Between Brothers*, ranked 117th out of 136 top shows watched by whites. And *Friends*, the number 4 show for whites, was number 118 for blacks.

Given our dissimilar experiences due to our races, blacks and whites have different perceptions of matters as diverse as law enforcement and the medical community. Many blacks, still haunted by the government's Tuskegee Experiment, view the medical community with suspicion. and the sense of security many whites feel in the presence of law enforcement officials is not mirrored by many blacks, whose experiences with police and the criminal justice system have been historically negative. To understand the black perspective one need only look at graphic images from the civil rights movement, where white officers physically assaulted peaceful protesters, or recall the trial of Emmet Till, the fourteen-year-old black teen who was abducted, tortured, and murdered for allegedly whistling at a white woman and whose killers were acquitted by an all-white jury. A 1996 Gallup Poll revealed that nearly two-thirds of blacks surveyed believed the criminal justice system was rigged against them.

It therefore stands to reason that blacks and whites would have opposite reactions to the O. J. Simpson verdict. Poll after poll showed the majority of whites believed Simpson was guilty while the majority of blacks believed he was not. Many whites, accustomed to a semblance of justice, were stunned by the verdict and called for reform of the jury system. Blacks, on the other hand, conditioned to expect Simpson's defeat, celebrated the surprising role reversal which allowed at least one black man to beat the system, even if he did so by virtue of his wealth. Many whites viewed the celebration in horror, seeing the widespread belief by blacks in Simpson's innocence as illogical.

Because perceptions of race and justice influence the way we see the world, it obviously matters who presents "facts" to the public. Ideally, the perspectives of different racial groups are meshed in order to cover the blind spots that each member of a racial group brings to his or her reporting. Even though good journalism calls for reporters to be able to transcend their own experiences and fairly reflect the lives and ideals of people from different cultures, classes, regions, and racial groups, each member of a racial group brings biases and perceptual voids to his or her reporting. With whites, however, the biases are often not detected by their white superiors because of their convergent worldviews.

Even so, white editors seem to have at least a subconscious understanding of the ways in which race influences news coverage, apparent from the ways in which reporters are assigned stories. At the *Daily News* in New York, black and Latino reporters have complained that no journalists of color were assigned to the O. J. Simpson trial. Of some sixty bylines on twenty-six stories in the paper's supplement on the case, fifty-eight went to white reporters and columnists and three to minorities. Two of the bylines by blacks were on a local reaction story that also included fifteen white reporters. Not a single minority was dispatched to the West Coast.[31] Implicit in much of the coverage was Simpson's guilt.

Black reporters at the *Los Angeles Times* have said that while they were sent to the streets to brave the violence during the Los Angeles riots, virtually all of the stories were in fact written by whites. In a report compiled by NABJ on coverage of the riots, *Los Angeles Times* reporter Angela Ford described a segregated newsroom where none of the assignment editors or those directing the field coverage were black or of color. Consequently, the coverage played up black lawlessness and clashes between blacks and Asians and downplayed the victimization of blacks and their profound sense of despair. Furthermore, the coverage focusing on black looters and black-on-white-and-Asian violence was not in line with police statistics: the largest group of people arrested in the days of upheaval were not black, but Latino, and the greatest number of victims were black, not Asian or white. Similar grievances were echoed by

African American reporters sent to Los Angeles from all over the country to cover the riots. The National Association of Black Journalists concluded that the contributions of African American reporters to their news organizations' coverage of the riots were largely undervalued or ignored.

In both of these high-profile stories, editors assigned people to direct the coverage whose perspectives and news judgment mirrored their own. To avoid debate and inconsistency, to simplify the process, white reporters were handed the reins, presumably because they could best gauge what white readers wanted to learn about the incidents.

Because of the baggage the members of different racial groups brought with them, the effect of tribalism on the coverage of events in which white subjects are pitted against blacks, as they were in the Simpson trial and the Los Angeles riots, cannot be ignored. The images of black-on-white violence—the sight of Nicole Brown's brutalized face and a prone Reginald Denny being battered by a group of black thugs in Los Angeles—played into the violent black male stereotype, and in the case of Simpson, intensified the presumption of his guilt. In contrast, black reporters, influenced by a mistrust of the criminal justice system and the media, could not dismiss, as so many of their white colleagues had, the defense lawyers' theory of a police conspiracy. What seemed preposterous to many whites made sense to black reporters because of the long and clandestine history of abusive police conduct toward blacks, which the Rodney King tape helped expose.

Even many blacks who believed that Simpson was guilty did not believe there was enough evidence to convict him. In addition, much of the media outrage over the verdict seemed to ignore that two of the jurors were white and one was Latino. Instead, the nine black jurors were characterized as racially biased, as questions lingered about whether some were fit to serve given their limited educational backgrounds. Despite the fact that whites with similar backgrounds had for decades served on juries, the verdict sparked serious discussions about the need to change the educational requirements for jurors. Similarly, black reporters did not come away from the Los Angeles riots with the same impressions as their white peers, many of whom focused on black-on-white-and-Asian violence while ignoring black victimization and the intense sense of hopelessness and despair in South Central Los Angeles.

However, as much as these colliding perspectives, and the reasons for them, could have added to our understanding of race, it was over-whelmingly the white perspective that was reflected in most of the news coverage in both cases. As a result, the news industry once again missed the opportunity to recognize the unique perspectives of different groups in society and to communicate the legitimacy of their conflicting views. Instead, white America was left with its blinders firmly in place, neither receptive to nor respectful of a viewpoint other than its own. Blacks were widely portrayed as irrational for believing there was enough reasonable doubt to acquit Simpson. African Americans and other people of color looked on from the shadows, further alienated from the media and society at large and disheartened by an ever-widening racial gap.

While the news media continue to report on the widening racial rift, they pry it still wider apart by failing to address the myriad ways they fuel black rage and pacify white indifference to it. Until whites and blacks are equally aware of the factors that lead both groups to contradictory conclusions as in the above two cases, they will neither understand the reasons for the other's misunderstandings and misperceptions, nor will they ever be able to move beyond them. As long as the perspectives of non-whites are deemed less valid, indeed less American, than those held by whites, we as a nation will remain fractured on issues that revolve around race.

The media have marginalized African Americans in a particularly interesting paradox in the case of Farrakhan. For nearly two decades, since the 1970s, Farrakhan has drawn thousands of African Americans to his annual Savior's Day speeches where he promoted his decades-old message of economic self-reliance, self-love, and discipline, which has helped to reform scores of drug addicts and criminals and has stabilized pockets of black communities across the country. Despite his enduring prominence in black America, Farrakhan's role has gone largely ignored, as were the even more dramatic contributions of Nation of Islam founder Elijah Muhammad decades earlier.

Farrakhan appears to have used his understanding of the media's narrow prism to gain a wider audience while casting himself as a victim of the (white) media. On the Friday preceding his historic Million Man March in October 1995, an interview with the Reuters news agency, taped earlier in the month, was released. In it he referred to Jews as "bloodsuckers." The controversy surrounding the disclosure, just days before the march, guaranteed him, and consequently the march, prominent media coverage. Prior to Farrakhan's statements regarding Jewish merchants, the march, which called for atonement, had only received scant media attention.

Some participants were uncomfortable that the media initially associated them with Farrakhan's views, even as these views assured the marchers and their cause national exposure. The intense interest in the days leading up to the march focused less on the marchers' noble concern for their communities and the black family, which was in itself compelling, than on Farrakhan's explosive remarks regarding Jewish merchants. Farrakhan seemed to understand that a single controversial black man would draw more media attention than a million black men who were marching out of concern for their families and their communities. In his address to the marchers, Farrakhan thanked the media for unwittingly helping to publicize the march.

Alan Keyes, a prominent black Republican, told the *Des Moines Register* that although the march was positive for those who participated, "it was disgraceful that the media focused on concern with family in the black community only when it was being raised by this hate-spewing, venom-filled bigot."[32] Keyes's comment suggests that the media coverage reflected an interest in the black family, when in fact the interest was only a by-product of their fixation on Farrakhan's inflammatory racial rhetoric. As Cornel West wrote in an essay in the *New York Times* published two days before the march, the media attempted to shift the focus of the march "from black pain to white anxiety" over Farrakhan.[33] It is also true that many whites in and out of the media were apprehensive about the possibility of violence given the massive gathering of black men in the nation's capital.

It is in part because of such limited, white-centered interest by the media that so many blacks, rightly or wrongly, refuse to assail Farrakhan even when his remarks are overtly anti-Semitic. While on moral grounds, a rebuke of bigoted views is appropriate, black leaders, resistant to paternalistic condemn-on-demand dictates, are caught in a catch-22. Routinely ignored, they are set upon occasionally to denounce a man who would be invisible to whites if not for his controversial racial views. And Farrakhan simply feeds on the media's fixation with superficial racial controversy, peppering his conservative pull-yourself-up-by-the-boot-strap message to black America with gratuitous anti-Jewish and anti-white statements which assure him sustained coverage.

As a result, Farrakhan's tentacles have extended far beyond his Chicago base. He has become the subtext in the news coverage of scores of political campaigns involving black candidates across the country. The trend may have begun with the Reverend Jesse Jackson's 1984 presidential campaign, during which he was pressured to distance himself from Farrakhan. Five years later, when Manhattan borough president David Dinkins vied to become New York City's first black mayor, he was pressured to repudiate Farrakhan, which he did in one of his television commercials.

Farrakhan has since been insinuated in dozens of campaigns, including the 1996 re-election campaign of Georgia Representative Cynthia McKinney. In the closing days of McKinney's campaign against John Mitnick, a white candidate, a vote she cast two years earlier against a House resolution to condemn a hate speech by Khallid Muhammad, a lieutenant of Farrakhan, again made news. Mitnick insisted that she "renounce the bigotry, racism, anti-Semitism and anti-Catholicism" of Farrakhan, even though he had played no role in her campaign. Two years earlier, McKinney had defended her vote against the resolution condemning a Farrakhan aide, saying Congress had never taken similar action and could set a dangerous precedent.[34] Her vote on the measure, which was overwhelmingly approved on February 23, 1994, is likely to trail her throughout her political career.

In 1997, the Reverend Al Sharpton, in his race for mayor, commanded headlines in the New York press for days because of his refusal to condemn Farrakhan, who he maintained played no role in his campaign. While the usage of Farrakhan is marginally more justified in Sharpton's campaign because they had had a high-profile association in the past, the media seems unable to distinguish between Sharpton and the far more moderate David Dinkins where Farrakhan is concerned. The inherent unfairness of the Farrakhan litmus test, and the persistent media coverage of its use, has provoked little self-reflection by the media. Even when members of the media acknowledge the double standard applied to black public officials, as did Clyde Haberman in the *New York Times* on April 11, 1997, their justification for it prevails. "Why do so many people—whites above all—take as a given that any black public figure, including one with a celebrated mouth like Mr. Sharpton, has to answer for Louis Farrakhan?" Haberman asked. He then effectively obscured the issue by asking: "Why do so many prominent blacks, when given the chance, tiptoe around the Farrakhan issue, raised fairly or not?"[35] Fairness is, then, beside the point. Black candidates should not have to answer for Farrakhan's views while white candidates are not held responsible for the rhetoric or actions of inflammatory whites. Central to the lapses in fairness and relevance is white interest—the desire by whites to know how black people regard Farrakhan and other controversial black figures, an obsession that is unflinchingly indulged by the media.

Long after the headlines concerning their views (or non-views) on Farrakhan fade, black leaders are haunted by their responses. Condemning Farrakhan inevitably results in the loss of some black support, because the act of white appeasement is viewed as weakness and betrayal by many blacks and a sign that the black leader, once elected, would serve interests other than those of blacks. But not condemning Farrakhan will mean certain censure and the loss of the goodwill of many whites, including those in the media. Even if the effect was not immediate, the reprisals could still come in the future. One is branded a Farrakhan supporter simply by virtue of not attacking him. Either way, the media's racial litmus test of black leaders eludes public scrutiny. Furthermore, Farrakhan's prominence in the media masks the pervasive marginalization of African Americans and their leaders.

Perhaps the greatest single source of bitterness by African Americans over the media's racial weighting system is due to the virtual news blackout of crimes against blacks, and the over-reaction by the media when comparable crimes are committed against whites, particularly affluent whites. At times, the significance of a victim's race is spelled out starkly, as it was on June 23, 1995, when a *New York Times* story presented brief profiles on the seven victims of a fatal shooting rampage by a depraved parolee. Beneath the headline, "Sudden End for Two Who Had Everything to Live For," were brief nuggets on the seven victims of the murderous rampage. As it turned out, the two who the paper told readers "had everything to live for" were white professionals. The other five victims were black or Latino, and the fifth was a reputed drug dealer of unidentified race.

What the story and headline patently implied was that the lives of up-scale whites had more value than the lives of others, particularly a thirty-eight-year-old Latino parking lot attendant, a thirty-year-old black blackjack dealer and her mother, an African livery cab driver, and an alleged drug dealer.

When the story was brought to the attention of the *Times* editors, William Borders, the news editor, wrote a letter saying the article "was an attempt to put a human face—indeed two human faces—on the terrible slaughter." He said it was not an attempt to evaluate the various lives or compare one with the other. "But on reflection, I can see how that inference might have been drawn, and I wish we had handled it differently."[36]

Borders did not say why, of seven victims, the paper only saw fit to put "two human faces" on the senseless tragedy. Whatever the reason, the story was an overt manifestation of the mainstream media's race-weighting system, which Borders excused as an unfortunate aberration.

One of the most prominent examples of coverage that told readers and viewers that white suffering has greater weight than that of non-whites is the media's reporting on the rape of a young white jogger in New York's Central Park by a gang of black and Latino teenagers in April 1989. For months, the unnamed woman's harrowing attack dominated the media, and exhaustive profiles were publicized on the accused, their families, their neighborhood, and on the barbarism of the crime. A week after the Central Park incident, a young black mother of four in Harlem went to the roof of her twenty-one-story apartment building to watch the sun set. She was raped at knife-point, brutally beaten, and thrown from the roof by a group of youths. The woman miraculously grabbed hold of a television cable, where she dangled, naked and seriously injured, until she was rescued by neighbors.

The Harlem woman survived to tell her tale, but it obviously was of little interest to the media gatekeepers. The story commanded only a news brief in one New York City tabloid, and no followup. One can only imagine how the media would have treated the story of the Harlem woman thrown from the roof if she had been white and affluent. In the meantime, the jogger's story captivated the media. A column in the *Washington Times* of August 23, 1990, by Suzanne Fields succinctly conveyed the way in which whites viewed the attack.

"The savage attack on New York's Central Park jogger touched the hearts and quickened the pulse of Americans everywhere. The victim became Everywoman, who innocently trusts that she's safe even when the sky is dark and strangers pass in the night. The attackers became the symbol of all violence that stalks our streets and parks and makes us fear for our sons and daughters, our mothers and fathers and for ourselves."[37]

Black readers and journalists knew the Central Park jogger was not viewed as Everywoman, but much more specifically as an affluent white woman. For many blacks, the blatant disparity in coverage was painful, their anguish compounded by their horror at the accused's young age and the heightening fear of black youth as a result of the unrelenting media coverage. As Fields said, the attackers came to symbolize all violence.

While the anguish of New York's black community was not included in much of the coverage, it was echoed in the commentary of black columnists across the country. Ellis Cose, in a *New York Times* essay on May 7, 1989, pointed out the uneven approach to news, depending on the race and class of the subjects. "While the incident is disturbing in its own right," wrote Cose of the Central Park jogger rape, "the news coverage is also disturbing for what it says about the media and the larger society."[38]

A week later, Clarence Page, a Pulitzer Prize–winning columnist at the *Chicago Tribune*, highlighted, as had the *Village Voice*, a New York City weekly, the uneven reporting. Seven murders and eight shootings had occurred in New York City on the April night that the Central Park jogger was attacked, but the crimes failed to make the headlines. Page made it clear that some of the crimes were as brutal as the attack on the young white jogger. One of the victims that week, a black woman, had been bashed with a cinder block, sexually abused with a pipe, and shot in the head. Her body was found under an elevated highway in the Bronx. Most New Yorkers never learned about this horrific crime.

Page also wrote that African Americans resented the media barrage of words like "wolves," "savages," and "mutants" to describe the young black and Latino defendants. The no-holds-barred labeling of the accused, who were frequently described as animals, was reminiscent of the hostile anti-black sentiments commonly expressed in the media in the pre–civil rights era. Page recalled how, during his early days as a reporter, his editors would bark "cheap it out" to dismiss crime stories in "the less white, less well-off parts of town."[39] While editors have bowed to more politically correct times, their news judgment, where race is concerned, remains largely unchanged.

Black reporters assigned to the Central Park rape story knew that the media hysteria that surrounded the case would not exist if the victim had been African American or Latino. As Curtis Taylor, a *New York Newsday* reporter, remarked: "They clear the news room when the victim is white. Everyone is on the story. You'd be lucky to get the police reporter to cover the story if the victim is black."[40]

The bitterness by blacks over the Central Park jogger coverage was evident as reporters, black and white, descended on Harlem for reaction stories. White reporters appeared stunned by the degree of anger over the news coverage. While they went to Harlem expecting to find outrage and compassion for the jogger following the brutal attack, they instead found contempt for her—who some black hecklers said should have known better than to go in a park late at night—and for news media that seemed to assign greater import to her suffering than to their own. The blacks who were encircled by camera crews in the housing projects knew that the media would not have been there if the Central Park jogger had been their mother, sister, daughter, or wife.

Outside the courtroom, a hard-core group of black supporters for the defendants showed up daily, many taunting the jogger and derisively shouting out her name. The media, adhering to the common practice of withholding the names of rape victims, did not identify her by name, although the *Amsterdam News*, a black weekly newspaper, did. Some of the courthouse provocateurs accused the jogger of going to the park to buy drugs and called her a whore. The disturbing antisocial display was, to be sure, an extreme reaction to perceived white racism and to the branding of the young black defendants and did not reflect a majority view. For black extremists, it was easier to direct their fury at a specific person, the jogger, than at the more nebulous media and society at large. But many blacks could relate, if not to their venomous invective, to the underlying rage. Many white reporters, on the other hand, could not get past the cruel remarks of the protesters to find the pain that lay behind them: the protesters knew that the media, which reflect the greater society, care more about white than non-white suffering.

Some editors defend the disparity in coverage, denying race as a factor. They argue that the uniqueness of a given crime could result in more prominent coverage. While many, they argue, are surprised when a person is attacked in a relatively safe environment, few are surprised, or find it newsworthy, when crimes are committed against people in neighborhoods already perceived as dangerous. The white jogger attack is a story of a man biting a dog, whereas the black woman being raped in Harlem is a simple "dog-bites-man" story. But if the Central Park jogger had been a black woman, even an affluent one, few believe that the media coverage would have been as prominent or as prolonged. Like the notorious Willie Horton ad in George Bush's presidential campaign, the Central Park jogger story played on white fears of black men violating white women, a centuries-old fear that provoked scores of lynchings of black men by white men during the Reconstruction era. As with the Willie Horton ad, there was no need to verbalize the threat the Central Park rape posed to the serenity of white life.

More importantly, the man-bites-dog argument denies the active role the media play in desensitizing people to black pain by undervaluing stories that convey their suffering. While this issue is raised time and again in the media, the media seem steadfastly committed to their race-weighted approach to covering news. Any acknowledgment of it is belated. In 1999, we were reminded of the racial disparity in coverage when on March 14 the *New York Times*, on the front page, noted the contrast between coverage of the murder of Amy Watkins, a twenty-two-year-old white woman who had come to New York from the Midwest to become a social worker, and of Marvin Watson, a Jamaican immigrant who was an electrician and saving money for the birth of his first child. Watson was stabbed to death trying to save his brother from an attack. Seven weeks later, Watkins was stabbed and left dead on the sidewalk on her way home.

Said the *Times*: "But if Ms. Watkins's death has attracted national attention, Mr. Watson died anonymously. Her death led Mayor Rudolph W. Giuliani to reassure the public, and more than two dozen investigators were assigned to the case, which remains unsolved, within a day. The police handled his case as an ordinary homicide and made an arrest a month later. Her death inspired sensational television reporters camped at the scene of the crime. His death went unreported by the tabloids and the *New York Times.*"

But attempting to explain the disparity in coverage, the article revealed traces of racial weighting. "Her photographs show a smiling, brown-haired woman; to many people, she looked too familiar, like a favorite friend or a relative in a picture on the mantel." Whose mantel, it did not say, but it was apparent the writer had primarily white readers in mind. It added: "Mr. Watson's death represents the immigrant's nightmare. He was a poor black man who died in the projects. A slender man who wore his hair in short dreadlocks, he came to New York to do better than his father and to have his son do better than him."[41]

Further, white defendants are more readily accorded sympathetic media coverage, as was Amy Grossberg, a New Jersey teen who in 1996 was arrested with her boyfriend Brian Peterson and charged with first-degree murder in the death of her newborn infant. Shortly before her trial, ABC Television's Barbara Walters conducted a cozy, tearful interview with Grossberg, who appeared with her parents and lawyer.

In the interview which aired on June 6, 1997, Walters asked no specific questions about the baby's death, but instead said she would focus on who Grossberg was, "how was she raised."

A voice-over preceding the interview told viewers: "Forty miles outside of New York City, in the suburbs of New Jersey, Amy Grossberg is a prisoner in her own home. Looking at Amy, it's hard to believe this eighteen-year-old honor student could, if convicted, be put to death for the murder of her newborn infant." Grossberg's aura of innocence by virtue of being white and living in the suburbs would almost certainly elude a black girl living in the innercity.

Walters then provided Grossberg national air time to pronounce her innocence. "I would absolutely never hurt anything or anybody," said a tearful Grossberg, who said she mourned her baby and visited her grave. Meanwhile, Grossberg's mother, Sonye, described her child as "warm, sensitive, and caring," noting that she was a camp counselor and never even had a parking ticket.

Walters closed the interview by saying there was "nothing in either Brian or Amy's past to point that they could commit this kind of cruelty. They seem to have been very responsible, caring people." The program was the highest-rated news-magazine show of the week.

It is difficult to imagine a black teenager accused of a similar crime being accorded a sympathetic interview on national television. In 1998, Grossberg pleaded guilty to manslaughter and was sentenced to two and a half years in prison.

Bryant Gumbel, who in January 1997 completed fifteen years as the host of NBC's top-rated *Today* show, was determined to take the race weighting system to task. He spent five years trying to convince NBC brass to take the show to Africa, the only continent other than Antarctica to which the show had not traveled. In his attempt, he had to find a way to overcome the prohibitive costs, but more significantly, the widespread disinterest in Africa by his superiors and many Americans. Just as many white Americans feel an ancestral connection to Europe, many African Americans, Gumbel argued, feel a similar tie to Africa that is often not shared by whites. Therefore, Gumbel's interest as an African American had to be filtered through a prism of white interest which made for a protracted struggle in some way akin to Sylvester Monroe's at *Time*. Like Monroe, Gumbel had to overcome prejudices amd stereotypes of blacks. But unlike Monroe, who was at least able to tap into the news value raised by Farrakhan's controversy, Gumbel had to overcome widespread indifference to his proposed subject.

Perhaps former president Jimmy Carter best summed up the challenge Gumbel faced as he explained the low level of interest in Africa by whites in and out of government. "It's not just government officials, it's the general American public," Carter told Katie Couric during a *Today* show interview. "We have much less interest in people who happen to be black or brown than we do in Europeans who are white. We become obsessed when a few dozen people are killed in Bosnia, but we ignore tens of thousands of people that might be killed at the same time in, say, Mozambique or in Sudan or increasingly now in Liberia. These are just kind of marginal notes on the political news scene."[42] A Freedom Forum study on Africa and the Media in 1991 reached a similar conclusion, saying that the paucity of coverage of Africa "speaks to the national character of the United States and the disproportionate attention and importance that American institutions assign to all things European; this has probably been exacerbated in recent years by the surge of dramatic news emanating from Europe." It added: "[U]nconscious racism remains a very serious matter in American newsrooms and needs to be addressed more frankly."[43]

A nationally televised program, then, had little to gain by fócusing on a continent so few Americans care about. But Gumbel was unwilling to accept the disinterest in Africa as a legitimate reason for journalists to ignore it. He began making a case to take the show to Africa in 1987, when he first presented a proposal, characterizing the show's failure to go there earlier as a glaring omission. He argued that there was more to Africa than the typical stories of gloom and doom, famine and civil war. "We only hear about Africa when people are starving or there are natural disasters, yet there are more burgeoning democracies in Africa than in Eastern Europe," Gumbel said.[44]

In spite of repeated proposals, NBC executives held firm, citing negative perceptions of Africa, the high cost of the endeavor, and the continent's lack of technology.

Gumbel, angered and surprised by the string of rejections, was also energized by the challenge to make Africa appealing to white viewers. For every political story, he would have to feature Africa's wildlife. Stories on metropolitan life would have to be balanced with stories on civil war and tribalism. And Gumbel continued to appeal to the network's sense of fairness and the news value of Africa.

"We had been everywhere else," said Gumbel. "Africa is routinely underrepresented and misrepresented."

In early 1992, Gumbel finally took his idea to Michael Gartner, then the president of NBC's news division. Since taking the reins of the network division in 1988, Gartner had presided over drastic cost-cutting and massive layoffs, which took the division from more than a $100 million in losses when he took charge to millions in profit near the end of his five-year reign. Gartner listened to Gumbel's proposal, then asked him to tell him how they would do it. "People are always saying 'Let's do this,'" said Gartner. "I said, 'Show me how we can.'"[45]

Gartner, the ultimate outsider from Iowa who often bashed elitist journalistic culture, said the two never discussed Gumbel's idea again, until months later, when Gumbel appeared in his office and dropped a thick, bound document on his desk. It contained close to one hundred pages and read like a doctoral dissertation. The proposal included story ideas emanating from a series of interviews Gumbel had conducted with

African and State Department officials, diplomats, and relief service workers. The document explored the technological limitations of different locations and the ways to overcome them, and it answered anticipated questions.

"It was a great work of journalism and research," said Gartner. "He even came up with ideas where I could find money in the budget to do it."

Gumbel's passion and commitment to the project convinced Gartner.

"He truly believed that nobody in this country knew anything about Africa, and NBC was the one that should explain it," said Gartner. "He was outraged by money spent on other things that were repetitious or boring. He felt it was his job to educate not only the viewers but guys like me. The thoroughness, the amount of effort that went into it, I had never seen anything like it. Never."

Gartner decided almost immediately to approve the project. "I went to his office and said, "'OK, go ahead.' He just looked at me and I thought he was going to cry."

More than two million dollars was spent on the series—the most the show had ever spent on such a venture. But Gartner, who resigned in 1993 in the wake of a segment of *Dateline NBC* in which a General Motors truck was rigged to explode, still insists it was money well spent. The critically acclaimed series also earned Gumbel the National Association of Black Journalists' "Journalist of the Year" award.

But the ratings told another story. The costly series lost the ratings war during the lucrative sweeps period. ABC's *Good Morning America* won with a trip to the Southwest. (ABC had a 4.7 rating, over NBC's 4.2, with each ratings point representing 931,000 homes.)

"It was my proudest moment at NBC and it was 100 percent Bryant: he conceived it, organized it, researched it, and anchored it," Gartner said. He said Gumbel handled every detail, down to securing visas for the NBC staff.

The week-long series was arguably the most comprehensive profile of Africa ever attempted on network television. (The Tyndall Report, published by a research group that monitors news broadcasts, said an average of 5.6 percent of the total time devoted to international news on the three television networks from 1988 to 1990 was on Africa. Another informal survey of network coverage found that Africa got less coverage than California whales trapped in arctic ice, a virus among North Sea seals, and the Time-Warner merger.) But given viewer response, the cost, and the persistence it required on the part of one of the most powerful journalists in network news, it is unlikely that a network would embark on another Africa project in the foreseeable future.

While journalists such as Monroe, Walker, and Gumbel make a difference in the way African Americans and other people of color are portrayed, their isolated achievements are often lost in the sea of negative images perpetuated by the media. With the daily parade of black stereotypes in the media—the welfare mothers, depraved criminals, and immoral youth—many black viewers and readers continue to view African American journalists as guardians of the status quo, as they had three decades ago. If they are to be measured by the results, it would be difficult, without direct knowledge of their individual, behind-the-scenes struggle, to hold even the most committed black journalists in high esteem.

Near the close of the twentieth century, pessimism, along with a tinge of bitterness, pervaded black-journalist circles. Even those who had shattered the glass ceiling wondered if the mainstream media was capable of meaningful change in the way it portrays people of color and the racial problems besetting our nation.

"Our country is as racist as it has been—arguably more racist than before 1980," says Gumbel. "As long as the public appetite wants to believe the face of crime has a black face, that's what we'll see."[46]

And until African Americans and other racial groups are integrated into the hierarchy that dictates news value, there is little reason to believe that the portrayals of blacks and other racial minorities will significantly change. Nor will the racial tensions in the newsroom subside, especially given the assault on affirmative action and other diversity efforts toward the end of the twentieth century. In 1998, the American Society of Newspaper Editors abandoned its 1978 goal of having newsroom staffs that reflect the proportion of minorities in the population by the year 2000. With only 11 percent of the newsroom jobs held by minorities, who represent nearly 30 percent of the population, it was clear the goal would not be met.

But equally troubling is how numbers have come to dominate the diversity debate, even though a darker hue does not necessarily change the newsroom culture. To succeed, a black editor or reporter can advance the media's race-weighting system as well as a white editor. This is where whites in the media need to redouble their efforts. True multiculturalism—an embrace of different perspectives—is the real challenge facing the news industry, a challenge that is infinitely more daunting than the one posed prior to the mid-1960s.

All-white newsrooms are easier to correct than multiracial newsrooms which still perpetuate a racial hierarchy that devalues the lives and experiences of blacks and other people of color.

Throughout the history of the media, white newsrooms have, more often than not, mirrored, and even fostered, this warped and damaging view of black life. To truly change, news organizations must confront a long history of pernicious attitudes toward blacks and other people of color which, while rarely addressed, are deeply enmeshed in the nation's subconscious. Our ongoing racial conflict must not be treated as isolated incidents that warrant one-day headlines. Rather, in their coverage of race, the news media must recognize the trajectory of oppressive conditions and demeaning attitudes that have resulted in a web of strife and mistrust of whites by African Americans.

| TWO |

Into the Mainstream

A History of Strife

> From the press and the pulpit we have suffered much by being incorrectly represented. Our vices and our degradation are ever arrayed against us, but our virtues are passed by unnoticed. —*Freedom's Journal*, 1827

The quest by Africans in America to be portrayed with dignity in an American press that, from its genesis, reflected society's view of black inferiority, has been a protracted and sometimes violent struggle that has always been rooted in racial strife. Many look to the 1960s as the period when African Americans began to influence the mainstream media's coverage of minorities, but we must make at least a cursory exploration of the black press's impact over nearly two centuries.

The black press reflects the quest by Africans in America to have a say in what Derrick Bell has aptly called "an alien place called home," and it underscores why it was—and still is in many quarters—critical to distinguish between a black and a white press. From the beginning, the white press mirrored the prevailing American view of black inferiority and used its news pages to provide information to white readers, with no regard for a black audience. The black press, on the other hand, was from the outset determined to challenge the ways in which the white media rendered blacks invisible or cast them as inferior to whites. In so doing, the black press served as the black counterpart and counterpoint to the white press as it reflected black tastes and sensibilities. However, unlike the white press, the black press was required to have a double consciousness and report on the activities of whites because of their profound effect on black life.

The crusade by black journalists to challenge a notion of white superiority began in 1827 when *Freedom's Journal,* the first black American
newspaper, was launched in the midst of a national debate over a plan to
return African Americans to Africa. The effort resulted in the expatria-
tion of 10,568 blacks to Liberia between 1820 and 1860. *Freedom's
Journal,* launched by the Reverend Samuel Cornish and John Brown
Russwurm, was staunchly anti-slavery and anti-colonization as it challenged the disparaging images of blacks in the popular press. The black
press, then, initiated the first serious foray into media criticism, a discipline that is now firmly rooted in the American discourse on the media.
Implicit in its mission was the desire for blacks to define themselves in
the face of a white media that was, at best, disparaging and, at worst, hostile to their plight.

"We wish to plead our own cause," said the first editorial on March
16, 1827. "Too long have others spoken for us. Too long has the public
been deceived by misrepresentations, in things which concern us dearly."
It added: "From the press and the pulpit we have suffered much by being
incorrectly represented. Our vices and our degradation are ever arrayed
against us, but our virtues are passed by unnoticed." More than a century and a half later, the complaint still resonates in many sectors of black
America.

Freedom's Journal operated in the epicenter of the American Colonization Society, which housed one of its most active branches in New
York City. Proponents of the measure argued that blacks would never be
integrated into the fabric of American life, while opponents countered
that blacks, by then two to three generations removed from Africa, were
more American than many of the immigrants who later settled in the
United States. This was, after all, some two hundred years after the first
slaves arrived in Jamestown.

Freedom's Journal not only addressed the callous portrayals of blacks,
but also the virtual blackout of issues of particular interest to African
Americans. The mainstream press's utter disinterest in African Americans
was underscored by the failure of most of New York's daily newspapers
even to mention the emancipation of New York State blacks on July 4,
1827. Only the *Albany Argus* recognized the momentous occasion by
printing Governor Tompkin's message, which carried out the legislation
that had been signed by his predecessor, Governor John Jay.

Freedom's Journal, which folded after only two years, nonetheless ushered in a succession of black newspapers. In the period between 1827, when *Freedom's Journal* was first published, and the signing of the Emancipation Proclamation in 1863, forty black newspapers were founded in northern states, eight of them in New York City. In addition, white-owned abolitionist papers like William Lloyd Garrison's *Liberator* in Boston, joined their struggle. The *Liberator* was first published on January 1, 1831, seven months before the slave revolt lead by Nat Turner in Virginia would claim the lives of sixty whites and result in Turner's death by hanging. Among the contributors to the *Liberator* was Maria W. Stewart, a black woman who was born free in Hartford, Connecticut. Her passionate anti-slavery articles were accompanied by a woodcut of a black woman in chains. In 1835, Elijah Lovejoy began publishing his *St. Louis Observer,* another abolitionist weekly that had twice been put out of business by pro-slavery mobs that vandalized its offices.

In 1837, as Lovejoy was setting up his third press, a mass meeting was called by citizens to devise a plan to suspend the paper. Lovejoy attended the meeting and vowed to continue publishing. Following the meeting, he was killed by a mob, becoming a tragic symbol of the abolitionist movement. Still, as noted by Jannette L. Dates and William Barlow in *Split Image: African Americans in the Mass Media*: "Even the most radical of the abolitionist papers—which were controlled by whites—were not prepared to go to the lengths the black press did of urging full citizenship for blacks. Freedom was one thing, but being equal was something entirely different. In many instances, blacks found that their agenda was not the agenda of their white friends."[1]

Dr. Martin Delany, Harvard's first black graduate, founded *The Mystery* in 1843, when Pittsburgh's regular dailies refused to publish articles by blacks. In 1848, it was purchased by the African Methodist Episcopal Church and renamed the *Christian Herald,* which, by 1970, was one of the oldest black weeklies.

But none of these papers was as sophisticated, eloquent, or famous as Frederick Douglass's *North Star,* which, beginning in 1847, he published in Rochester, New York, with his two sons. He launched the paper two years after his first autobiography brought him international acclaim. *Narrative of the Life of Frederick Douglass* chronicled his birth into slavery in 1817, his escape twenty one years later, and his return in 1845, when he bought his freedom from his Maryland owner. The dramatic story, coupled with Douglass's oratorial skills, established him as a leader of the abolitionist movement. He was in great demand as a speaker in the United States and abroad.

With correspondents in Europe, the West Indies, and throughout the United States, the paper's readership cut across racial lines, largely because of Douglass's eminence in the United States. Given his stature, Douglass's *North Star* influenced black and white public opinion more than any other black paper of that or, arguably, of any time. The *North Star*, whose masthead proclaimed, "Right is of no Sex—Truth is of no Color—God is the Father of us all, and we are all Brethen," was read in much of the United States and in Europe and the West Indies. The first issue, on November 1, 1847, explicitly stated the newspaper's mission: "The object of the *North Star* will be to attack slavery in all its forms and aspects, advocate universal emancipation, exact the standard of the colored people; and to hasten the day of freedom to our three million enslaved countrymen."

Douglass's immense popularity, however, did not spare him the wrath of his enemies, who burned down his house and destroyed his newspapers. But Douglass continued to publish. The *North Star* became *Frederick Douglass' Paper* in 1851, capitalizing on his celebrity. He finally suspended publication in 1860, the year Abraham Lincoln was elected to the White House and the South seceded from the United States.

Against this backdrop of activism in the black press, a handful of African Americans were already making their entry into mainstream journalism. With race a dominant national issue culminating in the Civil War, Thomas Morris Chester, born in Harrisburg, Pennsylvania, in 1834, became the first black correspondent for a major daily newspaper when he began contributing to the *Philadelphia Press* in August 1864. Between August and June 1865—the year the 13th Amendment abolished slavery in America—Chester filed dispatches on black troop activity near Petersburg, Florida. Thirty-two black infantry and calvary regiments were involved in General Ulysses S. Grant's siege of Petersburg and Richmond, resulting in the capture of up to three hundred rebels. It would be another one hundred years before black journalists would similarly be called upon en masse to report on civil unrest in urban areas throughout the country. Their ability to blend into the black world, chameleon-like, and to serve as invaluable informants for whites would make their eventual entry into mainstream journalism inevitable.

In 1889, Henry O. Flipper, the first black to graduate from West Point, became the first black editor of a mainstream newspaper, the *Arizona Sunday Herald*. He was, according to the U.S. Census of 1890, one of three hundred black journalists working in the United States, almost all of them working in the black press. Flipper's tenure was short lived, however, ending four months later, when the friend whom he had filled in for returned. The inclusion of blacks in the white media was still an anomaly.

By 1890, the number of black newspapers soared. But with the proliferation of black papers following the Civil War came their waning militancy, due, in part, to the sobering realities of emancipation. Scores of former slaves were left destitute and often worked as sharecroppers on the very plantations where they had been slaves. Increasingly, blacks were the victims of lynching, segregation, disenfranchisement, and brutal characterizations in the white press. While fear of retribution muted many in the black press, *Free Speech*, a black newspaper in Memphis, Tennessee, brazenly challenged the lynching of black men, many of them falsely accused of raping white women.

"Nobody in this section of the country believes the old thread-bare lies that negro men rape white women," said the May 21, 1892, editorial written by Ida B. Wells, the twenty-three-year-old editor and publisher. She charged that the lynching of three black businessmen was instigated by their white business competitors.

"If Southern men are not careful they will over-reach themselves and public sentiment will have a reaction and a conclusion will be reached which will be very damaging to the moral reputation of their women."

The editorial sparked calls for revenge in the local white press by writers unaware of Wells's gender. "Patience under such circumstances is not a virtue," said an editorial in The *Evening Scimitar* on May 25, 1892. "If the negroes themselves do not apply the remedy without delay it will be the duty of those whom he has attacked to tie the wretch who utters these calumnies to a stake at the intersection of Main and Madison Sts., brand him in the forehead with a hot iron and perform upon him a surgical operation with a pair of tailor's shears."

An editorial in the competing *Daily Commercial* that day said: "The fact that a black scoundrel is allowed to live and utter such loathsome and repulsive calumnies is a volume of evidence as to the wonderful patience of Southern whites. But we have had enough of it. There are some things that the Southern white will not tolerate, and the obscene intimations of the foregoing have brought the writer to the outermost limit of public patience. We hope we have said enough."

As part of a pattern of muffling voices sympathetic to the plight of African Americans, a mob destroyed *Free Speech's* office and print shop, and Wells was forced to flee the South. She went north to lecture against lynching and published her first pamphlet, "Southern Horrors," which documented the hangings. "Brave woman!" wrote Frederick Douglass on October 25, 1892, in a letter reprinted in Wells's "Southern Horrors." "You have done your people and mine a service which can neither be weighed nor measured." Wells would write articles for the *New York Age* and the *Chicago Defender*, which were among the most respected black weeklies of the time.

The vitriolic backlash against black gains made during Reconstruction continued to reverberate across the country, but nowhere as much as in the South, where white Democrats flagrantly castigated blacks from the House chambers and from the press. In 1900, a year marked by the recorded lynching of eighty-five blacks, U.S. Senator Benjamin Ryan Tillman of South Carolina bragged that ballot boxes had been stuffed and that blacks had been killed in 1876 to maintain white domination. He was referring to a year in which some forty-five black Republicans were killed in a series of white terrorist attacks in South Carolina, culminating in the dispatching of federal troops by President Rutherford Hayes just two weeks before the presidential election.

"The people of South Carolina, in their Constitution, have done their level best to prevent the niggers from voting," said Tillman in a *New York Press* article. Southerners, he said, "rose in righteousness and might. We took the Government. We stuffed ballot boxes, we bulldozed the niggers and we shot 'em. And we are not ashamed of it."[2]

In defending murder and intimidation as tactics to prevent blacks from voting, Tillman said that blacks, educated or uneducated, were a menace to good government.

That same year, with Charles Carroll's *The Negro the Beast*, being a national bestseller, even pro-liberal journals like the *Atlantic Monthly* published articles on the universal supremacy of the Anglo-Saxon. In 1901, as the recorded number of blacks lynched reached 105, and with *"The Negro, a Menace to American Civilization"* a national best-seller, President Theodore Roosevelt was denounced from the front page of the *New York Times* for inviting Booker T. Washington to dinner at the White House. By then, Washington—an international celebrity who had had tea with England's Queen Victoria and was entertained by dukes and earls—had emerged as the nation's most prominent African American due to his famous "Atlanta Compromise" speech in 1895. In that speech, Washington advised blacks to forsake their quest for racial equality and scholarly pursuits and instead seek work in agriculture.

According to press accounts of the speech, Washington received thunderous applause from whites in the audience as he assured them that segregation was acceptable, and quests for social equality were "extremest folly." In an illuminating dispatch by James Creelman of the *New York World,* he reported that while whites cheered wildly at the end of Washington's speech, "most of the Negroes in the audience were crying, perhaps without knowing just why."[3] That African Americans would despair over Washington's support of their inferior status was evidently beyond Creelman's comprehension.

Despite his stature in 1901 after the publication of *Up from Slavery,* which was read by millions, Washington's White House visit provoked a bitter reaction from whites across the country who were appalled that a black would be accorded such respect. Even so, Washington remained a forceful presence in black and white life, and, despite his anathema to black advancement, had few vocal black critics, particularly in the black press. As a major dispenser of Republican party patronage, Washington enjoyed support from many black newspapers, which liberally published his news releases while benefiting from his subsidies and advertising revenue. But William Monroe Trotter, a Harvard graduate who published *The Guardian* in Boston, was a vocal critic of Washington's accommodationist stance.

"The northern Negro has no rights Booker Washington is bound to respect," he wrote. "He must be stopped." In another editorial, he warned: "The Negro people will see the more clearly the need of repudiating Booker T. Washington as a leader." But it was apparent in Trotter's editorial of September 13, 1902, that his position had alienated him. "How long, O Booker, will you abuse our patience? How long do you think your scheming will escape us? To what end will your vaulting ambition hurl itself? Does not the fear of future hate and execration, does not the sacred rights and hopes of a suffering race, in no ways move you? The colored people see and understand you and they know that you have marked their very freedom for destruction, and yet, and yet, they endure you almost without murmur! O times, O evil days, upon which we have fallen!"

Trotter was among the thirty blacks at a historic meeting in Ontario, Canada, on July 10, 1905, to form the Niagara Movement, the forerunner of the National Association for the Advancement of Colored People. The effort was spearheaded by W. E. B. Du Bois, Trotter's Harvard schoolmate whom Trotter had previously criticized for his neutrality on Booker T. Washington. The group's Declaration of Principles bore none of that impartiality, but instead appeared to directly confront Washington's leadership.

"We refuse to allow the impression to remain that the Negro-American assents to inferiority, is submissive under oppression and apologetic before insults. Through helplessness we may submit, but the voice of protest of ten million Americans must never cease to assail the ears of their fellows, so long as America is unjust."

It added: "The Negro race in America, stolen, ravished and degraded, struggling up through difficulties and oppression, needs sympathy and receives criticism, needs help and is given hindrance, needs protection and is given mob violence, needs justice and is given charity, needs leadership and is given cowardice and apology, needs bread and is given a stone. This nation will never stand justified before God until these things are changed."[4]

With race at the forefront of the national dialogue, some of the nation's more liberal newspapers sought out black writers to lend their perspective to the discourse on race. By 1903, Du Bois's book *The Souls of Black Folk* had been widely and critically acclaimed, positioning him to rival Washington's solitary role as the nation's most important commentator on race. Like Washington, Du Bois understood the power of the press. In addition to contributing articles to liberal white publications, he invested in the *Moon Illustrated Weekly*, which debuted on December

2, 1905, but was out of business by the following August. From 1907 to 1910, he published *Horizon: A Journal of the Color Line*, which covered the lynching epidemic, national politics, and developments in Africa and Asia. But Du Bois's greatest forum came with the editorship of *The Crisis*, the monthly organ of the NAACP which Du Bois founded and began editing in 1910. Under Du Bois, *The Crisis* became the century's most influential journal of African American protest. During the twenty-four years in which Du Bois edited the journal, he took on the black clergy, public and elected officials and the black and white press.

John Edward Bruce, who wrote under the byline "Bruce Grit" for the *Negro World*, was also among the crop of black journalists whose fiery commentary was published by some of the more liberal white-owned newspapers. Unlike DuBois, whose scholarly articles and books on race were widely read and reviewed in mainstream publications, Bruce was a newspaperman whose lifework was journalism. Bruce became a regular contributor to the *Albany Argus'* Sunday paper, the *Albany Journal*, the *Times Union*, and *Press Knickerbocker*, for which he earned a penny a word.

Letters he received from U.S. senators, Rudyard Kipling, and President William Harrison's private secretary—the latter regarding a story he was writing on black White House employees—also underscored his prominence as a journalist. Bruce was well connected in black circles as well, with intimate letters from black luminaries like Du Bois, prominent New York Episcopal priest Alexander Crummel, and the president of Liberia found among his personal effects. An avid writer of newspaper letters to the editor, Bruce emerged as a vocal critic of the media. In 1905, upon Frederick Douglass's death, Bruce was assigned by the *Commercial Gazette* in Cincinnati, Ohio, to write a remembrance of a man Bruce had known for twenty-five years. Both men had been born into slavery in the same section of Maryland and had attended the same school.

Recalling his visit to the *Gazette's* newsroom, he wrote: "I had the occasion once to go into the room on the editorial floor, where are kept the biographical sketches and portraits of distinguished men and women. I worked the list over pretty thoroughly for the name of any Negro in the range of my acquaintance and found none."[5] Bruce was also annoyed that *Gazette* editors did not recognize Douglass's initials, which were well known to blacks, and he attributed it to the ignorance many whites had even of black figures as prominent as Douglass, whose death caused the North Carolina legislature to adjourn for the day in his honor.

Again, on November 30, 1911, in the *Negro World*, Bruce complained that white "cub reporters" were flippant in their articles about Marcus Garvey, the Jamaican-born black nationalist who organized the first mass movement of blacks and established a chain of enterprises, including stores, restaurants, hotels, factories, the *Negro World*, and the Black Star Line, a steamship company. At the peak of his power, in 1921, Garvey collected an estimated $10 million from blacks, with which he tried to form an African republic. He never did. Bruce condemned the New York media for misrepresenting the objectives of Garvey's organization, which recruited hundreds of thousands of blacks who answered Garvey's clarion call: "Up you mighty race." Between 1910 and 1940, Garvey published nine newspapers, and established the Universal Publishing House, the first independent black publishing company.

"Nobody expects that a prejudiced daily press is going to be fair to Negroes who are attempting to do something out of the ordinary and on their own initiative," wrote Bruce. "It is not in the interest of those whom these newspapers represent to encourage any movement among black people that is calculated to lift them to the commercial and industrial level of the white race."[6]

But not all black journalists wished to be activists or to operate outside the mainstream. In 1902, Lester Walton was hired to cover general news and sports for the *St. Louis Globe-Democrat.* Walton remained there until 1906, when he moved to the *Star Sayings*, which late became the *St. Louis Star.* While a journalist, Walton began composing songs on the side for Ernest Hogan, a famous musical comedy performer and writer. His interest in the entertainment world led him to New York, where he wrote songs for Hogan's show *Rufus Rastus* while writing for the *Colored American* magazine. In 1908, he was asked to be the drama editor of the *New York Age*, which had by then become one of the most influential black publications in the country, with contributions from the leading black religious and racial leaders, including Frederick Douglass and Booker T. Washington. At the *Age*, Walton's sophisticated critiques of black theater, which he held to unprecedented standards, made him a pioneer in the field. As he raised the expectations and, as a result, the quality of black theater, he became increasingly consumed by racial issues because of their pivotal force in black life.

In 1918, a year after America entered World War I, President Woodrow Wilson dispatched Walton to France to report on the conditions of black troops. He returned to France to cover the Versailles Treaty conference in 1919, the year of the "Red Summer," when twenty-six race riots erupted in Texas, Washington, D.C., Chicago, and Arkansas, resulting in more than seventy-six deaths and six hundred injuries. That year, seventy-six blacks were reported lynched.

Then in 1922, a year marked by the reported lynching of fifty-one African Americans and the exodus of another 500,000 from the South, Walton was commissioned by the *New York World*, one of the city's leading white dailies, to write a series of articles on racial conditions in the South. The series helped to secure him a regular staff position at the *World*, which helped to build a black readership despite the paper's otherwise white focus.

Over time, Walton became something of a media gadfly. In 1913, he began a lengthy campaign to convince newspapers to capitalize the "N" in Negro, arguing that it would put them on par with other ethnic categories that are capitalized. Walton first broached the subject in a letter to Samuel Bowles, the publisher of the *Springfield Republican*. At Walton's urging, Bowles brought Walton's letter before the annual meeting of the Associated Press in New York in 1913. The editors were unwilling to conform to his wishes. Undaunted, Walton fired off a flurry of letters to editors across the country, and to members of the city's Board of Education. In a letter to the *New York Times* dated October 13, 1918—five years after he first began his crusade—Walton wrote: "After reading the first two lines of your editorial appearing in Sunday's issue of *The Times* under the caption "The German Colonies" I am once more moved to respectfully ask you to adopt the policy of dignifying the term 'Negro' with a capital 'N.' You ask: 'Are negroes people? Are Chinamen people?'" He continued: "I note that you see fit to capitalize the 'C'; and the 'I' in 'Indian.' Why this glaringly obvious and painful distinction?"

"You do not look upon 'Chinamen' and 'yellow' as synonymous; neither 'Indian' and 'red.' But with a relentless persistency you insist that 'Negro' and 'black' are adjectives having the same signification. On what grounds other than moth-eaten custom is this queer rhetorical interpretation based?"[7]

In 1930, seventeen years after Walton launched his campaign, the *New York Times* became the first major newspaper to capitalize "Negro" and "Negress." Even through to the 1990s, the *Times* and other news organizations have still been grappling with the description for African Americans. It had, in its history, changed the description from negro to Negro, to black, and, beginning in the 1990s, to a combination of black (still lower case) and African American, reflecting, in part, African Americans' own quest for their identifying labels.

Walton also objected to headlines that identified crime suspects as Negro, saying they stigmatized the entire race. It took several more decades—until the 1980s—before most news organizations abandoned what had, for more than a century, been a standard practice of identifying non-white suspects by race. The practice heightened the perception that only people of color committed crime.

In 1929, when the *New York World* succumbed to the Great Depression, its demise was eulogized in the *Dunbar News*, a newspaper published by residents of the Laurence Dunbar Apartments in Harlem.

"The passing of Mr. Walton from Park Row, noted as 'newspaper row' of the city, removes the only Negro who rubbed shoulders with the best newspapermen of the city on even terms. . . . Mr. Walton was always a full fledged member of *The World* staff, working weekdays as well as Sundays. . . . In the course of his writings he covered nearly every important progressive movement, not only in Harlem, but of the race."

Implicit in the tribute was African Americans' pride that one of their own was writing for the mainstream media: it was a sign of racial progress that accorded ground-breaking status to those who achieved it. For their part, black journalists were willing to swap the psychological rewards of participating in the betterment of blacks in an unfiltered medium for the higher salaries and greater visibility and prestige of working in the white media. It would often require them to make the transition from informer to informant and interpreter. The interests, perspectives, and news values of the new audience would require black journalists to make fundamental adjustments which many were more than willing to do.

Walton would go on to write for the *New York Herald Tribune* while a handful of other blacks were also hired by mainstream newspapers.

These included Timothy Thomas Fortune, a legendary black editor who became an editorial writer at the *New York Sun*; Eugene Gordon, a feature writer at the *Boston Post*; and Noah D. Thompson, a feature writer at the *Los Angeles Express*. At the same time, many of the nation's leading publications continued to commission black journalists to write about race, with George Schuyler, a columnist for the black-owned *Pittsburgh Courier*, being among the most prolific.

Born in Providence, Rhode Island, in 1895, Schuyler was raised in Syracuse, New York. Beginning in 1925, after serving in the war, he began a forty-year career with the *Pittsburgh Courier*. Published by Robert L. Vann, the *Courier* stridently insisted on self-respect by African Americans and respect for them by others. In 1931, the paper launched a campaign against the *Amos 'n Andy* radio show. Hundreds of ministers heeded Vann's request to deliver self-respect sermons from the pulpit, and nearly 750,000 signed petitions demanding the cancelation of the show.[8] (The *Chicago Defender*, for one, favored keeping the program on the air.)

In 1931, while still at the *Courier*, the thirty-one-year-old Schuyler was assigned by the *New York Evening Post* to investigate and write a series of articles about allegations of slavery in Liberia, the African American colony in Africa that had been established nearly one hundred years earlier. Beginning in June 1931, he wrote six articles for the *New York Evening Post*, in addition to the *Buffalo Express*, the *Philadelphia Public Ledger*, and the *Washington Post*. It was a remarkable achievement for a black journalist of that time to work as a foreign correspondent for a mainstream newspaper, and to be greeted with such fanfare. The series was heavily advertised in newspapers and on newsstand placards in major cities.

Schuyler sought to bring to his work racial neutrality. He took pains not to appear racially biased, and, over time, became unabashedly conservative on issues of race. His work was devoid of any hint of racial cheerleading, even when he wrote about the absurdity of the Jim Crow south for the *American Mercury* in 1930, and about the abandonment of Liberia by the United States for the same paper in 1933. But his conscious efforts to downplay racial pride at times played into the attitudes of some whites in the media, who consciously ignored or derided blacks while extolling notions of white superiority. "In those days, what happened in the black community wasn't considered news," recalled Walter Cowan, a reporter and editor for *The Item, The States,* and *The States-Item* in New Orleans from 1936 to 1979.

"So the city editor had to know where the blacks lived. Say there was a police calling the 2200 block of Louisiana Avenue. If the city editor knew the street well enough, and he knew Louisiana Avenue was all black . . . he would know not to bother sending somebody out on the story." He said the dominant coverage of blacks was crime related. "The focus, of course, was on the white community."[9]

In his 1966 biography, *Black and Conservative,* Schuyler noted the commotion created by his series on Liberian slavery: "It was the talk of the town, especially among the Garveyites and the 'black nationalists' who expect a Negro newspaperman to lie to satisfy their egos. I have always refused to do this, regarding it as unworthy. I believe in calling the shots as I see them. This unchauvinistic approach may make many enemies but it engenders much respect for a writer."[10] It is also a strategy that white writers need never consciously consider and that places the burden on African American writers to *appear* racially neutral. That could, in practice, have the opposite effect by inducing black journalists in the name of neutrality, to give more weight to black corruption than to the disenfranchisement of blacks. In his coverage of Liberia, Schuyler highlighted the corruption of its leaders and citizens, making it clear to his editors and readers that his stories were untarnished by any racial loyalty.

By the end of his career in the 1960s, Schuyler had taken his stance against racial chauvinism to the extreme. He became one of the harshest critics of the most prominent black leaders of the time, including Dr. Martin Luther King Jr. The *Courier* refused to print a column he wrote in which he objected to King's receipt of the Nobel Peace Prize—probably because it feared a backlash given King's stature in the black community. The column was instead published by the *Union Leader,* a white daily newspaper in New Hampshire.

While King was revered in much of black America, he was, in Schuyler's view, the very cause of much of the nation's racial unrest. Nearly a year after King's death, Schuyler wrote that King "has left a legacy of race hatred that has divided much of this country into two fearful camps. Posing as a messenger of peace, the sanctimonious person did not soothe the passions but aroused them, injecting color consciousness as a catalyst to transform petty human squabbles into holy crusades." Of King's tactic of civil disobedience, he said he "concocted the intriguing principle of jurisprudence that it is permissible to disobey the law provided, of course, that after a conclave with yourself you decide that it is a bad law." A column he wrote blaming the Watts riots on civil rights "agitators" appeared in more than two hundred dailies and weeklies across the country.[11]

Schuyler was also rabidly anti-Communist and saw a Communist plot behind practically every major progressive cause, including the civil rights movement and anti-Vietnam War protests. "We have here a great big worldwide Red symphony orchestra which is playing on many instruments in many parts of the world," he said in a July 1968 interview.

In addition to appearing in the *Courier* from 1925 to 1966—reporting on stories throughout the world and across the country—dozens of Schuyler's articles were published in white-owned publications between 1923 and 1935 alone, including the *American Mercury* and the *Nation.* Many of his earlier articles provided a frontline perspective of the trials of being black in America. Beginning in 1953, his columns were circulated by the Spadea Syndicate, which distributed them to some sixty dailies with a combined circulation of six million. By 1965, his columns were distributed by the North American Newspaper Alliance, which served hundreds of dailies.

While Schuyler had an earlier start, his stature in the mainstream would eventually be rivaled by Earl Brown, a Harvard graduate who in 1940 became a staff writer for *Life* magazine. Before joining *Life,* Brown had served, for four years, as the managing editor of the *Amsterdam News,* a black weekly in Harlem, which, under the guidance of Dr. C. B. Powell, became, between 1936 and 1970, one of the nation's leading black newspapers. While at the *Amsterdam,* Brown evidently had his sights set on mainstream journalism, which represented a larger stage and a higher salary. Just as television news would usurp newspaper work as the pinnacle of success for many journalists, so too did the white media become the same for many black journalists. Brown began contributing stories to *Time* magazine early in his *Amsterdam News* tenure. A letter to him from a *Time* editor dated December 22, 1936, indicated that a Christmas check was enclosed and noted: "You have worked hard for us during 1936 and we appreciate the valuable assistance you have given."

In November 1940, Thomas Krug, a *Time* editor, wrote Brown to tell him that the national affairs staff was "delighted" with his report on New York City politics. "As you doubtless have heard, it's being held for a special story on Tammany Hall and the mayoralty situation." Brown was paid $40 for his contribution.

That same year, Brown was assigned to write a profile on Joe Louis for *Life* magazine, for which he was paid $500. In a letter that year to a friend whose help he sought in landing a job with the Democratic National Committee, Brown said he was fired from the *Amsterdam News* for writing the story. It was unclear if his firing was related to the content of the article or to the fact that he had a byline in another publication.

Shortly after leaving the *Amsterdam*, Brown was hired as a staff writer for *Life*, where he primarily covered labor, politics, and crime. Brown had boundless ambition. A letter dated June 19, 1941, to Brown from *Time* and *Life* publisher Henry Luce stated: "I am enormously interested in your proposal for a 'Black LIFE'—especially because of my respect for your judgment. . . . I am asking Andrew Heiskell to get in touch with you at your mutual convenience in order to pursue the matter further."

While *Black Life* never materialized, Brown's career flourished. In 1942, his article in *Life*, "Detroit Is Dynamite," chronicled the mounting racial tensions there and accurately predicted the riot of July 1943 that resulted in thirty-four deaths and the dispatching of federal troops. In 1942, Brown was also paid $200 to write an article for *Harper's* magazine on the plight of blacks in the military, an article that documented the growing resentment of black soldiers who were demanding the same rights in this country that they were fighting for on foreign soil. A year earlier, A. Philip Randolph had issued a call for 100,000 people to march on Washington to protest discrimination in the armed forces. He called off the march only after President Franklin Roosevelt issued Executive Order 8802, which forbade racial and religious discrimination in government training programs and the armed forces.

That same summer, on August 6, 1941, a fight between black and white soldiers in North Carolina resulted in the fatal shooting of a black private and a white military policeman. This incident marked the first in a series of violent racial clashes between black soldiers and white soldiers and civilians that persisted throughout the war.

An editor's note preceding Brown's article in the April 1942 issue of *Harper's* said: "As we go to press, few white citizens of the United States are aware of the extent to which their Negro fellow countrymen are—in the words of this article—'angry, resentful, and utterly apathetic about the war.' In order to focus public attention upon a critical problem we have asked Mr. Brown, one of the ablest Negro journalists, to state frankly what and why the feeling is." By then, it was apparent that the role of the black journalist was to interpret the thoughts and aspirations of blacks for whites, which put them in the same league as some of the nation's most prominent black leaders.

In 1944, Brown wrote another article for *Harper's*, this time on the importance of the black vote. In that article, Brown noted the scars left by the race riots in Detroit and the prevailing disappointment of blacks by the Roosevelt administration's response to the riots, particularly the attorney general's recommendation that southern blacks stop migrating to Detroit to prevent more racial trouble. He said positions such as that, compounded by the campaign for white supremacy advanced by southern Democrats in Congress and the continuing discrimination in the military, could result in a shift by blacks back to the Republican party.

In 1946, amid mounting racial hostility as war veterans returned home, white mobs in Atlanta killed six black veterans in one three-week period in Georgia. It was Georgia's first multiple lynching since 1918 and prompted the NAACP to urge President Harry Truman to intervene. Truman appointed a special commission to recommend legislation that addressed Negro rights. The NAACP issued a report that called 1946 "one of the grimmest years in the history of the National Association for the Advancement of Colored People." The report deplored the blow-torching and eye-gouging of returning black veterans, adding: "Negroes in America have been disillusioned over the wave of lynchings, brutality and official recession from all of the flamboyant promises of post-war democracy and decency."

A year later, a Truman Commission report entitled "To Secure These Rights" condemned racial injustices suffered by blacks, and brought the term "civil rights" into common usage. That same year, a report commissioned by Luce examining the American press was released. It contained the first major indictment of press coverage of minorities by a mainstream panel. The study, "A Free and Responsible Press," was led by Luce's friend Robert Hutchins, the chancellor of the University of Chicago. The panel was comprised of legal scholars, political scientists, philosophers, and a poet, but no journalists.

The report by the Hutchins Commission on Freedom of the Press concluded that the press was more concerned with "scoops and sensations" than the social significance of the news. It recommended, among other things, the projection of a representative portrait of the constituent groups in the society. In other words, it called on newspapers to report on issues affecting blacks and other non-whites more fairly. The report also expressed concern about the growing concentration of media ownership—a concern still valid today due to the large concentration of ownership by a handful of major companies—and complained about the quality of news reports. The study found the media more concerned with stories of "night-club murders, race riots, strike violence and quarrels among public officials" than in stories on public education and other issues of greater social significance.[12]

Foreshadowing by two decades the even harsher condemnation of the media's treatment of minorities, the report recommended "the projection of a representative picture of the constituent groups in the society." Confronting the harmful effects of racial stereotypes, it warned: "Even if nothing is said about the Chinese in the dialogue of a film, if the Chinese appear in a succession of pictures as sinister drug addicts and militarists, an image of China is built which needs to be balanced by another. If the Negro appears in the stories published in magazines of national circulation only as a servant, if children figure constantly in radio dramas as impertinent and ungovernable brats—the image of the Negro and the American child is distorted. The plugging of special color and 'hate' words in radio and press dispatches, in advertising copy, in news stories–such as 'ruthless,' 'confused,' 'bureaucratic'—performs inevitably the same image-making function."

It added: "The truth about any social group, though it should not exclude its weaknesses and vices, includes also recognition of its values, its aspirations, and its common humanity." These ideals, which hearken back to the mission statement of *Freedom's Journal*, would be revisited twenty-one years later by a presidential commission.

The report, progressive for its time, was widely dismissed by white journalists, with much of the criticism aimed at the composition of the panel, made up mostly of academics, including Columbia University history professor Arthur Schlesinger, Sr.

While widely assailed, the report nonetheless sparked serious self-reflection by the press about its social responsibility. The March 29th issue of *Editor and Publisher* carried seven articles and an editorial on the report. While mainly critical, the thirteen pages dedicated to the Hutchins report spoke volumes about the seriousness with which it was greeted in the journalism community. While quick to dismiss it as the work of a removed group of academicians, some, like the editor of the *Quill*, felt it "too important to be subjected to some of the sniping that has passed for criticism."

In the months and years that followed, efforts to improve press performance were launched. In the face of growing public dissatisfaction with the press, many acknowledged the need for improvement. In June came *CBS Views the Press*, followed the next month by the formation of the National Council of Editorial Writers. On January 1, 1948, the editor of the *Boston Herald*, perhaps reflecting a growing acknowledgment by his peers that the press needed to get its house in order, was quoted in the *ASNE Bulletin*, the organ of the American Society of Newspaper Editors: "We should be neither mad nor smug. We should act constructively."

In 1949, the American Society of Newspaper Editors set up a committee to discuss self-criticism, and in 1950 it established a permanent body to monitor press activities. That same year it appointed ten journalists and educators to investigate the state of newspaper journalism. The group rejected the Hutchins Commission's findings and suggested that it would be open to "intelligent criticism" of the newspaper-reading public. While unwilling to acknowledge the Hutchins Commission's role in sparking needed self-reflection, editors and publishers readily admitted the need to improve, even though it would be years before media executives would expend energy exploring the coverage or hiring of minorities. This period of self reflection, then, did little to advance the mainstream media's relation to African Americans and other minorities.

In the meantime, race continued to make headlines. In February 1948, Truman became the first president to address an NAACP convention, and he sent to Congress a special civil rights message calling for a federal anti-lynching law. *Atlanta Constitution* editor Ralph McGill, considered a liberal on racial issues, attacked the bill as too radical. That same year, Alabama and Mississippi Democrats bolted from the Democratic convention following its adoption of a civil rights plank, and the California Supreme Court voided a state statute banning interracial marriages.

Against this turbulent racial backdrop, Brown, by then a prominent journalist, was convinced he could have a greater influence in government. He entered New York City politics while continuing to hold on to his job at *Life*. He would later successfully run for a City Council seat in Harlem occupied by Benjamin J. Davis, an avowed Communist who was expected to win. Brown defeated Davis by a 3 to 1 margin.

That same year, Ted Poston, who in 1936 joined the staff of the *New York Post*, was awarded the prestigious George Polk Award for his series of articles on the trial of three young blacks charged in the rape of a young white woman in Florida. Beneath front-page banner headlines, Poston related how the three young men were beaten and tortured, and a fourth killed, for an alleged rape that he said was never proven and probably never occurred. After the woman implicated the young men, Poston said, three days of terror gripped Groveland, the small black community outside of Orlando, Florida. Mobs of angry whites burned down houses and fired guns indiscriminately. Many blacks escaped to the woods, including Ernest J. Thomas, one of the accused. He was found shot to death in the woods ten days after the alleged rape.

After a three-day trial, the remaining three defendants were convicted. Two were sentenced to death and the third to life imprisonment. Poston wrote that prosecutors had not presented "one bit of evidence to support Mrs. Padgett's story. Conversely, the record indicated strongly that the prosecuting witness had not been raped at all."

On September 7, 1949—nine days after the first of two riots prevented Paul Robeson from performing in Westchester County, New York—Poston, under the headline "Negro Reporter from Up North Put in 'His Place' by the South"—reported that he was turned away from the water fountain outside the courtroom; that blacks were relegated to the Jim Crow section of the courtroom; and that he was pushed and tripped by white deputies.

"You are jostled regularly on the stairs to the third floor courtroom, and finally one day two crackers suddenly jostle and trip you on the marble stairway, laughing when your glasses drop and break, admonishing you: 'Look where you're going, nigger.'"

Poston was also unable to eat at restaurants in Tavares, where the trial was held. He said black residents began bringing him and the legal team home-cooked meals.

Perhaps his most gripping account came on September 8, when he reported that he was pursued at ninety miles per hour by a "blood-thirsty mob" in three cars as he, the defendants' two NAACP attorneys, and a *Chicago Defender* reporter drove away from the court house following the guilty verdict. The white spectators were angry that one of the defendants had escaped the death penalty.

Poston chronicled the hair-raising escape through Tavares in a ninety-mile chase to Orlando as the white men pursued them in cars and a pick-up truck. "Really scared people don't think much of anything, but getting away," wrote Poston. "You try to deny the existing situation, you tell yourself 'It's only somebody trying to scare you' and you close your eyes and nurse the thought even when you know it isn't true. You curse yourself, of course. You recall that you really didn't have to be in this spot. Hadn't the city desk three times turned down your request to cover Florida's 'Little Scottsboro Case?' But, oh no, you wanted to be a big shot."

Finally, on September 14, the *Post* wrote an editorial calling on Attorney General J. Howard McGrath to step into the case. "We have informed McGrath that Poston, whose courageous on-the-scene reporting produced the memorable series published within the past week, is ready to meet with him or any Justice Department official at any hour."

A day later, a headline blared "M'Grath Calls Poston on Florida Terror." In that story, it was reported that Poston was invited to Washington to meet with the attorney general. On September 20, the *Post* reported that McGrath had launched an "intensive federal probe" into the trial, the three-day reign of terror and the murder of Ernest Thomas.

Poston, who was nominated for a Pulitzer Prize in 1949, continued to report on events throughout the South. He traveled through five southern states to report on the impact of the 1954 Supreme Court *Brown vs. Board of Education* decision that ended official segregation in public education. In 1961, Poston was nominated for a Heywood Broun Award. In 1989 he was posthumously inducted into the National Association of Black Journalists' Hall of Fame.

But the successes of journalists like Poston did not, by all indications, ease the passage into the newsroom for other black journalists. Prior to the 1960s, most African Americans in the newsroom operated as an 'only,' and the overall number at mainstream papers was still low. The first black full-time reporter for the *Mirror,* a tabloid owned by the Chandler family (which also owned the *Los Angeles Times),* was Chester Lloyd Washington. He was hired to cover superior court cases in 1949, a year after the afternoon tabloid was launched. In 1950, Marvel Jackson Cooke would become the first full-time black woman reporter at a mainstream newspaper when she was hired at the *Daily Compass,* where she was a colleague of I. F. Stone. When the paper folded, however, she was unable to find another daily newspaper job. In 1950, Carl Rowan was hired as a copy editor at the *Minneapolis Tribune,* eventually becoming a reporter and foreign correspondent.

Two years later, in 1952, Simeon S. Booker would become the first black full-time reporter for the *Washington Post.* However, as an indication of the difficulties he encountered, he was instructed not to use certain restrooms out of deference to white colleagues who didn't want to share facilities with a black man. He left a year and a half later, in June 1953, discouraged over news coverage and his inability to make a difference. He later said: "God knows I tried to succeed at the *Post.* I struggled so hard that friends thought I was dying. I looked so fatigued. After a year and a half, I had to give up. Trying to cover news in a city where even animal cemeteries were segregated overwhelmed me."[13]

For Booker, there was no getting around his race. He said he was almost arrested while covering a hold-up because police assumed he was one of the bandits. In the newsroom, he was mostly relegated to unrewarding tasks, such as obituaries and weekly roundups. "Every so often they'd give me a story," he said. "Sometimes they gave me a story on blacks." More often than not, he said, they wanted him to write critical pieces on black leaders including Mary Church Terrell, the outspoken leader who, according to Booker, "they wanted to badmouth."[14]

In 1953, Booker jumped at the opportunity to work for Johnson Publications, which was founded by John Johnson Jr. in 1945 and became the most successful African–American publishing empire in history, with publications including *Ebony, Jet,* and *Black World.* "It was more beneficial than sitting in the city room at the *Post,*" he said. In 1999, Booker was still working for Johnson Publications, based in Washington, D.C.

That same year, in 1953, the first of Chicago's four daily newspapers was integrated when Ben Holman, a brash twenty-one-year-old college graduate, was hired as a police reporter for the *Chicago Daily News* as riots continued to plague Chicago's Trumbull housing project a year after the first black families moved in. Holman, a native of Bloomfield, New Jersey, said he applied to nearly one hundred newspapers before he finally landed a position as a police reporter at the *Daily News.*

More than four decades later, Holman recalled his first day of work, when he walked into the police bureau to greet his new colleagues. "I said 'Hi,' and they all got up and literally walked out of the room," he said. "There was no veneer of the hypocrisy you get today. I sat there stunned. I sat at my desk. I didn't know what to do."[15]

For weeks Holman, the only black reporter in the bureau, was shunned by his colleagues, who, he said, would "go down the hall and get a lead and they'd come back in the newsroom and no-one ever spoke to me. I would have to check every single beat on my own. I was shocked, I was hurt, but I had come a long, long way." But Holman, who was raised by his single mother and had never known his father, was the first in his family to graduate from high school. He refused to be broken. "I was an ex-welfare kid who worked my way through college and none of these son-of-a-bitches would get to me."

Holman said he was shut out for several weeks, until one of the men broke the ice and apologized for his behavior. "He took me aside when no one was looking and said he feels rotten inside," he said. Holman said that while he was isolated in the newsroom, he always enjoyed the full support of his editors.

As a promising college student at all-black and male Lincoln University, which he entered in 1948, Holman had already decided to forgo the dreams of his mother and professors that he become a doctor, and decided instead on a career in daily journalism. He transferred to the University of Kansas, where he was the journalism school's valedictorian in 1952. As a journalism student, Holman had heard of only a handful of black journalists working at mainstream newspapers, including Poston and George Brown. Brown, a writer at the *Denver Post* and a University of Kansas alumnus, had belonged to the same Greek fraternity as Holman. Brown, who later became lieutenant governor of Colorado, had graduated a year before Holman. But blacks at mainstream newspapers were still rare. "People kept saying, 'You're crazy. Do you see any black folks working in newspapers?'" recalled Holman nearly fifty years later. "I said somebody's going to have to break this down. It may as well be me."

Upon graduating at the top of his class, Holman spent the first few weeks working as a yard boy as he awaited replies to his letters to editors around the country. Most did not bother to respond, realizing, he presumes, that he was African American. He did manage to get a reply from the *Oregonian* in Portland, Oregon, but in the end, he did not get an interview. Asked why he persisted in the face of overwhelming rejection, Holman replied: "The black press didn't pay that kind of money. And in those days, I was pretty much an intergrationsit. I believed that I ought to get as good a job as any white person. I was truly idealistic. I really did think I would live to see the day when race wasn't an issue in this country."[16]

To Holman, the white press represented the pinnacle of success. "I never gave up hope," he said. "I always felt strong, 'Don't settle for anything less. Train for the top.'" But finally, after a flood of rejections, Holman responded to an invitation to go to Chicago to meet with publisher John Johnson to discuss a position at *Ebony* magazine.

Holman said Johnson offered to pay him $40 to $50 a week as a staff writer. "I said, 'Is that all?'" Holman recalled. He said Johnson ordered him out of the building, but the two later became friends. Holman immediately followed up on letters he had sent to the editors of Chicago's four daily newspapers by calling to inform them he was in Chicago and would appreciate an interview. A week later, he was hired by the *Daily News.*

Similar stories have been shared by other black reporters who attempted to secure newspaper jobs in the 1950s. Robert Maynard, who eventually worked at the *Washington Post* and became the first black publisher of a major mainstream daily, once recalled an interview at a

White Plains, New York, newspaper. He said the interview was held late at night, when most of the news staff had already left. He said the editor told him that while he had no problem hiring him, "he didn't think his employees would accept it."[17]

Maynard said he applied to more than three hundred newspapers over a ten-year span and was turned down by all, he believed, because of his race. He said when he deleted the names of black newspapers for which he had written, he got an interview, but not the job. Throughout the 1950s and early 1960s, a long list of blacks were becoming "firsts" in the news industry, but being black was still a solitary affair.

As racial unrest simmered in cities across the country, north and south, news organizations realized the growing need to hire people who could connect with the anger festering in black communities. With the civil rights movement turning the South upside down—beginning with the Montgomery bus boycott of 1955, which was prompted by the refusal of a black seamstress named Rosa Parks to give up her seat on the bus to a white passenger—even southern papers found the need to employ black stringers. A month into the boycott by blacks, Grover Hall, editor of the *Montgomery Advertiser*, realized the action by the city's blacks warranted special attention. He called on a black reporter named Tom Johnson to find out who was leading the movement. On January 19, Johnson's profile on Martin Luther King Jr. was the first full portrait of a black person in the paper. The coverage of the bus boycott, which threatened to put the city's bus companies out of business, was the first time the paper had treated black life as a serious subject. And, once again, the employment of a black journalist was born of necessity.

During this period, the South convulsed with racial hatred and fear as blacks rose up against injustice. In the midst of the boycott, King's home was bombed. Around that same time, white students at the University of Alabama rioted against the court-ordered admission of the first African American student, which prompted the university to suspend Autherine Lucy for her own safety. King was arrested and tried for organizing the boycott, and, after a four-day trial, was found guilty and ordered to pay a $500 fine or face a one-year prison sentence. The largest segregation rally of the century was staged by the Mississippi and Alabama White Citizens Council, which brought 10,000 people to the Montgomery Coliseum, where the keynote speaker was Senator James Eastland of Mississippi. Meanwhile, the Southern Manifesto, signed by ninety southern congressmen and all but three senators—two of them Al Gore and Lyndon Johnson—pledged fierce resistance to integration, which they equated with subversion of the Constitution. A month later singer, Nat "King" Cole was attacked on stage by white supremacists during a performance in a Birmingham theater.

While many southern papers stubbornly refused to cover the movement, northern papers such as the *New York Times* took a keen interest in the racial upheaval. Not many black journalists were yet holding regular staff positions at daily newspapers, even though the prominence of journalists like Brown, Walton, and Schuyler must have fueled the ambitions of other blacks who longed for higher salaries in the white press. The movement toward newsroom integration, glacial though it was, was clearly seen as a sign of racial progress, even as black editors and publishers complained of the talent drain. Lamented *Chicago Defender* publisher John Sengstacke: "Over the years, we have been training them and they have been stealing them."

But as white newspaper and television reporters began paying closer attention to racial issues, with hordes of reporters from across the nation sent to the South to cover the growing movement, the black press began losing ground. Contributing to their decline may have been their conservative position on civil rights during a time of growing impatience with the glacial racial progress, particularly in urban areas. Many urban blacks instead turned to more outspoken papers which grabbed the militant mantle of the early black press.

The black press also had difficulty competing with the extensive coverage of the well-staffed mainstream publications, and, like the daily press, with the immediacy of television. The growing reliance of black readers on the mainstream media was eased by the hiring of black reporters to news organizations which, in hiring black reporters, sought to win the confidence of black newsmakers. In 1962, Mal Goode became the first black network correspondent when he was hired by ABC. CBS and NBC soon followed suit, hiring Benjamin Holman and Bob Teague, respectively, as network correspondents. "ABC had Mal Goode, NBC had Bob Teague. CBS had to have their black too," quipped Holman, who went to the network just months after taking a job at WBBM-TV,

Chicago's CBS affiliate. In quick succession, he had integrated the *Chicago Daily News*, WBBM, and then CBS. He said that the day he left WBBM, "They said they had to hire another black. 'We need another Negro.' It was strictly tokenism. You had to have your token Negro."

At CBS, Holman was among the reporters dispatched to Birmingham in 1963 to cover the bombing by white supremacists of the Sixteenth Street Baptist Church which killed four black girls. He was teamed with Dan Rather, the network's Atlanta correspondent. He said when they arrived in Birmingham, he was turned away from the hotel where the rest of the television crew was staying. Instead, they placed him in the modest hotel where Martin Luther King Jr. had stayed. "Dan took it worse than me," Holman said, referring to Rather. "He was staying at a beautiful downtown hotel and I was staying at a little motel. . . . Everywhere we went, they would not put me up. As the correspondent, I was in charge but the first thing they wanted to know was whether I was a servant or the driver."[18] He added, "The [station] V.P. called me and said if it gets too bad, come home."

Elsewhere, blacks were trickling onto the staffs of daily newspapers and local television stations. Robert McGruder was hired in 1963 to work for the *Journal Herald* in Dayton, Ohio.

That same year, Steven Duncan, the Newark bureau chief for the *Baltimore Afro-American*, became a reporter for the *World Telegram and Sun* in New York. "I had just gotten married and I needed more money," Duncan said. He joined Dale Wright, the paper's first black reporter who had been an editor for *Jet* magazine and who eventually left the *Telegram and Sun* to work for Governor Nelson Rockefeller. In 1964, McGruder left the *Journal Herald* and became the first black reporter at the *Cleveland Plain Dealer*, which had been pressured by black leaders to integrate its staff. In 1966, as riots engulfed Cleveland, McGruder was there on the front lines to cover them. That same year, Duncan was hired by the New York *Daily News* as the momentum toward integration mirrored the growing unrest in urban America.

The black press, then, became a victim of the very integration it had so vigorously advocated. With the crumbling of segregation came the hemorrhaging of talent from black newspapers, coupled with a decline of black patronage and advertising revenue. Newspapers that were well written and staffed with national correspondents increasingly became thinly staffed and poorly written, with an overreliance on crime stories, news wire reports, and government press releases that lacked relevance. By 1970, many black newspapers were only a shell of their former selves. At the *Chicago Defender,* the circulation, which had reached a high of 257,000 in 1945, sagged to 33,000 by 1970. At the *Baltimore Afro-American,* circulation dipped from 137,000 in 1945 to 28,000 in 1970. And at the *Pittsburgh Courier,* circulation dropped from 202,000 in 1945 to 20,000 in 1970. As their numbers dropped, the more militant papers published by the *Black Panthers* and the *Nation of Islam* gained a wide readership. In 1970, the *Black Panther* claimed a weekly circulation of 100,000, and *Muhammad Speaks,* 600,000.[19] By the late 1990s, many of the legendary papers were struggling to survive or had already folded. In 1998, the *Call and Post,* which had been Cleveland's black voice since 1919, joined a long list of black papers that folded. Other legendary newspapers, like the *Chicago Defender,* were struggling to survive.

In New York, the historically significant *Amsterdam News* was a bare bones operation, dominated by press releases and society and church news. In contrast to its staff of widely regarded writers and national correspondents of the past, in 1999 the paper had just one full-time staff writer and operated from an antiquated newsroom. In a city of some two million blacks, its circulation hovered around 26,000, down from 58,905 in 1977. The *Chicago Defender,* along with the *Tri-State Defender,* the *New Pittsburgh Courier,* and the *Michigan Chronicle,* all owned by the Sengstacke Enterprise group, were left reeling from the $4 million in estate taxes levied against it following the death in 1997 of John Sengstacke. The *Defender's* mid-1940s circulation of 300,000 was down to 25,000. Sengstacke's flagship paper no longer attracted such luminaries as Langston Hughes and Ida B. Wells who had been regular contributors. In 1999, the Sengstacke group was working feverishly to raise money to hold on to the papers without selling them.

Meanwhile, by the late 1990s *Emerge,* the nation's only black news magazine, had captured the irreverence and militancy of the early black press, but, like other news-oriented publications, struggled to gain a readership. In 1999, circulation for the eight-year-old monthly hovered around 160,000, despite a population of some 20 million African Americans nationally and the magazine's biting editorial edge. A 1994 cover story on Clarence Thomas, for example, portrayed him wearing a kerchief on his head, in a derisive reference to a handkerchief head, which, in the parlance of blacks, mean's a sellout. *Emerge* contributors include some of the most high profile journalists in the country, including *Time*'s Sylvester Monroe, *Newsweek*'s Vern Smith, and a host of writers from the *New York Times* and the *Washington Post*. Often, these writers had submitted articles their own white-centered news organizations would not publish. The editor, George Curry, was a former *Chicago Tribune* bureau chief. But in 1994, there were already tremors over the bottom line. Owned by Black Entertainment Television, the public cable company founded by Robert Johnson, it was losing $1 million a quarter.

Many blacks, like whites, were increasingly turning to the entertainment media, with magazines like *Ebony* boasting a nearly two million circulation. But still, the need for a black press persisted. Even in its decimated state, the black press highlighted issues that the white press ignored or underplayed. In 1989, for example, the *Amsterdam News* ran 104 consecutive front-page editorials calling for the resignation of Edward Koch, a popular mayor who was nonetheless viewed by many in the city's African American community as insensitive to their needs. The editorials helped galvanize black voters against Koch and set the stage for the upset victory of David Dinkins, the city's first black mayor. At its best, the black press provided and continues to provide the most definitive social history of the African American experience. But as the civil rights movement gave way to convulsive urban unrest in the North, the black press became a victim of its own advocacy as the mainstream media began hiring black journalists to tap into the fury that was gripping black neighborhoods.

Ben Bradlee arrived at the *Washington Post* as deputy managing editor for national and international affairs on August 1, 1965, ten days before the Watts riots. At the time, several black journalists were already on staff, including Jesse Lewis and Dorothy Gilliam, who was on leave, and Bill Raspberry, who that year was feted as Journalist of the Year by the National Press Club. A year later, his column in the *Post* became nationally syndicated.

Others, including Booker, Luther Jackson, and Wallace Terry, had, as legendary *Washington Post* editor Bradlee wrote in his memoir, "moved on after comparatively short stays on the horns of their own painful dilemmas." Bradlee noted that they were treated suspiciously by black activists and "denied the years of training and experience which would have made them truly competitive."[20] (The latter point may have been overstated, as Clint Wilson points out in *Black Journalists in Paradox*, since many black journalists were highly educated and honed their skills at high-quality black papers.) But Bradlee acknowledged that racism was a significant barrier to their progress. Referring to the period between 1965 and 1971, Bradlee wrote: "I was not sensitive to racism or sexism, to understate the matter. The newsroom was racist. Overtly racist in a few isolated cases; passively racist in many places where reporters were insensitive and unsensitized. This racism would slowly and painfully subside, if not vanish, over the next ten years. But at the time, such racism at the *Post* (and other papers) stood in the way of excellence."[21]

Robert Maynard, the esteemed black journalist, said that most black journalists owed their jobs to the terrifying, televised images of the Watts riots, which resulted in millions of dollars in property damage and thousands of casualties. More precisely, he attributed the hiring of blacks to the image of an overturned, burning KNXT news mobile unit that had been broadcast around the country on August 11, 1965.

"It was that frightful scene in south central Los Angeles that made most editors across the country aware for the first time that there might be an imperative for even the token desegregation of their newsrooms. Something like that incident would occur in nearly every major city in which there was an uprising. The smart editors had received the earlier message from Watts and had a black reporter or so in place. The slower ones promoted a copy aide, a librarian's assistant, in one instance a circulation truck driver. . . . In hardly any instance was their assignment to sit in the office and interpret what was happening and help answer the complaint of the Watts residents by explaining this riot. No, the job was to blend with the crowd and report back to the office so that others could write a story they had not in most instances witnessed and whose causes they could only dimly perceive."[22]

Thus, even as their numbers grew in the mainstream, black journalists were often not integrated into the hierarchy of news decisions, nor were they playing lead roles in much of the coverage. More often than not, they were feeders, providing information from the frontline, while white reporters were spared the danger of entering urban war zones.

With riots spreading like wildfire in black urban neighborhoods across the country, including Newark, Detroit, and Harlem, President Lyndon Johnson, in 1967, commissioned a panel, led by Senator Otto Kerner, to study the nation's racial problems. Part of their charge was to examine the role the media played in fueling the unrest. The findings of that study would trigger the most dramatic hiring of black journalists to date.

THREE

The Bumpy Road into
the Newsroom

Our nation is moving toward two societies, one black, one
white—separate and unequal.
> —The National Advisory Commission
> on Civil Disorders, 1968

The findings in March 1968 of the National Commission on Civil Disorders exploded like a bomb at news stands around the country. After a
year of study, the presidential panel unflinchingly blamed systemic white
racism and decades of discrimination in housing, employment, and education for the festering black rage that erupted into riots across the country. It warned that the growing racial divisions, if not addressed, could
destroy the fabric of American life. Not since the Civil War and the
Emancipation Proclamation had race been so candidly addressed on a
national level, and never before had a body with the weight of a presidential panel leveled such a searing indictment of American white racism.

The report extended its criticism to the news media, which it faulted
for their distorted and inadequate coverage of black America and race relations which, according to the panel, contributed to black alienation
and despair. In a critical chapter devoted to the media, the report said
that in reporting the unrest, the media exaggerated the degree of violence and destruction and the level of black-white confrontation. For example, it said some papers, at the height of the Detroit riot, put property
damage in excess of $500 million, when the actual figure was between
$40 and $45 million. It said television coverage in particular tended to
define the events as black-white confrontations, when almost all the

deaths, injuries, and property damage occurred in black neighborhoods. Perhaps news organizations were attempting to justify the immense coverage by finding in the story relevance for whites. They also gave greater weight to property damage, presumably because of its relevance for white property owners, than they gave to the devastating impact that damage had for the people who remained in decimated neighborhoods. Underreported was the wave of fires allegedly set by white landlords eager to flee inner-city neighborhoods and cash in on insurance policies.

While the panel addressed the role the media played in the racial unrest, its most forceful commentary was reserved for the media's daily failings where blacks were concerned. "The Commission's major concern with the news media is not in riot reporting as such, but in the failure to report adequately on race relations and ghetto problems and to bring more Negroes into journalism." The report said the disorders "are only one aspect of the dilemmas and difficulties of race relations in America. In defining, explaining and reporting this broader, more complex and ultimately far more fundamental subject, the communications media, ironically, have failed to communicate."[1]

It added: "Far too often, the press acts and talks about Negroes as if Negroes do not read the newspapers or watch television, give birth, marry, die and go to P.T.A. meetings."[2]

It said: "By failing to portray the Negro as a matter of routine and in the context of the total society, the news media have, we believe, contributed to the black-white schism in this country."[3]

The panel also condemned as "shockingly backward" the news media's record of hiring, training, and promoting blacks, and said that the claim by many editors that qualified blacks could not be found "rings hollow from an industry where, only yesterday, jobs were scarce and promotion unthinkable for a man whose skin was black."[4]

It concluded: "Along with the community as a whole, the press has too long basked in a white world, looking out of it, if at all, with white men's eyes and a white perspective. That is no longer good enough. The painful process of readjustment that is required of the American news media must begin now. They must make a reality of integration—in both their product and personnel. . . . In all this, the commission asks for fair and courageous journalism; commitment and coverage that are worthy of one of the crucial domestic stories in America's history."[5]

The Kerner report was not groundbreaking to the extent that it merely echoed the criticism African Americans had directed at the news media as early as 1827, when *Freedom's Journal* was published as an antidote to the demeaning and Euro-centric portrayals of African Americans. But even coming nearly a century and a half after *Freedom's Journal*, it was striking for its unblinking candor, considering that race was rarely explored in the public sphere in such depth or with as much urgency and sensitivity to African Americans. Not since the Hutchins Commission raised the issue of stereotypical portrayals of racial minorities had a panel of influential whites so seriously examined media bias. As prestigious as the Hutchins Commission panel had been, it could not compete in prominence or in magnitude with a presidential panel, particularly given the release of its findings in the midst of a national crisis. Even if whites could dismiss some of the findings as radical, no one could deny the conclusion that the news media were Euro-centric and overwhelmingly staffed by whites. Once the bias was publicly acknowledged, it would be difficult for many media executives to ignore the inherent unfairness of media apartheid, and the danger of fueling black alienation by maintaining the status quo.

For many editors and news directors, the first step was momentous: they would have to open their doors to a group of people who were more like aliens than fellow citizens. Their disinterest in, and ignorance of African Americans was evident from the kind of pervasive media coverage described by the Kerner Report. Only a handful of news organizations had, prior to the mid-sixties, ventured down the bumpy road of employing blacks, and, when they did, they rarely hired more than a token black or two. The burden to conform fell squarely on the lone black in the newsroom. In northern newsrooms, it was easier to dispatch reporters like Ted Poston south to report on blatant instances of racial injustice there than it was to expose the more subtle, but still injurious, racial injustices close to home. Increasingly, even so-called liberal northern whites were stung by charges of racism from urban black leaders, who were more confrontational and impatient than the civil rights leaders of the past. Driven by the fear brought on by violence, and in some cases by guilt, news organizations finally swung open their doors primarily to African Americans, but also to other people of color.

They would soon learn how much like changing a leopard's spots would be the task of integrating an institution that, from its inception, had been white in tone and perspective. It would not be enough to merely hire blacks. The new hires would have to be given space to assert their unique cultural values and norms, and also the freedom to reflect ideas and attitudes that could contest mainstream—meaning white—thought. The hiring of African Americans would mean that the assumptions of white America could be challenged from within the very institution that reflected and sustained America's identity as a white nation. But given the gravity of the racial crisis, metropolitan news executives knew they would have to try to build bridges to a community seething with rage.

The panel's searing observations struck a chord, if the major media's painstaking coverage of the report findings was any indication. Papers like the *New York Times* and the *Washington Post* candidly reported the panel's criticism of the media, and, in lead editorials, embraced the study's major findings. "The report of the Riot Commission splits the darkness like a flash of lightning," began the editorial in the *Washington Post* on March 3. "It is a distinguished, powerful and potentially useful document not because it presents any startling revelations or novel solutions but because it tells the truth with stark candor, exposing the hideous cancer of racial discrimination and injustice which must be excised from the American system if it is not to prove fatal to American life."

It concluded: "When this truth is genuinely and unstintingly accepted by the Nation's leadership—when it can really be made the first order of business for the American people—it may afford the margin of hope that will restore the national health."

On March 2, the *New York Times* editorial stated: "The report of the President's National Advisory Commission on Civil Disorders must have an effect on all Americans as electrifying as the summer riots that brought it into being. It is a warning that transcends all considerations of partisan or group interest—a warning that total national commitment and sacrifice in the cause of genuine racial equality is the price of America's survival as a society built on order and justice." All that is needed, said the *Times*, "is the will—and the sense of urgency—and the leadership in the nation's capital."

Action was swift and sweeping, particularly in large urban areas where minority journalists were hired in record numbers. Acel Moore, who had been hired as a copy boy for the *Philadelphia Inquirer* in 1962 was, within a month of the report, promoted to reporter. "That contributed greatly to my hiring," said Moore, who would eventually win a Pulitzer Prize and become a columnist at the Inquirer.[6] In the days following the report's release, *Inquirer* editors engaged in serious soul searching as they discussed mistakes they had made in news coverage, and looked for ways to avoid them in the future. In addition to Moore, the *Inquirer* hired several other blacks in a scene that was replicated at metropolitan newspapers and television stations across the country.

In broadcasting, minority hiring was fueled by a federal policy announced in 1968, but adopted in 1969, which held that broadcast operating licenses would not be granted to stations practicing deliberate employment discrimination. A year later, the policy was broadened to require stations to file annual reports outlining their minority recruitment efforts. Under the guidelines, stations with five to ten employees were expected to hire women and minorities at a rate of at least 50 percent of the work force. In adopting the policy, the Federal Communications Commission relied on the broad mandate of the Communications Act of 1934, which empowered the agency to protect the public interest by reflecting the tastes and viewpoints of the community it served.

The United Church of Christ, long active in the struggle to desegregate the airwaves, had petitioned for the new ruling, which the Department of Justice supported, contending that it could be a major impetus for social change. The exclusion of blacks on the airwaves both underscored and served to justify their exclusion in all public discourse. The invisibility of African Americans on the airwaves was less an omission than affirmation of their relative unimportance in the dominant culture.

In a letter to FCC chairman Rosel H. Hyde, Stephen J. Pollack, assistant attorney general in the Civil Rights Division, wrote: "Because of the enormous impact which television and radio have upon American life, the employment practices of the broadcasting industry have an importance greater than that suggested by the number of its employees. The provision of equal opportunity in employment in that industry could therefore contribute significantly toward reducing and ending discrimination in other industries."[7] Indeed, the presentation of intelligent

African Americans participating in meaningful roles in the media could begin to counter centuries of negative portrayals perpetuated by newspapers, television and radio programs, movies and in advertising.

In 1970, it was also announced that the FCC would use statistics to monitor compliance. The commission said that while statistical data for any given year would not necessarily demonstrate employment discrimination, it would be used "to show industry employment patterns and to raise appropriate questions as to the causes of such patterns."[8]

Among those to reap the benefits of this era of inclusion was Joe Oglesby, a student at Florida A&M who was hired during the summer of 1968 as a television news intern at WFLA-TV in Tampa, and John Johnson, a twenty-nine-year-old associate professor of art at Lincoln University who was hired to work in ABC News's documentary unit in 1969. But if federal policies eased their entry into the industry, the individuals themselves had to find a way to fit into a culture unaccustomed, and at times resistant, to diverse perspectives.

At ABC, Johnson was the sole black associate producer in the documentary unit, where one of the first documentaries he produced was about welfare. The series was an attempt to look at the misconceptions of welfare, including the prevailing notion that blacks were the greatest beneficiaries. After months of working on the series, which included interviews with a university professor, several U.S. senators, and welfare advocates, the package was ready to air, but, somehow, both the air tapes and the protection copies had been erased.

"They had been destroyed," Johnson said, still disturbed by the incident nearly three decades later. While an investigation into the episode found that the erasure was accidental and several people were fired, Johnson called such a possibility "remote" given the care given to avoid such mishaps. Both tapes, he stressed, had been boldly labeled and stored in the library. Johnson, who had entered journalism infused with optimism, revealed that the incident nearly "destroyed" his desire to work in the industry. "It was a catalytic experience for me," said Johnson, who had been raised to believe that—despite rigid racial barriers—with hard work, talent, and passion he could overcome racial hurdles.[9] The incident was a painful reminder that, despite Johnson's best efforts, race would continue to obstruct his path. Johnson nonetheless stayed in the business until 1997, when, at age fifty-nine, he walked away from a four-year, $3 million contract as an anchor for NBC's New York City affiliate to care for his ailing father.

During the course of three decades, Johnson would have other negative experiences that would color his view of the news industry. But the incident which most altered his perceptions of race in the news industry occurred while he was covering the 1971 Attica uprising while employed as a network correspondent. Johnson was among those present during negotiations between prison officials and inmates, and he was there during the uprising, when he witnessed the killing of inmates. During the ordeal, Johnson was pepper gassed and said a white guard at one point pointed a gun at him while yelling, "Nigger! Nigger! Nigger!"

Johnson said he pleaded with the guard not to shoot and managed to escape the anarchy. But when he reported his harrowing experience, ABC News, he said, chose not to broadcast his report, including his account of the slaughter of prisoners by the guards. Early on, Johnson had questioned the other reporters' allegations that they had witnessed inmates slitting hostages' throats, something Johnson said he never saw.

What he did see, however, was a full-scale massacre by the guards. "But it was hard to take a black man's word," he says.

The specific reason why ABC failed to broadcast Johnson's account is not known. But the network did send other reporters to the scene, and Johnson said his credibility was called into question. While Johnson was questioned by his own network, he was interviewed by other news services about his eyewitness account. His experience inside the prison walls was also featured some twenty-five years later in the PBS documentary *Eyes on the Prize*. In it, an emotional Johnson is shown reporting on the uprising, still shaken from his harrowing ordeal. And Johnson's contention that the guards, and not the prisoners, were the aggressors was later borne out by investigations which showed that all of the dead and injured were victims of the guards, not the inmates.

"In the early days, it was a constant state of proving oneself," recalled Johnson, who ended his career as one of New York City's most popular newsmen, having worked at all three network affiliates. "I said to myself, 'My God, if the people in the news business have negative attitudes towards blacks and minorities, how is there going to be fair representation of who we are?'"[10] The question is particularly troubling in a society that routinely characterizes the men and women in the media as liberal. Given that perception, many white Americans are prepared to dismiss the heartfelt stories of racial anguish by successful African Americans as either bellyaching, hypersensitivity, or insincerity. This is particularly true since many whites will never reach the level of success enjoyed by Johnson, and therefore have little sympathy for his plight. While the burden of race falls most often on blacks, it is often assumed by whites that their race served as a ladder rather than a hurdle.

Johnson's experiences in the North would pale compared to those endured by black journalists in the South, where civil rights activists waged a fierce battle against segregated airwaves. FCC policies, coupled with a decades-long effort by civil rights activists in Jackson, Mississippi, resulted in the hiring, in 1972, of the nation's first black news director. When William Dilday entered the troubled Jackson market as news director of WLBT-TV, the station had a checkered history and was the target of several lawsuits over the years for espousing segregationist policies and for discrimination in programming.

Jackson's African American community had complained that the station openly advocated segregation while refusing to air opposing views by civil rights organizations. The first complaint against the station was filed in 1955 by the NAACP, which claimed WLBT deliberately cut off a network program about race relationships on which NAACP general counsel Thurgood Marshall appeared. A sign flashed across the screen, alerting readers: "Sorry, Cable Trouble." Two years later, another complaint was filed by civil rights activists after the station broadcast a program advocating the maintenance of racial segregation, then refused requests to present opposing viewpoints. The Office of Communication of the United Church of Christ began monitoring the station to accumulate evidence that it was using the public airways to promote segregation while ignoring the views of the community's African Americans, who comprised 40 percent of the population.

One of its findings in 1962 was that the station broadcast editorials and advertisements sponsored by the Jackson White Citizens Council supporting segregation at the University of Mississippi while refusing to allow opposing views to be aired. WLBT-TV responded that it refused to broadcast pro-integration positions in order not to provoke violence. The church became one of the groups that finally challenged the station's FCC license renewal on the grounds of discrimination.[11]

While a license renewal hearing was required in light of the petition, the FCC renewed the license without a hearing, saying that the petitioners would not suffer economic injury as a result of the renewal. However, it granted a one-year license, as opposed to the customary three, and required station officials to meet with local civil rights groups.

The United States Court of Appeals for the District of Columbia Circuit ordered a hearing, while determining that all listeners had standing to file petitions to deny a license. "A history of programming misconduct of the kind alleged would preclude, as a matter of law, the required finding that renewal of the license would serve the public interest," the court found.

The FCC still proceeded, however, to grant a three-year renewal of WLBT's license, saying that it had indeed served the public interest. But in a landmark ruling in 1964, the District of Columbia Circuit Court ordered the agency to revoke WLBT's license, upholding the requirement for broadcasters to serve their local community. Despite a series of legal challenges, the petitioners prevailed when, in 1969, the FCC was ordered by the Court of Appeals to revoke the station's license, which it did on December 3, 1969. With WLBT's license revoked, interim control was granted to the locally based Communications Improvement Inc., which, after a series of legal challenges, eventually hired Dilday to manage the station.

Dilday made dramatic changes during his first six months, hiring minorities into key posts and covering issues of concern to Jackson's black community. Before Dilday's arrival, no one had addressed inferior medical facilities and housing conditions in black communities. Dilday, plucked from a Boston station where he was the public relations director, quickly provoked the wrath of Jackson's white community with his on-air editorials, in one of which he lashed out at the governor for vetoing a bill that would have earmarked $8 million to open community health centers in poor, rural areas. By the time he concluded the editorial, the switchboard lit up, with many whites demanding the station to take Dilday off the air. For months, Dilday said he received threats on his life and harassing letters and phone calls, and he was monitored by the Federal Bureau of Investigations. But in a year and a half, Dilday built WLBT into the market's number one station, attracting more than a million prime-time viewers from parts of

Mississippi, Louisiana, and Alabama. In that time, he also oversaw the coverage of stories that garnered major journalism awards, including the prestigious Peabody Award.

These sobering experiences aside, the number of minorities in broadcasting increased to 9.1 percent by 1970, according to Federal Communications Commission statistics. But these gains did not come without vigilance by the FCC and various civil rights organizations as white broadcasters were resistant to government-sanctioned racial inclusion. Prior to the federal mandates, however, the same broadcasters obviously found little reason to change on their own. A number of measures adopted by the FCC intended to enhance minority hiring efforts—including a ten-point program in 1977 which required licensees with more than fifty full-time employees to file detailed employment profiles—were challenged by the National Association of Broadcasters, which argued that the guidelines were discriminatory and unrealistic. The broadcasters were unsuccessful in their federal court challenge.

Meanwhile, the progress in newspapers, where no such federal hiring policies were in place, was not nearly as great. Between 1968 and 1978, the percentage of minorities—who, prior to Kerner, were primarily black—increased fourfold, from less than one percent to 3.9 percent.[12] Many of these minority hires were graduates of the handful of programs that were aimed at minority training, a response to the still common refrain that qualified minority journalists could not be found. This claim, as explored in the previous chapter, ignored the legions of well-educated, experienced, and talented black journalists who worked at high-quality black newspapers across the country. Many were unemployed or underemployed as a result of the sharp circulation declines at black weeklies, intensified by the growing competition from the mainstream media's intense coverage of the civil rights movement and the increasing popularity of television.

Even so, a number of programs aimed at minority training were established. Among the most ambitious was an eight-week summer program founded and directed by Fred Friendly at Columbia University and funded with a $250,000 Ford Foundation grant. The program had twenty-two graduates in 1969 and thirty seven in 1970, the year Friendly chided his colleagues at an American Society of Newspaper Editors meeting. Noting that no blacks were on the panel, he said, "We come here where the agenda is set for the American newspaper people, and there is a deficiency in black voices, in young voices."[13]

One of the early graduates of the program was Joe Oglesby, who in 1968 had interned at WFLA in Tampa, and a year later, while in his junior year at Florida A&M, was an intern at the *St. Petersburg Times.* Oglesby was the only black intern of twenty selected from around the country, and he was one of five who received scholarships to complete their final year of school. Upon graduating, Oglesby was offered a full-time position at the paper provided he completed the summer program at Columbia. Oglesby, who in addition to his news internship at the paper and at the television station was also editor of his weekly college newspaper, jumped at the opportunity. He harbored no resentment that several white interns were hired without additional training.

"The way I looked at it, it was a great opportunity," reasoned Oglesby, who joined the second class of Friendly's summer program, which continued to train minority journalists until 1974.[14] While the training of minorities was the primary objective of the program and it enabled minorities who—unlike Oglesby—had no prior journalistic training to enter the field, programs such as these were also symbolically significant. For the first time, minorities were being summoned into a profession that had routinely excluded them.

In 1975, a grant by Gannett enabled a group of journalists, led by Robert C. Maynard, a *Washington Post* national correspondent and later its ombudsman, and Earl Caldwell, a *New York Times* reporter, to reestablish the program at the University of California at Berkeley. Renamed the Institute for Journalism Education, the program was directed by some of the African American pillars of mainstream journalism, including Maynard, Ellis Cose, and *Washington Post* columnist Dorothy Gilliam. By 1979, the program claimed that its 120 graduates represented 10 percent of all minority journalists employed at daily newspapers.

Meanwhile, other programs aimed at minority training were launched by a number of news organizations and press institutes, including the American Press Institute, the Poynter Institute, the Gannett Center for Media Studies, Times Mirror, and Knight-Ridder. Many of the incoming minority journalists graduated from these programs, joining papers with only a handful of black, Latino, and Asian journalists. When Oglesby was hired by the *St. Petersburg Times* as a full-time reporter in 1970, he joined two other minorities, Peggy Peterman and Sam Adams. For the South, during that time, three blacks on the same paper was remarkable.

"You could look all over the South and not find that," Oglesby said, crediting Nelson Poynter, publisher of the progressive paper that aggressively covered the civil rights movement and championed desegregation long before other papers in the region.[15]

Augmenting these programs was the increase in the number of African Americans studying journalism in college. In 1968, under 2 percent of the 24,000 journalism majors in U.S. colleges and universities were black. At the time, blacks comprised about 11 percent of the U.S. population.[16] By 1978, the percentage of blacks studying journalism more than doubled, with African Americans comprising 4.6 percent of the 61,000 undergraduate journalism students.[17]

Given the dramatic inclusion of minorities in the newsroom and the hiring of pioneers like Dilday, it was easy to hail the obvious signs of progress in the news industry, particularly given the homogeneous picture prior to the Kerner report. It was far more difficult to comprehend the anger of some of the journalists who seemed to be excelling. While many focused on the growing number of minorities, few recognized the rockey transition into the mainstream, particularly for African Americans, who historically have had difficulty being absorbed into white cultural institutions. The unspoken expectation was for blacks and other minorities to fit into an established culture that was not expected to bend to accommodate them. So even while the new arrivals were not greeted in the blatantly discriminatory manner of their forebears in the 1940s and 1950s, some bitterly complained that they were expected to leave behind any traces of their culture and ethnicity and adopt the mannerisms and attitudes of whites. The consequences for those who would not conform could be severe. Kerner-inspired hires like Karen Howze, a graduate of the University of Southern California's journalism program, says her early years were spent undervalued and underutilized, with few opportunities to do the kind of important stories she had envisioned. "Their attitude was just wait until we need you for the next riot," said Howze, one of two black reporters at the *San Francisco Chronicle* in 1972.[18] That year, the American Society of Newspaper Editors counted 253 minority journalists, and estimated that 300 existed at mainstream newspapers across the country. Many were already voicing their frustration over their inability to make a difference at their respective newspapers.

Howze covered police and crime and made the most of the mundane aspects of it by paying close attention to municipal court. After her request to be moved to civil court was denied, she enrolled in law school while working the police beat at night and on weekends. When she graduated in 1977, she again requested to cover civil court, but again her request was denied. "They ended up assigning it to someone who didn't want it," she complained.

On television, the issues affecting African American journalists moved well beyond news content. There was the requirement for African Americans to mimic whites not only in their behavior and attitudes, but also in appearance. As such, the African Americans on television spoke in the same clipped diction as their white counterparts and bore no traces of African American culture in their mannerisms or appearance. These became, for some black viewers, a source of contention and alienation, although most accepted the affectations of black television journalists as prerequisites for middle-class achievement.

But while their speech and mannerisms conformed to the dictates of television, some African Americans attempted to assert their African American uniqueness in other ways. Melba Tolliver was a young television reporter at New York City's ABC-TV affiliate when she was assigned to cover the White House Rose Garden wedding of Tricia Nixon, the president's daughter. But the day before she was to travel to Washington to cover the wedding, Tolliver showed up at work with her hair styled naturally in an Afro, which, particularly during the 1970s, was both fashionable and associated with the "Black Power" movement. Some thus equated the hairstyle with a political statement. But the simple fact is that the Afro is the natural state of hair for most people of African origin. Just as most white women were not required to process their hair with chemicals, or transfigure its texture with hot irons or perm rods as a condition of their jobs, some blacks began to see their natural hair as a logical and esthetically acceptable option. When Tolliver appeared at work, the producer, clearly surprised by her new hairdo, called the news director at home, who summoned Tolliver to the phone. "He asked 'would I like it?'" Tolliver recalled. Tolliver replied that he should watch the show and see for himself. Once he did, Al Primo told her the hairstyle did not look feminine, and that she should change it. He told her that if she did not, she could not be shown in the film footage doing stand-up.[19]

Tolliver proceeded with her travel to Washington, D.C., to cover the wedding. Once there, she and the cameraman disobeyed Primo's orders and included her image in the footage of Tricia Nixon's wedding. However, Tolliver was told that her scheduled appearance the next morning on a morning local show, "A.M. New York," was canceled. Upon her return, she was summoned to a meeting with the vice president and general manager for news and the news director, where both insisted that she straighten her hair. Implicit in their dictate was that only those hairstyles that conformed with European sensibilities and esthetic ideals were appropriate for television newswomen.

During a series of meetings that followed, the two men, according to Tolliver, suggested that even a scarf or hat would be preferable to her closely cropped Afro. In the end, she was told that failure to change her Afro would result in her being sent to Staten Island to cover landfills. For three days, as Tolliver dug in her heels, she was not seen on the air. "I don't recall ever having considered straightening my hair," insisted Tolliver, who, while tough before her superiors, wept in private and while relating her ordeal to friends. "That [changing her hair] would have been humiliating. It was the principle and it was the esthetic—I thought my hair looked great."[20]

The three-day deadlock was broken when, finally, a *New York Post* reporter, tipped off about the standoff, called her for comment. Tolliver declined to discuss it, saying that she was "petrified" over the prospect of media attention over what she considered a private personnel matter. "I was going to stick to it, but I was afraid of being splashed across the paper."

But the story in the *Post* provoked viewers, black and white, to write letters supporting Tolliver's right to wear an Afro. Tolliver recalls at least one viewer, who identified herself as a white woman, writing that while she did not personally like her hairstyle, she supported her right to wear it.

"It proved them wrong, that their fears were wrong," Tolliver said, referring to station executives. "They desperately feared they'd lose part of the audience because people would see me as a Black Pantherette. They were just wrong. They didn't lose ratings. They probably gained."[21]

Tolliver would later do a half-hour show on African influences on American style for the station. And, ironically, when Tolliver left Channel 7 to go to Channel 4, the NBC affiliate, the general manager wanted assurances that Tolliver *would* wear an Afro, which they intended to promote. Tolliver was not the last African American reporter to be disciplined for wearing ethnic hairstyles. Nine years after her battle, Dorothy Reed, then thirty-one and a television reporter and co-anchor at KGO-TV, the ABC affiliate in San Francisco, was suspended for two weeks for wearing her hair in cornrows. Reed decided to wear the cornrows to attend the gala opening of the San Francisco Ballet, which had, for the first time, hired a black dancer and board director. "So I wore them in celebration of the new black presence in the San Francisco Ballet," she recalled.[22]

But Reed could not have anticipated the reaction from her supervisors when she reported for work one Monday morning. As Reed recalls, her news director was "shocked" by her appearance, but he said he would reserve judgment until he saw how she appeared on air. Reed's first day at work with braids was memorable for other reasons. That Monday was President Ronald Reagan's inauguration, and also the day American hostages were released by Iran. Reed's assignment was to go to a local Iranian-owned restaurant for a local sidebar. From the scene, she was called in the car by her supervisor and told that the interview should be filmed in a way that insured that her face would not be in the footage.

At the end of the day, her manager told her the braids were unattractive, and that she should take them out.

"I was verbally warned that I had to change my hair," she recalled. But for a week, Reed did not, telling her supervisors that, at the very least, she should be given an opportunity to appear on air. All along, Reed believed that San Franciscans, known for their progressive attitudes, would accept her hairstyle. But her public would not be able to judge because by Friday of that week, Reed was called in by the news director and told that she must take the braids out by Monday or face suspension without pay.

Over the weekend, Reed consulted with Assembly Speaker Willie

Brown, friends, and colleagues as she explored her options. In her heart, Reed was wedded to keeping her braids.

"I felt they didn't have the right to tell me to do that, not without cause, without explanation. I said the issue was racism," she said.

Most people advised Reed to simply conform, given the high stakes. Recalling her talk with Brown, then the most powerful black politician in California, she said he told her, "Personally, I don't like it," referring to her braids. "If you want to do this, I'll support you, but this is the end of your career and you'll be blackballed. You know that. You'll win the battle, but, in the end, you're going to lose. Are you prepared to do this?"

Reed weighed the advice and her personal circumstances: she was a single mother, earning a substantial income in one of the largest television markets in the country. She realized the battle she was about to wage could cost her both short-term income and, in the long term, an entire career she had been building for seven years. But Reed said she also thought of all the times she had conformed, dutifully wearing tight little jackets with the station's pin affixed to her lapel and speaking in a low, unintimidating voice to please her employers. She thought of all the stories she was unable to cover because news directors were not interested in most aspects of the black experience. And she also thought of the time she spent at WTVR-TV in Richmond, when, despite having the highest ratings, she was passed over for an anchor position in 1976. She said she was told that no station in the country had a black woman anchoring prime-time news, and they weren't about to be the first. The job went to a white male.

But equally important for Reed was her own self-worth, the battles she faced overcoming white ideals of beauty, ideals that a brown-skinned woman with brown eyes and curly hair could never hope to meet. "I was always insecure about my personal beauty," she said. "This sort of attack hits you very deeply. Some people don't realize how deep an issue that is for black women." So on Monday, Reed appeared at work wearing braids.

"I had this opportunity to take a stand, to get people to look at an issue and deal with the racism. I had bitten my tongue many times. It was just the one time I said, 'No, this is as far as I'm going to go.' Everybody black I knew had taken a lot, had swallowed a lot, had compromised and compromised, and, for what? This was a chance to say, 'Look, this is what you're doing.'"

That Monday, January 26, 1981, Reed was suspended and told her hair was inappropriate and distracting. Unlike Tolliver, Reed took her fight with her employer to the media, telling reporters that the incident was "a case of white male-dominated management deciding how I should look as an acceptable black woman."[23] She told reporters that the hairstyle "gives me a tremendous amount of pride and reflects my heritage," and she enlisted the support of the local chapter of the NAACP, which accused the station of racism and staged several demonstrations outside the station offices. Reed also filed a grievance with her union, the American Federation of Television and Radio Artists.

Over the next two weeks, several hundred people marched in protest, and the story garnered front-page headlines. Inside the newsroom, Reed's colleagues were divided, and some were extremely angry over the negative publicity she had brought to the station. For two weeks her telephone rang incessantly as she granted an endless stream of interview requests. "The stress was overwhelming," she said. "I couldn't sleep. The interviews, going over it, over and over again. I have tremendous sympathy for people who get dragged into the public light. I had no idea it would become the issue that it did."

After two weeks in the center of the maelstrom, Reed, with the help of the union, reached a settlement with the station. The station agreed to pay her for the time she was suspended if she dispensed with the colorful beads adorning her hair. She returned two weeks later on air with the braids, but no beads.

On the Monday that she was to return, the general manager asked her to meet him at a local hotel for breakfast so they could walk into the newsroom together as a sign that the issue was behind them. He warned her that she might face some hostility from colleagues, but even that did not prepare her for the cold reception that awaited her. In addition to the hostile stares and stony silence of some of her peers, Reed returned to a ton of mail, some of it chilling and epithet-laced. She was called a nigger and told to "go back to Africa. "Really, really ugly racist things were written and it scared me enormously," said Reed. "And the mail kept coming. It's like everyday, somebody calling you a nigger. That's what it was like for those months."[24]

And even with the settlement, Reed knew that her days at the station, and in the industry, were numbered. She had a standard twenty-six-week contract, which would expire that September. Once it expired, she was simply told the station was exercising its option, and she was, without cause, let go.

"I knew that the station would let me go as soon as the station felt comfortable," she said.

Reed, who in 1998 was in an English doctoral program while teaching at the State University of New York at Stony Brook in Long Island, never sought another job in television. "I knew that was the end. I don't think people like to be called racist. I was seen as a troublemaker."

She wrote freelance articles, earned a master's degree, and, in 1991, was hired as news director at KBLX Radio, where she worked from 1991 through 1996, making less than half of what she earned on television. More traumatic than the loss of a career and lifestyle was the illness that beset her following her ordeal. She was diagnosed with lupus, an illness that progressively worsened, and which Reed attributed to her stressful ordeal at work. For a year after leaving the station, Reed was unable to work. But even given the toll that the episode had on her life, Reed said her only regret was not filing a lawsuit.

"When I look back on it and look back on the pain and suffering, my illness became so much worse. I suffered in a way that could be documented. But also, when I was let go, I could have demanded a reason. I didn't have to let that go but at that point it was so painful I just wanted to get away from it."

Reed insisted that she would do the same all over again. "I don't know many other reporters who have a chance to say those things. I had the cameras on me. You have the opportunity to take a stand, to get people to look at an issue and deal with the racism."

But whether her battle made a substantive difference in television news is open to debate. Most television reporters still conform to white ideals of beauty, although that is slowly changing, with notable exceptions like ABC News's Farai Chideya, who wears twists, and Michelle McQueen, whose hair is styled in a short Afro. Reed noted her satisfaction in seeing Charlayne Hunter Gault of PBS occasionally wear braids. But it is important to Reed that the episode made a difference to Bay Area blacks. "I know when I die, it will be 'Cornrow Lady died,'" she said.

"I don't regret it at any stretch, but I had no idea how high the price would be. It was extraordinarily traumatic. You're talking about trauma."

A month after Reed waged her battle, Max Robinson, the dashing newsman who in 1978 became the first African American to anchor a network news program, ABC's "World News Tonight" with Peter Jennings and Frank Reynolds, caused a stir in a now famous speech he made at Smith College in Northampton, Massachusetts, on February 8, 1981. Robinson reportedly told his audience that the news media were a "crooked mirror" through which white America viewed itself. He said that "only by talking about racism, by taking a professional risk, will I take myself out of the mean, racist trap all black Americans find themselves in."[25]

Robinson also complained that he and other black journalists had been excluded from covering the presidential inauguration and the hostage crisis. He later said he did not mean to single ABC out for criticism, and ABC later countered that three black reporters had worked on those stories. But as a result of Robinson's stinging criticism, it came to light that only four of the network's sixty five correspondents were black. The other networks, NBC and CBS, reported that they each employed eight black correspondents.

According to reported accounts of the speech, Robinson said the network expected him to "speak like any old white boy," and not incorporate his unique cultural perspective into his work.

In spite of his meteoric rise from a top-rated news anchorman in Washington, D.C., and Chicago to a network anchor, Robinson continued to be an outspoken critic of racism in and out of the news industry. Throughout his short and sparkling career, Robinson, one of the founders of the National Association of Black Journalists, served as mentor to scores of African Americans in the newsroom and seemed always consumed by the nation's racial problems. Near the end of his life he would say that he was plagued by feelings of deep-seated insecurity. "I think one of my basic flaws has been a lack of esteem," he told a *Washington Post* reporter months before his death. "I never could do enough or be good enough. And that was the real problem."[26]

But none of these insecurities were evident as he read the news in his commanding, charismatic style, becoming, for many blacks, the embodiment of black pride and professional integrity. Robinson's talent was already apparent during his senior year in all-black Armstrong High School in segregated Richmond, Virginia, when, in 1957, he was voted "Boy Most Likely to Succeed." He attended Oberlin College on an academic scholarship but soon dropped out. After a number of odd jobs, he landed a position in 1964 as a newsreader on a UHF station in Portsmouth, Virginia, where he read the news off camera during station breaks while the screen said "News."

One day, Robinson convinced the cameraman to remove the slide so that he can be seen on air. The next day, he was called in and fired after irate callers complained about the black man on the television. The following year, he was selected for a trainee program at WTOP in Washington, D.C., where he initially was the floor director, responsible for erecting sets, cueing the talent, and cleaning the studio. One day, during a visit by John Hayes, the president of Post-Newsweek Stations, program director James Silverman secretly tested him.

He asked Robinson to read the newspaper for a microphone check. Both men were awed by his telegenic looks, authoritative and smooth delivery, and resonant voice. They immediately transferred him to the news division where, in 1965, he held his first reporting position. A year later, he was lured to WRC, the competing station, where he became its first black reporter, winning six awards, including a national Emmy for a series on life in the black Anacostia district. In 1969, he returned to WTOP, becoming the first black newsman to anchor a local television news program. He reigned over the local ratings until his departure for the network job in 1978.

Robinson's tenure at ABC News was marked by both his soaring achievement as a newsman, covering high-profile stories including the 1980 political conventions, and his tragic fall five years later. Robinson privately battled depression and alcohol abuse, while he publicly battled the pressure of being a pioneer with the weight of race on his back. He was often torn between his role as a network television icon who was expected to conform and avoid controversy, and his outrage over racial injustice both within and outside the news industry. He often complained about the portrayals of blacks, and about the exclusion of a black view-

point in the newscast. He was once quoted as saying: "I remember someone saying to me that I wasn't a team player. And I said, 'I'd be happy to play on the team if the rules were not structured against me and my people.'"[27]

By the time Robinson made his "Crooked Mirror" speech at Smith College in 1981, the signs of personal problems were already apparent. Colleagues said he sometimes showed up for work intoxicated or failed to show up at all. By the end of his life, he admitted he had battled alcohol abuse and depression throughout his career.

Following publication of his remarks at Smith College, Robinson was summoned to New York for a three-hour meeting with Roone Arledge, president of ABC at the time. While Robinson told Arledge he was quoted out of context and misrepresented, the reported remarks, for many in the industry, had the ring of authenticity, and the short-term damage to ABC, and long-term damage to Robinson's career, had been done. Compounding his woes, some of the people who had been heartened by his candor expressed disappointment in Robinson's attempt to distance himself from the remarks.

Dorothy Gilliam, a black columnist at the *Washington Post*, wrote: "If we must totally check our cultural and historical identities at the doors of our workplace, how much do we really bring to these workplaces?" she said, equating Robinson's $210,000 a year job with a "cultural straight-jacket."[28] Robinson was, then, unable to please blacks who encouraged his expressions of outrage, or whites who expected his silence.

Two years after his "Crooked Mirror" remarks, Robinson's fate at the network was all but sealed when he failed to appear at the funeral of *Worlds News Tonight* colleague Frank Reynolds, where he was to sit next to First Lady Nancy Reagan. Two months later, Peter Jennings was named the sole anchor and senior editor of *World News Tonight*. Robinson ended his career at ABC doing weekend reports and some reporting. In 1984 his descent was complete when he left ABC to become co-anchor of the NBC affiliate in Chicago. He left the station several months later, citing exhaustion, and checked into a Cleveland hospital for alcoholism and depression. He died four years later after secretly battling AIDS.

Several thousand people attended Robinson's funeral, where he was celebrated for so valiantly using his vaulted position to raise issues of racism in the industry. Many of the lions of journalism, including Dan Rather, Peter Jennings, Roone Arledge, Ed Bradley, Bernard Shaw, and Sam Donaldson paid their respects. He was eulogized by the Reverend Jesse Jackson, who, following his 1984 and 1988 presidential races, was arguably the most prominent black American. "Max Robinson never adjusted," Jackson said. "He was not a TV thermometer who measured things and spilled them back out. He tried to be a thermostat—to change the temperature."[29]

While a long line of journalists had also left the industry because of a similar inability to adjust, perhaps none left as tragically, or publicly, as Robinson. The vast majority of black journalists waged their battles for more inclusive coverage and equality in assignments and hiring behind closed doors. Their struggle was assisted by the National Association of Black Journalists, which in 1975 was formed by forty-four journalists at a meeting in Washington, D.C. Among the founders were Max Robinson, Robert Maynard; Acel Moore of the *Philadelphia Inquirer*, DeWayne Wickham of the *Baltimore Sun*, Mal Johnson of Cox Broadcasting, Les Payne of *Newsday*, Vernon Jarrett of the *Chicago Tribune*, and Chuck Stone, the *Philadelphia Daily News* columnist who was elected the first president. The founders also included members of the black press, such as *Essence* editor Marcia Gillespie.

Many of the founders had met one another while covering national conventions of civil rights organizations, or at some of the private briefings with black reporters convened by Urban League chairman Whitney Young. NABJ would do what no other minority press association had done, and that was to walk a racial tightrope in which they took on their white employers on the explosive issue of race while working in an industry that required neutrality. Previous minority press associations comprised men and women of the black press who could operate without concern about how their racial views would affect their job security. While NABJ focused on minority hiring, an easy priority given the paucity of black journalists, it also looked at issues of coverage and promotion.

The organization held its first conference the month before the 1976 presidential elections, and on October 2 it released a statement that underscored its advocacy role. "NABJ is disturbed by the media's benign neglect of issues affecting the black community in this campaign. Our professional colleagues . . . have only responded to the issues articulated by Gerald Ford and Jimmy Carter. Both candidates are assiduously by-passing black voters." On another point, it objected to the exclusion of blacks on a presidential debate panel. "While NABJ commends the inclusion of a woman panelist on the presidential debate we deplore the fact that the same sensitivity was not extended to blacks."[30] By 1999, the organization had some three thousand members and its conventions attracted world leaders and presidents.

In 1978, as the American Society of Newspaper Editors took stock of minority hiring in the ten years since the Kerner report, its minority committee reported that while minority hiring had been significant, it was insufficient. The committee reported that minorities, who comprised 17 percent of the population, held 3.95 percent of newsroom jobs. The report also noted that the number of minorities in supervisory positions was "pitifully small," and that 68 percent—over two-thirds of the nation's newspapers—employed no minority journalists. One-third of all minority journalists were concentrated at thirty-four newspapers.[31]

The report also noted that while the Kerner report had focused on blacks, ten years later the newspaper industry had necessarily broadened the definition of minorities to include Native Americans, Latinos and Asians. Of the 1,375 minority journalists identified in the survey, 844 were black; 300 were Hispanic; 165 were Asian; and 48 were Native American. The total number of minorities in the workforce was said to be 1,700.

Blacks, who at the time comprised roughly 10 percent of the population, were said to hold 2 percent of the newsroom jobs. Similarly, Latinos were 5 percent of the population and one percent of the newsroom workforce. Four percent of those studied held traditional management positions, and one minority executive editor and three minority associate editors were identified by the survey.

Meanwhile, the visible movement of blacks and other minorities into mainstream journalism attracted a growing number of minorities to college journalism programs. As already noted, in 1978 blacks alone accounted for 4.6 percent of the 61,000 undergraduate journalism students. But that same year, a survey by the Dow Jones Newspaper Fund found that only one in five minorities who earned journalism degrees was hired for reporting jobs between 1974 and 1978. The survey also found that their unemployment rate was nearly three times greater than that of their white peers.[32] That same year, a University of Michigan study, "Kerner Plus Ten," authored by Melba Tolliver and Professor Marion Marzolf, concluded that the drive to hire, train, and promote minorities slowed to a trickle following the decline of urban violence. The stagnation was due in part to the great number of minorities leaving the field because of their inability to make a difference. Robert Maynard, a *Washington Post* reporter and director of the Institute of Journalism Education at the time, told attendants at the Kerner Plus Ten symposium that most of the twenty five minority journalists he knew in 1968 had left the field. So while the complexion of newsrooms had changed, many of the journalists were being made to conform to the values and perspectives of news organizations that were still identifiably white. And as violence subsided, so too, it seemed, did the will to diversify newsrooms.

"Despite an early spurt in the hiring of minorities to report for daily news organizations," the report said, "by 1974 there had been a leveling off in hiring and this trend continued in 1977." It estimated that in 1977, minorities still accounted for less than one percent of the 40,000 print journalists and 3 percent of broadcast journalists.

Sobered by the industry's ten-year report card, some in the news industry acknowledged that they had not done enough to hire or fairly report on minorities. "In the matter of hiring minorities, of covering minorities, we've found a lot of excuses to do something else," John Quinn, a Gannett executive and ASNE program chairman, bluntly told colleagues that year. "We must find a way to recreate the feeling that there is a moral reason to do the right thing—to get ourselves fired up to right a wrong the same as we get fired up to right a wrong we've uncovered at city hall."[33]

Before the conclusion of its annual meeting, the ASNE board unanimously approved its minority committee's recommendations to rekindle the commitment to recruit, train, and hire minorities, and to place emphasis on increasing the number of minority executives. It also set a goal of minority employment equivalent to the percentage of minorities in the population by the year 2000, characterizing the goal as "fair and obtainable."[34]

But the high-profile push to hire minorities through job fairs, training programs, and job postings specifically calling for minority candidates created hostility in the trenches. White reporters complained that minorities—who some already assumed were less qualified—were unfairly taking jobs away from them. In essence, their fear that blacks and other minorities were taking away their jobs was well founded. Minorities were finally being hired for jobs in the news industry that had historically been reserved for whites. So the affirmative action, while unacknowledged, had for decades—even centuries—benefited whites. But contrary to perceptions that African Americans and other minorities were ill-prepared for these jobs, many were as qualified, and in some cases more qualified, than their white peers since they were being hired during a time when the industry had raised its standards. Unlike in years past, by the 1970s a college degree requirement for newsroom jobs was de rigueur. And for African Americans, the requirement was not unusual, since journalists had historically been among the most educated members of their race, attracting Harvard-educated men like Martin Delany, W. E. B. Du Bois, Monroe Trotter, and Earl Brown.

In 1978, Karen Howze, armed with journalism and law degrees, the latter earned while a reporter at the *San Francisco Chronicle*, entered the Institute for Journalism Education. She was placed at *Newsday* on Long Island to learn copyediting skills. By the end of her stint, the *Rochester Times Union* offered her a job as a special projects editor, which she accepted. Within a month, she was promoted to assistant managing editor for local news. What Howze did not realize was that the Gannett Company had made diversity a top priority, and she was hired under a plan that called for a black and a Hispanic to fill two assistant managing editor jobs. At the time, minorities held one percent of news management positions, according to ASNE figures. She learned about the company's initiative after a bulletin board announcement on her promotion noted that she was being hired under the company's "Partnership in Progress" plan.

The resentment from whites in the newsroom was palpable. "I had to spend a lot of time trying to figure out how to get these white people to work for me," recalled Howze. "I was twenty-seven and wasn't good as a manager, but I was good as a reporter and editor."[35]

Howze, for a variety of reasons, clashed with her superiors over story selections and her efforts to more aggressively cover the Hispanic community. At the time, Rochester had the state's second largest Hispanic population. "They never even acknowledged that there was a Hispanic community."

She confronted superiors over what she believed was insensitive coverage, noting that a headline on a story on the pope's visit to a Brooklyn neighborhood was "Pope Goes to Ghetto." Howze was eventually removed from her job and, during the midst of a hiring freeze, was assigned to develop an internship program. In time, Howze had alienated herself from many of her white supervisors. But she understood their resentment.

"Here I was an African American woman and someone outside of [my editor's] jurisdiction said he had to hire me," she reasoned.[36]

While the assumption of racial preference trails most black journalists, even in newsrooms where there are few, there cannot even be an assumption of merit when news organizations tell their white workers someone was hired because they are black, or Hispanic, or Greek. But assumptions of inferiority are continually fueled by suggestions that blacks need not be as qualified as whites to succeed. Conversely, whites have not borne negative consequences from the decades of blatant racial preference in the news industry and elsewhere. In all of the years that blacks were denied jobs in mainstream journalism, few if any were told the jobs they were applying for were being reserved for whites, even as they were. Even today, most whites assume other whites are hired because they are competent, not because they are white, even if minority journalists may suspect otherwise.

However damaging some of the minority recruitment efforts were to race relations in the industry, they bore results. Between 1978 and 1988, the number of minorities working in the newspaper industry more than doubled, from 1,700 to 3,900.[37] Where minorities represented 3.95 percent of the workforce in 1978, they represented 7 percent ten years later. And a handful of blacks were making major strides in the industry. One was Robert McGruder, who began his journalism career as a reporter at the *Journal Herald* in Dayton, Ohio, in 1963 before becoming the first black reporter at the *Cleveland Plain Dealer*. In 1978 McGruder became one of the first black executive editors when he was promoted to city editor of the *Dealer*. His hiring, no doubt, was inspired by the politics of the city, which for ten years had been led by a black mayor.

But by the mid-1980s, it was clear that McGruder would remain an exception and hiring alone would not sufficiently address news coverage or the hue of the work force, given the large turnover of black journalists and the small number in decision-making positions. In addition, the emphasis on minority hiring brought to the forefront the growing hostilities of white journalists, who were mirroring the backlash to affirmative action in the greater society. White journalists complained that they were being squeezed out—that they were a dying species—even as they held, twenty years after Kerner, 93 percent of newsroom jobs. It was clear that the will that had spawned the dramatic, albeit glacial, entry of minorities was fading. The industry leaders most responsible for the change could not have been inspired by the growing disillusionment voiced by the National Association of Black Journalists over the pace of hiring and the continuing stereotypical coverage.

For myriad reasons—the inability to influence coverage and to move up—minorities were leaving the field almost as quickly as new ones were being hired. In 1985, "Quiet Crisis," a ten-year survey conducted by the Institute of Journalism Education (IJE), concluded that more than 40 percent of minorities tracked in a ten-year study expected to leave the industry, largely because of a perceived glass ceiling. In that report, one unnamed black managing editor was quoted as saying: "Too many publications consider that in hiring minorities or women they satisfied the requirements they have to meet. They haven't considered the question of opportunities for the person to grow and move along." Despite aggressive minority hiring, the percentage of minorities in the media increased by less than one percent between 1980 and 1985, largely because of their high turnover rate.

Another report, "Musical Chairs: Minority Hiring in America's Newsrooms," published in 1986 by IJE, noted that about 91 percent of the senior editors hired the previous year were white, and three-quarters were men. "As much as in hiring, it is on the battleground of retention that the struggle for full parity . . . will be won or lost," argued Ellis Cose, the study's author and IJE president at the time. This battle would increasingly move from the newsroom to the courtroom as a growing number of black journalists accused their employers of racial discrimination. Just as the bloody civil rights movement and the urban uprisings had fueled the industry's will to be more racially inclusive, another kind of battle, it seemed, would have to reignite the embers.

FOUR

Slaying the Dragon

On April 15, 1987, in a verdict that rocked the news industry, a six-member federal jury determined that the New York *Daily News* discriminated against four African American journalists who, because of their race, were given less important assignments, lower salaries, and fewer promotions than their white counterparts. The jury, comprised of four whites, one Asian, and one African American, said discrimination had been proved in 12 of 23 incidents cited in a lawsuit that took seven years to wind its way through the legal system before landing in Manhattan's Federal District Court.

For the first time in history, racial attitudes in the American newsroom were put on trial, and no one was spared intense public scrutiny as charges of racism, sexual harassment, ethical breaches, and incompetence were hurled across the aisle. During a nine-week trial, the plaintiffs described a newsroom where racial epithets were freely dispensed and where African Americans were shut out of coveted posts such as the state capital, the national desk, and top editing jobs. They also claimed that the news retaliated against them after they filed their complaint.

In response, the defense portrayed journalists David Hardy, a forty-four-year-old reporter; Causewell Vaughan, a forty-four-year-old copy editor; Steven Duncan, a sixty-three-year-old assistant news editor; and Joan Shepard, a forty-five-year-old cultural editor, as mediocre malcontents who did not deserve to be promoted. The bitterly contested trial took on David-versus-Goliath proportions, and pitted the four plaintiffs and their scrappy lawyers against the mighty Tribune Company, the nation's largest general circulation newspaper, and its blue-chip law firm. As an indication of the high stakes involved, the *News*'s witness list of forty people read like a *Who's Who* in journalism. Included were legendary *Washington Post* editor Benjamin Bradlee; Thomas Winship, the former editor of the *Boston Globe* and a major proponent of news diversity; and a host of editors, reporters, and columnists from other elite news organizations, including the *New York Times* and *Newsday*.

While the *Daily News* alone was on trial, editors from around the country evidently saw the case as a test of their news organizations' own racial policies, which they were eager to defend.

"I felt like a young David going against Goliath with a sling shot," recalled Steve Duncan, one of the plaintiffs.[1] Indeed, the parallels were striking. Danny Alterman, a rumpled, self-described radical of New York's Alterman & Boop, P.C., had cut his teeth defending the Black Panthers and the Attica inmates following the prison uprising. His associates were Pia Gallegos of Alterman & Boop, and Susan S. Singer of Newark, New Jersey's Brown & Brown, P.C., whose principal was Raymond Brown, a charismatic and nationally renowned black criminal lawyer. At the eleventh hour, Brown handed the case off to his associates. Led by Alterman, the plaintiffs' team squared off against lead attorney Thomas C. Morrison of Patterson, Belknap, Webb and Tyler, whose principal partner was Harold "Ace" Tyler Jr., a well-connected former federal judge and deputy attorney general who had taken an active interest in the case. With 139 lawyers and a revenue of nearly $40 million in 1987, the firm's prominent clients included Nelson and Laurence Rockefeller.[2]

"They had unlimited resources," said Alterman of the firm that occupied two floors in a Rockefeller Center office building while Alterman and his associates toiled in a cramped office in lower Manhattan or across the bridge in Newark. "They had assistants who did all the work. We had none," Alterman complained.[3] He noted how a bevy of assistants carrying boxes and books trailed behind members of the legal team. Given the overwhelming odds, the plaintiffs, who for many black journalists became folk heroes following their victory, received little support in the heat of battle. At every turn, they were turned away—in part, they believed, because of the Tribune Company's long tentacles. "We sought help from the NAACP, the Urban League. Nobody helped us," Duncan recalled.[4] Causewell Vaughan, another plaintiff, recalls seeking the support of black elected officials, some of whom said they feared taking a public position against the *News*, whose endorsements they sought for their elections. Even the *Amsterdam News*, the city's leading black news-

W.E.B. Du Bois, the scholarly black social scientist, author, and activist who turned to journalism to voice his ideas. He founded and edited *The Crisis*, the journal of the NAACP, which during his tenure from 1910 to 1934 was the nation's most important black journal. *(Photographs and Prints Division, Schomburg Center for Research in Black Culture, the New York Public Library, Astor, Lenox and Tilden Foundations)*

Portrait of John E. Bruce, known as "Bruce Grit," a well-known turn-of-the-century journalist whose articles were published in both the black and the white press. *(Photographs and Prints Division, Schomburg Center for Research in Black Culture, the New York Public Library, Astor, Lenox and Tilden Foundations)*

FEBRUARY, 1931

REPORTER

POLICE DEPARTMENT
CITY OF NEW YORK

THE BEARER Lester A. Walton

REPRESENTING The World

is entitled to pass all Police and Fire Lines
wherever formed.

SUBJECT TO CONDITIONS ON BACK

POLICE COMMISSIONER

FIRE COMMISSIONER

CITY EDITOR

No. 1304

EXPIRES
FEB. 28, 1931

Left: Lester A. Walton's press pass for the New York *World,* February 1931. Lester A. Walton was hired to cover news and sports for the *St. Louis Globe Democrat* in 1902 and was a prominent fixture at *The World* in New York in the 1920s and 1930s. *(Photographs and Prints Division, Schomburg Center for Research in Black Culture, the New York Public Library, Astor, Lenox and Tilden Foundations)*

Right: George S. Schuyler, a prolific writer whose articles were widely published in leading mainstream publications in the 1930s and 1940s, in addition to the *Pittsburgh Courier.* By the 1960s Schuyler, then a syndicated columnist, became one of the nation's most outspoken black conservatives. *(Photographs and Prints Division, Schomburg Center for Research in Black Culture, the New York Public Library, Astor, Lenox and Tilden Foundations)*

In 1936 the legendary Ted Poston was hired by the *New York Post* where his daring coverage of the civil rights movement throughout the South won him acclaim. *(Photographs and Prints Division, Schomburg Center for Research in Black Culture, the New York Public Library, Astor, Lenox and Tilden Foundations)*

Above: Earl Brown, the former *Amsterdam News* editor whose freelance articles were widely published in leading mainstream magazines throughout the 1930s, including *Time.* In 1941 he was hired as a staff reporter at *Life* magazine. *(Photographs and Prints Division, Schomburg Center for Research in Black Culture, the New York Public Library, Astor, Lenox and Tilden Foundations)*

Left: Max Robinson became the nation's first African American network television anchor when he was hired by ABC News in 1978. *(Courtesy of Randall Robinson)*

Left: Janet Cooke, who was forced to return the Pulitzer Prize in 1981 after admitting her story was a hoax. *(Copyright 1981, Washington Post. Reprinted by permission.)*

Below: New York television journalist Melba Tolliver, shortly after she was suspended for appearing on air with an Afro in 1971. *(Courtesy of Melba Tolliver)*

Above: Bryant Gumbel, the former co-anchor of NBC's *Today Show* on the set in Africa. *(Reprinted by permission)*

Left: In 1997 Gumbel was one of the highest-paid newsmen in the country when he left NBC for CBS News. *(Copyright 1997, CBS News. Photo: Craig Blankenhorn.)*

John Johnson reporting out of Sowesto, South Africa for WABC-TV in New York. Johnson worked as a broadcast journalist for thirty years, until 1998. *(Reprinted by permission)*

paper, paid little attention to the trial, and whole weeks passed by without any mention of it. Some privately speculated that the *Amsterdam News* was afraid to antagonize *Tribune* executives, on whom it relied to help distribute the weekly paper.

However, coverage in the Brooklyn-based the *City Sun*, a plucky black weekly published by Andrew W. Cooper, more than made up for the *Amsterdam News*'s hands-off posture. The *City Sun*, a throwback to the early black press, was well written, irreverent, and steeped in the black nationalist spirit that held sway in the 1960s. The paper provided extensive and prominent stories on the case, replete with plaintiff profiles and lengthy pieces by former *Daily News* journalists, including Clinton Cox, one of the twelve original plaintiffs, who settled his case out of court before the trial. From the pages of the *City Sun* he issued a blistering attack on his former employer's treatment of black employees.

The plaintiffs also garnered the support of Gil Noble, a crusading black journalist who produced and hosted *Like It Is*, a weekly public affairs show. Broadcast on New York's ABC affiliate, *Like It Is* had won numerous local Emmy awards and scores of community citations for its ground-breaking programs on issues such as police brutality and its documentaries on historic black figures. Percy Sutton, who had come to prominence as Malcolm X's attorney and New York City's first black Manhattan borough president, also regularly highlighted the plaintiffs' plight on WLIB and WBLS radio stations, which he owned. The plaintiffs were also given air time on WBAI Radio.

But the foursome had trouble mustering the support of their black colleagues in the mainstream media. "We were looking around for witnesses," said Duncan. "A lot of them were just afraid. They probably thought we were crazy." Added Vaughan: "It was every man for himself."

The plaintiffs were particularly troubled by the way in which *News* managers had positioned Bob Herbert, one of the original members of the *News*'s disgruntled black caucus who broke from the group. Herbert, who in 1985 became a city editor and then a columnist and member of the editorial board, was held out as an example of the rewards of talent and hard work, an argument obviously intended to seriously impair the plaintiff's lawsuit. Of all the prominent journalists on the *News*'s witness list, Herbert was the one the legal team most feared.

"He was the first everything for the *Daily News*," said Alterman, noting how, in quick succession, he had, after the lawsuit was filed, become the *News*'s first black investigative reporter, editorial page writer, and city editor before getting his own column. While no one disputed Herbert's evident talent, the implication was that the four others had not risen through the ranks for reasons other than race. More than a decade later, Alterman could barely contain his resentment over Herbert's willingness to shield his employer from charges of racial discrimination. "The perception was that he had benefited from his connections with the black caucus and sold out. He reaped the benefits of the rewards and never advanced the cause," said Alterman.[5]

Herbert's support for the plaintiffs would have been admirable, indeed courageous; but the expectation for him to throw himself on the sword for four colleagues, thereby risking his own fragile advancement in the big leagues, seemed overly idealistic. While Alterman had little reason to expect Herbert's support, he had every reason to attempt to neutralize him since Herbert's testimony could have proved devastating to the plaintiffs' case. Alterman's public posture, however, belied his private fear. The judge fined him $500 for heatedly challenging the *News* to put Herbert on the stand. "They kept saying Bob Herbert was this, Bob Herbert was that," said Alterman. "I would have attempted to show he benefited from the black caucus and that there was racism at the paper that he wasn't copping to. He would say he got it all on merit. . . . He wouldn't stand up [for the plaintiffs] because he was more concerned about his self interest."[6]

Silent, too, was the National Association of Black Journalists, which took no public stance on the case. Les Payne, a founding member of the organization, said the lawsuit was widely viewed by black journalists as a personnel matter affecting four individuals, rather than as one that would send a neon message to the news industry on behalf of all black journalists. It was easier for African Americans, out of self-interest, to support actively the kind of class action challenges that galvanized journalists at other news organizations. Payne and others also pointed out that the four plaintiffs had few, if any, ties to NABJ that might have spawned greater interest in their plight.

It should also be noted that in 1987, NABJ did not yet enjoy the prominence and relative clout it would by the mid- to late-1990s, when presidential candidates and other national and world leaders addressed its convention, nor did it have a mechanism to support legal challenges by black journalists. It was only after the trial's successful conclusion that the prospect of organizational support for such litigation was considered. So, while the lack of support by NABJ appears, in retrospect, to be a glaring error of judgment, the unprecedented nature of the trial, coupled with the infancy of the organization and the nonexistent ties between the plaintiffs and the organization rendered the expectation of vigorous support impractical. Only in hindsight would NABJ recognize what their white colleagues had apparently grasped in the heat of battle: that the landmark case had implications for the entire industry.

While the plaintiffs failed to capture the imaginations and support of civil rights and journalism organizations, several prominent African Americans became actively involved in their struggle. Among them was Payne, an assistant managing editor of *Newsday*, which at the time made him one of the nation's highest-ranking black news executives. Payne, one of the founders of the National Association of Black Journalists, also wrote a weekly column, had garnered a Pulitzer Prize and a George Polk award, and during his 20-year career at Newsday was one of the industry's fiercest advocates for newsroom diversity. Sometime in 1985, Payne received a call from Raymond Brown, who was preparing the plaintiffs' court case. Brown asked Payne to provide his expertise on industry standards for promotion and performance.

Many Saturdays for nearly two years, Payne consulted Brown on every aspect of the newsroom, including the roles of the various editors, the ways in which salaries and promotions were determined, and the significance of specific assignments and beats. "I began to explain to the lawyers the industry of journalism," said Payne. "We went over the files of everyone who worked at the *Daily News*," recounted Payne, who examined the files of reporters and editors who were promoted, including their level of training and education. "We looked at theories of the case, every aspect of the case."[7]

By sifting through the personnel records, they were able to detect income and assignment disparities between black and white reporters with similar backgrounds. Payne, unbeknownst to his employer, had become an integral player in the plaintiffs' legal strategy. He was paid $100 an hour for his efforts.

But shortly before the case went to trial and after attempts by the *News* to settle out of court failed, Brown dropped a bomb by announcing he would not try the case in court because of obligations to other cases. "I was stunned," recalled Payne, who had fully expected Brown to handle the court case. With Brown out of the picture, that responsibility fell to Alterman, an experienced trial lawyer who, nonetheless, lacked Brown's charismatic presence. Alterman at the time primarily handled landlord-tenant cases and was representing Clinton Cox in a separate racial discrimination lawsuit against the *News*. The plaintiffs speculated that Brown never intended to try the case in court, but rather to settle it. Alterman said the *News* had offered Brown under $500,000 to settle the case out of court, an offer that was rejected by the plaintiffs.

From the first day of the trial, which opened on a bitterly cold day on February 9, the plaintiffs realized what they were up against. Even before the opening arguments, Alterman recalls feeling intimidated by the phalanx of *News* editors and lawyers—all polished and commanding in dark suits—on the *News*'s side of the courtroom. "Everyone was big and looked tough and confident," said Alterman. "We had a couple of people on the other side of the room. . . . We didn't get any support."

A *New York Times* article that day offered clues to the *News*'s strategy and quoted Jim Hoge, publisher of the *News*, as saying: "We're going to have to talk to the issue of competence and appropriateness for individual jobs, and we're prepared to do so." The article said the *News* will "critically question the journalistic performance and abilities" of the plaintiffs, and noted that Thomas Winship, the highly respected former editor of the *Boston Globe* with a reputation for promoting newsroom diversity, was one of its witnesses.[8]

With jury selection completed on February 9, the next day's opening arguments by *News* attorney Thomas Morrison devastated the plaintiffs and their lawyers. "We are very, very unhappy being in this court," said Morrison. He assailed the competence, and the very employability, of the plaintiffs. "The reason these plaintiffs are in court is because they cannot accept the fact that they are not as good as they think they are." The *News*, he said, "has refused to bow down to demands of the plaintiffs to be given assignments and promotions they are not entitled to." He added: "They have taken every event that happened to them in the last ten years and twisted them into the fabric of racism."

One by one, the competence and credibility of the journalists was assaulted.

"They portrayed us as some wild group of malcontents," said Vaughan. "They were punching away at our credibility, our professionalism, our employability. . . . We didn't expect it. It was quite brutal."

Said Alterman: "I could barely stand up after the opening," recounting the charts and graphs that highlighted every transgression each plaintiff had committed during the course of his tenure at the *News.* "It took the wind out of us."[9] Alterman's opening statement was passionate, but, in light of the serious assaults on the plaintiffs' credibility, predictable. "These people have had their career paths ended, their dreams shattered. Simply speaking, they didn't advance because of their race." The cry of racism had, for many, long before lost its resonance. But while the *News* had dealt a major body blow to the plaintiffs, the battle had just begun. Alterman's strategy remained the same. He would put on the stand three of the *News's* most racially inflammatory editors while counteracting the characterization of the plaintiffs with evidence of their journalistic accomplishments. He would show that despite Morrison's opening remarks, the four were more than "average" journalists who were lucky to work for the *News.* The plaintiffs hung on to the certainty that they were right. "Once I made the decision, I felt I was obligated to stay in it until the end," said Duncan.

David Hardy, the lead plaintiff in *Hardy et al. vs. The Daily News Inc.,* was more philosophical: "If black people like Fannie Lou Hamer and Muhammad Ali had the moral courage to risk life and limb, and eschew material gain, to stand for the principles of racial equality, then we had a moral obligation to carry on our struggle. After all, we only stood to lose a job."[10]

Of course, the plaintiffs also stood to lose careers they had spent years, and in the case of Duncan decades, building. His first job after graduating from the University of Illinois was with the *Argus* of St. Louis in 1952, and then with the *Baltimore Afro-American,* for which he covered the Emmett Till trial in a segregated courtroom, where black reporters were relegated to a card table off to the side. Duncan had also integrated the press table in Montgomery while covering the trial of Martin Luther King Jr. and garnered national attention by securing an exclusive interview with Cuban leader Fidel Castro. While at the *News*, Duncan taught both at Columbia University and Brooklyn College.

In 1963, Duncan secured his first job in the mainstream press writing for the *World Telegram and Sun*, a job he secured with the help of Dale Wright, the paper's first black reporter. Duncan joined the *Daily News* staff in 1969. "When I moved to New York, I didn't let the *Daily News* in my apartment because of the way they handled blacks," Duncan said. "I decided to accept the job at the *Daily News* . . . to demonstrate that there were blacks capable of holding these positions." It would prove a difficult and ultimately futile course for Duncan and scores of black journalists who not only sought to do their jobs to their best ability but also to disprove a negative: the notion of black inferiority. It was tantamount to a devoted husband having to prove he did not commit adultery. Even as the accused lived a model life, the accuser laid in wait for a transgression that would lend credence to a false premise. Duncan, like other African Americans in the mainstream media, would eventually question whether he could serve the interests of blacks while serving his white employer since, in the context of a racially polarized society, the two goals were often mutually exclusive.

In five charges against the paper, Duncan alleged that, despite his experience, he was never considered for promotion, while less qualified whites, several of whom he had supervised, were promoted over him. "Many times I didn't know these jobs were available until they were filled," Duncan testified. "I'm convinced this happened because of my race." In June 1980, after filing a grievance with the Equal Employment Opportunity Commission, Duncan was transferred from his job as a New Jersey section editor to the makeup room, which was a clear demotion. He alleged the *News* had retaliated because of the complaint.

In opening arguments, Morrison described Duncan as a "marginal, undistinguished" journalist who was "in the twilight of his career," and defended Duncan's transfer by saying the New Jersey section was scaled down and jobs were eliminated. Duncan was only promoted to assistant news editor after the case was set to go to trial.

Joan Shepard had joined the *News* staff as a general assignment reporter in 1973 after stints at *Women's Wear Daily* and WINS Radio as a consumer affairs reporter. Shepard filed eight claims against the paper, which she said refused to allow her to work on consumer and fashion stories, for which her background had prepared her. She also alleged that her editor, Dick Blood, made disparaging remarks about her race and gender. Shepard testified that he had once called her a "streetwalker" and that she was reassigned to the captions department when she protested. "In many instances, a vacancy became open and I was never told about it until it was filled," she testified. "I was never considered despite my qualifications and experience because I'm black." She said she was named cultural affairs editor only after the lawsuit was filed.

Katherine Vanzi, a white reporter at the paper from 1974 to 1980, testified that Blood had derided the qualifications of blacks at the paper. She said Blood, while he was the night city editor, had told her: "Blacks are not well suited for journalism. They didn't have the background and education." She added: "He would say we didn't have any qualified minorities. He would make snide comments about Afros and cornrows and daishikis."

She also testified that she challenged Blood's decision to demote Shepard to caption writing, and that she heard Blood call Shepard a "streetwalker" after Shepard returned from a walking tour with a politician. She said she told him: "If Joan is smart, she'll sue."[11]

In his own testimony, Blood denied using racial epithets in the newsroom and said he could not recall calling Shepard a streetwalker, but if he had, "it would have been said in some humorous context." He said such a comment would not be out of character in the newsroom.

"This was a rough-and-tumble place," he said, "a place with a lot of black humor."

Asked specifically if he had used the word "nigger," Blood said: "It is not a word which I would use, and not a word I've heard often in the world in which I travel." Given the blue-collar, hard-drinking, "rough and tumble" world of the *News*, his testimony must have already struck black and white jurors alike as implausible. Alterman then presented a deposition by a news executive that indicated that Blood had been reprimanded for calling a black reporter a nigger. On the witness stand, the executive, former editor Michael O'Neill, said he was mistaken, and that it was actually a white financial writer who uttered the epithet.

Under cross-examination, Blood contradicted previous testimony in which he said he did not know about the plaintiffs' allegations of racism when Duncan was transferred from one bureau to another, or when Hardy was pulled off a high-profile story.

Alterman presented a 1981 affidavit that contained Blood's remarks about the plaintiffs' allegations. "You've been lying to us about a lot of things, haven't you, Mr. Blood?" asked Alterman. He pressured Blood to concede that, contrary to earlier testimony, he did not know any reporter other than Shepard who was transferred from a regular staff reporting job to caption writing. In contrast, Phil Roura, a white reporter whom Blood had cited as being transferred from reporter to captions, was actually promoted to reporter and then editor after it was learned he was on the payroll of a New Jersey assemblyman.[12]

Given his turn to comment on Shepard's work, former *News* editor James Weighart testified that Shepard "had a real writing problem" and was a "sloppy writer." In a flash, Shepard's entire career as a journalist had been irreparably damaged.

Causewell Vaughan joined the *News* staff as a reporter in 1973 after numerous jobs in newspapers, including copy boy at the *New York Post* in 1962 and 1963, as a stringer for the *Buffalo Evening News*, a copy editor at the *New York Times*, and then, for six years, as a reporter for the Associated Press, with posts in Newark, Atlanta, and Washington, D.C., all cities plagued by urban rioting.

"I was an asset," Vaughan said of his time at AP. There were, to be sure, obvious advantages for mainstream news organizations to have black reporters cover urban rioting. Not only could they seamlessly flow with the scenes of unrest, but they would have access not accorded white reporters. In addition to the riots, Vaughan also covered the Black Panthers, who did not allow white reporters to attend its press conferences. Suddenly, white news organizations found themselves shut out of one of the biggest stories of the era, the rise of black nationalism and the wholesale rejection by blacks of the notion of white supremacy. These news organizations would turn to their underutilized black reporters to gather intelligence that could, in turn, be used by the government and the media against the very organizations that had befriended black reporters. Unlike the reporter in the black press who was reporting information for people whose interests converged with organizations or individuals committed to black advancement, the black reporter working for the mainstream media delivered the information to an audience acutely threatened by it. The reporter, then, became, in some respects, less a conveyor of ideas and information than a paid informant. Most hurtful for Vaughan was that his efforts were not rewarded. While his white colleagues were, after the Newark riot coverage, promoted to overseas posts, or to Washington or New York, he was offered a job in Madison, Wisconsin. "Guys were going to Rome, Washington, New York, and I'm going to Madison," he recounted three decades later.

Once at the News, Vaughan, by then age thirty, made his ambition to be an editor clear. He began as a federal court house reporter, and then as a general assignment reporter. In five claims against the paper, Vaughan charged that the *News* disregarded the experience of its black employees when filling editing jobs, and that he, like the others, was demoted after he joined the lawsuit in 1980.

Vaughan said that after proving himself for two years on the federal courthouse beat, he reminded editors of his wish to be an editor. He was instead placed on general assignment while he waited for an editor's job to open. In 1977, the Manhattan regional editor slot opened, and Vaughan made his wishes known again. Over the course of time he had been at the *News*, he had, on numerous occasions, filled in on editing posts, including as night city editor. He spent six months working as acting night city editor, and suddenly "from left field" they hired a reporter who didn't want the job, he bristled. "I would be his assistant," he recalled. "I said 'I don't understand. He doesn't even want the job. He doesn't have the experience.'"

Editors replied that the reporter had been under consideration longer. "By now, I'm seeing the handwriting on the wall," Vaughan said.

But three years later, the Brooklyn section was expanded to a pull-out and Vaughan was named editor. With the 1980 census came the recognition that Brooklyn had usurped Harlem as New York City's black political power base as its black population swelled, partly the result of the influx of Caribbean immigrants. The borough had the most black elected officials of any of the city's five boroughs. Editors increasingly saw Brooklyn as a place to send its black reporters.

By late 1980, Vaughan was reassigned out of Brooklyn and told he would become editor of the Manhattan section, which had greater prestige because of Manhattan's allure as a cultural mecca. But again, someone else was named to the job. "That's when I decided to file a complaint," Vaughan recounted. By then, the black caucus was meeting regularly, but Vaughan had, before then, been too absorbed by his responsibility of putting out a section to attend.

In his February 10 opening arguments, Morrison launched a blistering attack on Vaughan's competence and professionalism. He said Vaughan, while a Brooklyn editor covering the campaign of Representative Fred Richmond, had the congressman co-sign a personal loan for him, which is a clear and serious breach of journalistic ethics. The revelation of the financial arrangement became public during a federal investigation of Richmond, who was charged, and later convicted, of fraud.

Vaughan had already suffered the humiliating consequences of his egregious error when the *News* published a lengthy page 3 story on Richmond's financial woes, which included an account of how Richmond had, in 1979, co-signed the $2,400 loan for Vaughan, whom the article identified as a *Daily News* editor. The article also noted that Vaughan defaulted on the loan, leaving Richmond to repay $1,832. Richmond was quoted as saying: "He said he needed $2,400, but his credit was no good, so I went to my bank, Manufacturers Hanover, and got him the money. He made a couple of payments and then nothing, and I finally paid it off. You know, it is a source of embarrassment."[13]

Vaughan declined to comment for the article, which quoted *Daily News* executive editor James Weighart as saying that Vaughan had been suspended "and the matter is under investigation."

Vaughan was stunned. He said at least one of his superiors had known of the financial arrangement six months earlier, but editors only chose to suspend him for three weeks and demoted him to a copy-editing position, after he was quoted in the *Amsterdam News*, the black weekly newspaper, as criticizing the *News*'s racial policies. Vaughan also said *News* editors had investigated all of the stories he had written following the loan and could not find any coverage of Richmond that could have been deemed inappropriately favorable. Vaughan was suspended two days before the story ran in the *News*. In opening arguments, Morrison said Vaughan had been a "major disappointment to the *Daily News*," adding that he should have been fired for having Richmond co-sign the loan.

Sam Roberts, the city editor when Vaughan was suspended, echoed that sentiment from the witness stand. "I did not give it the weight I should have because if I did, I would have had Vaughan fired," said Roberts, who, by then, was a *New York Times* urban-affair columnist.[14] According to Vaughan, Roberts learned about the loan in the spring of 1981, but Vaughan was not suspended until December 1981.

Under cross-examination, Roberts conceded that he had offered Vaughan the job of assistant night city editor after he learned of the loan, which called into question Vaughan's belated demotion and suspension months later. Roberts explained that Vaughan had acknowledged his error in judgment and had told him his father had been ill and that he was broke as a result of the newspaper strike of 1978. On the witness stand, Vaughan elaborated.

"I was still having financial trouble in 1979–80," Vaughan said of the period, when he stopped payments on the loan. He said he eventually decided to allow the bank to take the money from his paycheck, but learned that Richmond had already paid off the loan. "It was never my intention to involve Mr. Richmond in my personal affairs."[15]

Like other *Daily News* editors, Roberts was hard pressed to show how Vaughan's transgression was worse than the serious offenses of two white *Daily News* reporters, Phil Roura and Harry Slagle, both of whom were, while working for the *News*, on the payrolls of elected officials. Roura, in fact, was promoted to reporter and then editor while working for a New Jersey assemblyman between 1974 and 1979. Roberts testified that the standards had changed from the 1960s to the late 1970s, but when it was pointed out that the violations occurred during the same period, as Vaughan's he replied that he did not know enough about those cases to comment.[16]

An article in *Editor and Publisher* in February 1982 quoted Vaughan as calling his transfer to a copy-editing position a demotion, and saying: "If there was a question about racism at the *Daily News*, it's been dispelled by the action taken against me. There are so many glaring examples of conflict of interest in the city room."

Meanwhile, Hardy was quoted as saying the penalty reflected a clear double standard, "one for whites, a more severe one for blacks." In light of the available information, it was certainly difficult to argue that the transgressions had been dealt with evenly.

Alterman also put Richard Oliver, a former metropolitan editor, on the stand to underscore the lighter penalties meted out to white offenders. Alterman asked Oliver to explain why he had the Fire Department illegally install, at taxpayers' expense, a light and siren in his personal car. Oliver conceded he had done a "dumb thing" but insisted he had never used it. Alterman presented a pretrial deposition in which he said he had "rarely" used it, then exploded: "Were you lying today, or were you lying. . . ." Before he could complete his question, Oliver admitted he had used it, but only when the car was parked. Oliver was neither suspended nor demoted after the issue was reported in local newspapers.

However, James Weighart said the two incidents could not be compared. "Vaughan never intended to pay back the loan. It was a shakedown," he said. Oliver, on the other hand, "was a dumb cluck who had a siren put on his car like a jerk."[17]

The *News*'s harshest assault was reserved for David Hardy, the lead plaintiff in *Hardy vs. the Daily News*, considered by all concerned the driving force behind the lawsuit. Even his critics begrudgingly admired his dedication to the lawsuit. "He could have been a great reporter if he had put as much energy into developing his craft as he has into this lawsuit," Alex Michelini, Hardy's former supervisor at the *News*, told the *Columbia Journalism Review*.[18]

Alterman considered Hardy's input vital to the case. "He scouted out witnesses, he bugged the Equal Employment Opportunity Commission (EEOC). He helped raise some of the money. He was the guy who got up in the middle of the night, the guy who was fearless. He went to every conference with the judge. He did all of the work that needed to be done to continue the momentum. He never got depressed. He was there. He was a dynamic force that was essential."

Hardy, perhaps more than the other plaintiffs, was perfectly groomed for the epic battle with the *News*. Hardy joined the *News* as a reporter in 1967 after working as a sports reporter for the *Plainfield Courier* in New Jersey. He attended some of the early meetings of black journalists who, in 1968, began discussing the formation of the National Association of Black Journalists and in 1969 left the *News* to become a reporter for the *Washington Post*, the industry leader in the number of black staff reporters. He was still at the *Post* in March 1972, when black reporters—labeled the Metro 7—filed a discrimination complaint with the federal Equal Employment Opportunity Commission office against the *Post*.

Leon Dash, one of the seven *Washington Post* metro reporters, recalled that Hardy consulted with him often on the status of the claim. And on March 23, 1974, when the seven reporters held a press conference at a church directly behind the *Post* to announce the EEOC complaint, Hardy was there in a show of support. Dash said when a reporter asked him if the complainants were afraid of management retaliation, he replied that they were not afraid of anything. "David raised his fist and smiled," Dash recalled.

Dash, upon graduating from Howard University, joined the *Washington Post* staff in 1968 in the midst of vocal demonstrations by blacks over home rule in the District of Columbia, which denied residents equal representation in Congress. Instead, the district, which, population-wise, is as large as several states, has a nonvoting delegate to Congress. "I was hired because they were afraid that there would be a riot that summer," said Dash. "I was not seen as being on a career track. The white males were being mentored and brought along by editors. They were being steered to stories that editors knew would make the front page. Black reporters had to struggle. . . . If we didn't take action, we wouldn't move up."[19]

The Metro 7 were protesting equal opportunity "with respect to job assignments, promotional opportunities, including promotions to management positions and other terms and conditions of employment," according to their statement.[20] They complained that there were no blacks in top editorial management, foreign news reporting and editing, or in reporting or editing of sports and financial news. Dash called the national and foreign desks, which had no minorities, the "white highlands."

"The lack of black participation in the shaping of the news reported by one of America's most prestigious newspapers is to us an insult to the black community of this city and an insult to black Americans around the country," the statement said.

In its coverage of the conference, the *Post*, through its attorney Joseph Califano, a former Kennedy administration official and future Cabinet secretary in the Carter administration, replied that it employed twenty-one black reporters, photographers, and editors, more than any other newspaper in the country, and that it implemented a plan to hire more blacks after five weeks of meetings with the Metro 7 reporters. Califano said the paper had already hired one black reporter for the national staff, named another to the city desk, and appointed two additional black reporter interns. But the Metro 7 said talks broke off because of management's refusal to agree to increase black participation in vital news decisions. The group also noted that while 71 percent of Washington was black, only 37—or 9.3 percent—of the *Post* newsroom's 396 employees were.

Time magazine provided a glimpse of the industry's resentment over the protest, when, in an article on April 10, 1972, it noted the irony of the nation's most racially liberal paper being sued by black reporters. The article pointed out that blacks on the news staff included an editorial writer, columnist, two assistant city editors, two cultural writers, and fourteen reporters and photographers. In contrast, the *Los Angeles Times* had four blacks out of 437 editorial employees. And in typical circle-the-wagon fashion, *Time* dismissed the merits of the black journalists' grievances.

After stressing that blacks represented nearly 10 percent of the editorial staff, the article went on: "Not enough, say seven of the *Post*'s black city-desk reporters. . . . They demanded to know, among other things, why there were no blacks in senior executive positions, why there have traditionally been only one or two blacks on the prestigious national staff. Another grievance concerns the *Post*'s coverage of black affairs, which some staffers consider too stereotyped."

Time was unsympathetic to the plaintiffs' cause. "But that charge and the one accusing the *Post* of discrimination seem overdrawn," concluded the article. "The paper frequently runs stories sympathetic to black problems, and articles that treat blacks as individuals. The *Post* supports an all-black intern program at the Washington Journalism Center. The paper also has sent a black editor around the country scouting for black recruits." The article, which seemed more a defense of the industry than an objective account of the news, seemed to suggest that since the paper could count more black journalists on its staff than other news organizations, the black journalists should feel satisfied that they were hired at all. They should not concern themselves with issues of glass ceilings and underutilization or stereotypical coverage. It was the same attitude that fueled the *Daily News* lawsuit. Like white journalists, black journalists want more than simply to be hired by premier news organizations. They want their talents and aspirations to be recognized and rewarded. Unfortunately, in too many instances, this has not occurred without some form of protest.

To the group's demand of 35 percent minority representation, the article noted that many publications were having problems getting beyond "a few token blacks" because of the dearth of candidates. While even that point could be argued, it failed to address the ways in which blacks were utilized and the prevailing perception by blacks in and out of the media that much of the news coverage of African Americans was stereotypical. The *Time* article ended by noting that the hiring of two black interns and promotion of a black reporter to the national staff "did not satisfy the seven dissidents. They gained the support of 26 other blacks on the paper and went ahead with their formal complaint. At the *Washington Star* last week, black staff members met to consider what action they should bring against their management."

The press column evoked an industry under siege by ungrateful black journalists.

A year later, the EEOC issued a report that determined that the *Washington Post* was a discriminatory employer. The *Post*, still represented by Califano, said there would be no mediation unless the EEOC retracted its report, which the agency refused to do. Management refused to agree to a goal of 35 percent minority representation, which it called a quota. The reporters, represented by Clifford Alexander Jr., who in 1969 had resigned as EEOC chair, were unable to foot the expense of a court challenge, so they embraced their partial victory, and moved on.[21]

Six years later, Dash became a foreign correspondent with three separate assignments to Angola. The following year he was sent to cover the Ivory Coast. Nonetheless, he said the battle for racial parity in the newsroom continued. In 1995, Dash went on to win the Pulitzer Prize for "Rosa Lee's Story," a series of articles in the *Washington Post* on a black woman in Washington, D.C., who had a long history of family dysfunction. He left the *Post* in 1998 to become a journalism professor at the University of Illinois. He remained convinced that none of the progress made by himself and other blacks would have occurred without agitation. "Race was an issue. Race is still an issue," he said twenty-seven years after challenging the *Post*.[22]

The courage displayed by the black reporters left an indelible impression on Hardy, who returned to the *News* in 1972. According to Hardy, Michael O'Neill, then the editor, insisted he had changed the newsroom to one that was more tolerant of blacks.

But Hardy recalled returning to a place where blacks were racially taunted by white supervisors who failed to recognize their abilities. That year, black reporters at the *New York Times* had filed a class-action suit, alleging many of the same problems as the Metro 7 had. One of the complainants was Earl Caldwell, whom Hardy and others would later lure to the *News* to work as the paper's first black columnist; and C. Gerald Fraser, who had previously worked at the *News* before going to the *Times*. Hardy had filed an affidavit in support of the *Times* plaintiffs, which would later undermine his own case.

"Certainly my education about racism in the media and how to most effectively combat it came from my proximity to both episodes," Hardy said.[23]

When black reporters first raised the prospect of a lawsuit to Caldwell, he opposed the idea. At the time, Caldwell was building a national reputation with his coverage of the Black Panthers from the paper's San Francisco bureau. He had already been embroiled in a high-profile battle with the government, which resulted in shield laws that allow reporters to keep their notes confidential without legal ramifications. The 1970 statute that first brought Caldwell national prominence was drafted to protect him from a California grand jury that subpoenaed him to turn over boxes of notes on the Black Panther party sought by the U.S. Department of Justice. In a case that became a national cause célèbre, the Supreme Court held that under certain conditions, reporters must, like other citizens, testify to crimes they witness, but nothing else.

Caldwell destroyed fourteen months of notes on the Black Panther party. The same year, the New York State legislature passed the state's shield law, which was signed into law by Governor Nelson Rockefeller.

The *New York Times*'s class-action suit did not interest Caldwell until he was shown the paper's salary roster, which revealed that whites made far more than their black colleagues in similar positions. "I didn't know reporters were making that kind of money," he said, noting that many were earning more than double his salary. He said he was infuriated to learn that a white intern who had on occasion served as his go-fer made more than he. Caldwell confronted the national editor, Gene Roberts, telling him, "I can't believe you would treat me so shabbily. I'm running through walls for you."[24]

According to Caldwell, Roberts replied that his salary was too low to bring up to the level of his white peers. "He said 'I'd have to take all the money in my budget to give you a raise.'"

Until then, Caldwell was content with his position at the *Times.* "I got the assignments, bylines, everything except the money. Once you realize it, then you're walking around angry all the time. I joined the lawsuit after that."

In 1979, the *Times* reached a settlement with its black reporters—out of the glare of the public. Leonard Harris, a *Times* spokesman, told reporters that the paper did not admit to discrimination but agreed to abide by a minority hiring policy. Caldwell called the settlement "a rip-off." He said he received several thousand dollars. Another reporter, Pamela Hollie, who had been a business reporter for the *Wall Street Journal* before going to the *Times,* reportedly received a check for $400 a year. For the black journalists, the settlement was more a moral victory than a case of financial reparation.

Meanwhile, in 1978 women and blacks at the Associated Press filed a joint complaint against their employer, making many of the same claims. Their case, in 1979, was joined by the Equal Employment Opportunity Commission, which filed a class-action suit based on race, gender, and national origin. Janice Goodman, their attorney, said the major argument was that there were no women or black bureau chiefs, executives, or editors. "That was a statistical fact," said Goodman, who in the late 1970s also handled a sexual discrimination lawsuit on behalf of women at NBC.[25] The AP case, which was the first to enjoin the issues of race and sex discrimination, was, like other lawsuits at other news organizations, including ABC and *Newsweek,* settled out of court in the early 1980s.

Around the same period, John Johnson, a prominent black investigative television reporter in New York, sued the ABC affiliate for race discrimination. Johnson's battle with ABC stemmed from its refusal to promote him or allow him to break his contract to accept a more lucrative offer to become an anchorman at Cable News Network (CNN). "I said if you're not going to promote me, then let me go," Johnson recalled. Instead, the station sent a cease-and-desist letter to CNN, saying it would not allow Johnson to violate his contract. "They basically said, 'You'll stay here and that will be that,'" Johnson recounted.[26]

Johnson filed discrimination charges in federal court, which, during the discovery process, drew several of the station's prominent television personalities to the courtroom to testify about his role at the station. "I had one little lawyer and his assistant. There was little ol' me up against this powerful corporation. It didn't make me popular with my agents. Who does this make you popular with in that food chain?"

For the station, the publicity from such a case, in the midst of the class-action lawsuits at the Associated Press and the *New York Times*, had to make executives uneasy, especially given Johnson's high "q" rating—which measures viewer popularity. Johnson reached a settlement with ABC that stipulated that he could not work for another station in the New York market for five years. Johnson decided to stay at ABC after the station surpassed the CNN financial offer, promoted him, and gave him a say in minority hiring and review. Bernard Shaw, an African American who would become one of the most recognized faces in television news around the world, was instead hired for the CNN job. "From that point on, in a way, I was a trouble-maker," Johnson concluded many years later. "I wasn't going to go anywhere at ABC, up the network ladder." Johnson remained in local television until 1997, when he retired to care for his ailing father. Until the *Daily News* lawsuit, all of the challenges against major news organizations were, for the most part, waged and set-tled out of the public eye. "That's why I admired the plaintiffs in the *Daily News* lawsuit," said Caldwell. "They stood up and they fought."[27]

The *Daily News* battle began in 1977, when Hardy and other black staffers were united in their disillusionment and anger over the promotions and prestige assignments that eluded black writers. No blacks were assigned to Capitol Hill or Albany, New York's state capital, nor were there any blacks in management. Clinton Cox, who in 1978 became the first black reporter assigned to the *News*'s Albany bureau, said that when he initially asked for the assignment, executive editor Michael O'Neill told him he could open a bureau in Harlem, Bedford-Stuyvesant, or any other black community in New York if he'd forget about Albany.

"I insisted, and after an incredible amount of hassle was transferred to Albany," Cox recounted. "Once I was there, however, the *Daily News* took stories away from me, dropped my byline so many times I lost count, saw that I was excluded from social functions involving the job, and never gave me another raise."[28] He charged that he was shut out of coverage of the gubernatorial campaign.

Cox also alleged that during the entire fourteen months he worked in the Albany bureau, Oliver never spoke to him. "He had the *News*'s operator make phone calls routinely to every other reporter assigned there during my tenure," he wrote. "Every time I answered the phone, however, Oliver would have the operator leave a message for one of the other reporters to call him back."[29]

After a series of meetings between the caucus and management, the group decided in 1980 to file a complaint with the New York City Human Rights Commission. Unable to reach a settlement, the caucus filed a federal court suit in 1982, which was joined by the Federal Equal Employment Opportunity Commission. According to the Commission report, the discriminatory patterns at the paper "in all likelihood could not have been obtained by chance. On no measure did black or Hispanic salaries equal or pass those of the whites."[30] A class-action lawsuit filed by the U.S. Equal Employment Opportunity Commission on behalf of all black employees of the *News* was to go before Judge Cedarbaum following the four plaintiffs' trial.

On February 8, on the eve of the trial, the plaintiffs were offered $500,000 to settle the case, which they declined. It was a decision that would forever change the course of their careers, and indeed their lives. In opening arguments, Hardy was characterized as emotionally unstable, violent, and an instigator of the lawsuit whose "monumental ego" would not allow him to see his shortcomings.[31] Morrison said Hardy had a "warped" view of race and exercised poor judgment when, in 1976, he was involved in a fight with an attorney while covering a trial.

In an attempt to cast him as someone who was out of touch with reality, *News* attorneys presented a document in which Hardy had described himself as a better writer than *Washington Post* reporter Bob Woodward, and a better reporter than Carl Bernstein, the two reporters who achieved fame for uncovering the Watergate scandal. The very notion struck the lawyers, and Hardy's editors, as preposterous. "Bettered

Woodstein," chided a March 5, 1987, *Daily News* headline over the coverage of Hardy's testimony.

Hardy also testified that he could have been hired by the *New York Times* "any time up to the time I left the *Washington Post.*" But *News* lawyers undermined his credibility by presenting a sworn affidavit Hardy had filed in support of the *New York Times* reporters in 1979, which said: "I have applied on three occasions for a position with the *New York Times*. For the reasons set forth below, I believe my rejection for these positions was based upon my race. This discriminatory rejection was so discouraging to me that I did not make a formal application again."[32] Undaunted, Hardy responded that he had been offered a job as a sports copy editor and as a reporter-trainee on the metropolitan staff, both which he said he declined.

News attorneys also produced a letter that Hardy had written to Judge Richard Conners of Superior Court in 1975 while he covered Jersey City courts. The judge had instructed attorneys not to speak with Hardy concerning an upcoming trial. In his protest letter, Hardy wrote: "I am still trying to decide if your actions and words were the insipid gyrations of a bigot, the irrational ravings of a jurist unable to bear weighty responsibility or a specious effort by an arrogant and ignorant man to intimidate a free press."

Asked by Morrison if the letter was a misuse of his power as a journalist, Hardy replied that he wrote it "to defend the free press, to defend my ability to work in that county."

Joseph McNamara, deputy city editor at the time, disparaged Hardy's work, which he said was often late, overwritten, and wanting for attribution. "I thought Mr. Hardy was an average reporter," he said. "I thought that he was slow with copy . . . and tended to overwrite."[33] But McNamara conceded that he had never put his assessment of Hardy's work in writing and could not recall ever discussing his concerns with his superiors.

Wrote Alex Jones, who closely covered the trial for the *Times*: "Mr. Hardy seldom lost his composure and seemed to relish the parry and thrust of cross-examination, which he described off the stand as 'playing Ping-Pong with Thomas C. Morrison.'"[34]

Hardy also testified that the fight with lawyer Mike Reilly outside the courthouse was sparked by a racial put-down by the lawyer, that

Reilly took the first swing, and that he had merely defended himself. He stressed that he was not disciplined after informing his editors of the skirmish.

Hardy testified that blacks and Latinos were routinely called "bongos and banjos" by white *News* editors; that Tony Marino, while an assistant editor, had, in his presence, referred to two African American women as "nigger broads," an allegation that Marino denied; and that black reporters were consistently denied merit raises and promotions. He also charged that he was taken off the Abscam story—in which several elected officials were convicted of bribery after attempting to sell arms and airplanes to Saudi Arabia—and replaced by white reporters after the story garnered national headlines.

In 1980, Hardy uncovered information that implicated former U.S. Senator Harrison Williams of New Jersey, who was later convicted in the scandal. Hardy's information linked Williams to a company that sought a casino license in New Jersey. But Richard Oliver, then the metropolitan editor, testified that Hardy had greatly overstated his role in the story, which NBC broke on February 2, 1980. The *News* countered that Hardy had interesting details about New Jersey senator Harrison Williams—who was later nabbed in an FBI sting—and his secret interest in a casino, but that they were unrelated to Abscam.

Oliver also alleged that Hardy had filed a false story on the scandal, which Hardy insisted wasn't false but tainted by a *News* rewrite man who neglected to include portions of his report that he telephoned in. Under cross-examination, Oliver conceded that Hardy could have been the victim of a bad source. Meanwhile, city editor Arthur Browne refused to divulge the source who, he claimed had disproved Hardy's account. Alterman challenged Browne to admit that he had not contacted the New Jersey sources Hardy had used. Browne later said he could not recall if he had contacted sources in New Jersey used by Hardy. He also conceded that he had not talked to Hardy, or the rewrite man who typed Hardy's story dictated by phone. He became visibly agitated when Alterman asked if he had checked the sources of a white reporter whose story had also come under scrutiny.

In what emerged as a critical issue in the trial, Hardy claimed he was taken off the story and transferred to New York only after he and the other caucus members filed their June 1980 complaint despite *News* editors' insistence that he was removed because of a false report. Alterman produced an internal memo which showed that *News* management wanted Hardy "out of Trenton" even before the flawed story was filed. Oliver contended that Hardy had essentially removed himself from the story by taking a one-month sick leave, which Hardy attributed to stress over the way he was marginalized in the coverage. Hardy revealed he believed he might have a nervous breakdown.

Hardy testified that his removal from the story—the biggest story to emanate from his beat—was devastating. The *News* tapped John McLaughlin, the paper's chief political reporter, to direct the coverage. Joseph Barletta, the *News*'s general manager between 1977 and 1980, testified that Hardy became "unbalanced and out of control" when he was taken off the story and had threatened to kill Blood, his editor, during a meeting at a restaurant between newspaper executives and black caucus members. "He was very angry," he testified.[35] Newspaper executives no longer met with the paper's black caucus after Hardy's outbreak.

The *News*' attempt to characterize Hardy as a loose canon and to disparage Hardy's journalistic track record instead lent credence to the pressures he endured as a black reporter at the white-managed newspaper. In a letter of recommendation for Hardy to *Washington Post* editor Ben Bradlee, Rolfe Neill, a former *News* assistant managing editor, wrote: "At the *News*, Dave's responsibilities have not given him a chance for leadership. But because he is Black and bigotry has frequently come his way in the office, I have a number of times observed him under stress. He comes off well." He went on to describe Hardy as a "loyal, sensitive, intelligent, young reporter who has the potential for substantial accomplishment."[36]

Retired associate editor Jack Smee, who had testified that Hardy's stories were often slanted, under cross-examination conceded that there were never negative letters or memorandums from *News* executives about the performance of Hardy or the other plaintiffs. He also acknowledged that in 1975 and again in 1978, he had written two letters recommending Hardy for a prestigious Nieman fellowship at Harvard University.[37]

Another letter, which the jury would not see, also offered evidence of Hardy's journalistic ability. In that letter, News editor Gilman Spencer recommended that Hardy be nominated for a Pulitzer Prize for his coverage of a former New Jersey senator David Friedland, who had mysteriously disappeared after his conviction in a $20 million scam. While the rest of the media reported that Friedland had drowned while scuba diving in the Bahamas before his scheduled sentencing, a skeptical Hardy went to the Bahamas and concluded he had manufactured his supposed death. Months later, Friedland contacted Hardy and agreed to an interview, which resulted in a front-page story.

"David Hardy's reporting on the Friedland case typified the work he has done for this newspaper during his 16 years here," wrote Spencer in the letter dated January 28, 1986. "I am delighted to recommend it for Pulitzer consideration for Investigative Journalism."[38] That letter, however, could not be entered as court evidence because it fell outside of the period covered by the lawsuit. But in testimony that could have been equally devastating to the plaintiffs' case, the judge excluded evidence that Hardy had, beginning in 1973, written stories about two landlords without informing his editors that the pair were *his* landlords, with whom he was involved in a dispute. Hardy had described the landlords as having mob ties. The *News* claimed to have paid an estimated $200,000 to settle the libel lawsuit.

But despite the controversies swirling around Vaughan and Hardy, the evidence overwhelmingly showed that blacks were excluded from top newsroom positions because, according to *News* editors, no qualified blacks could ever be found. Bob Herbert was promoted only after the lawsuit was filed. However, Caldwell testified that he had, as cofounder of the Institute for Journalism Education, provided a list of potential black candidates to *News* editors and months later learned that not one had been called. The point of the testimony was to debunk the *News*'s contention that the paucity of black reporters was due to their small supply.

Sal Gerage, an associate metropolitan editor when the suit was filed, testified that the plaintiffs had been targeted after they sued the paper. Blood testified that retaliation could not have entered his mind because he was not aware of the caucus complaints until 1984, as he was preparing for his court appearance, However, during cross examination Alterman presented documents prepared by Blood in 1980 and 1981 referring to some of the plaintiffs' charges. "You have been lying to us, have you not, sir," demanded Alterman. Blood said his memory had failed him.[39]

During the final days of testimony, James Wieghart, the former executive editor, said he attempted to derail the lawsuit by promoting Duncan to assistant news editor, "in part because of the pending matter, the racial bias suit." Duncan testified that, until he became a party in the lawsuit, "I was not considered material for promotion."

Particularly damaging to the *News'* defense were findings by the Equal Employment Opportunity Commission, which studied the *News's* salary and promotions between 1979 and 1981. "We found whites as a group were paid more than blacks. White employees were likely to get merit increases and the increases they got were likely to be higher," said Vincent Donato, an EEOC manager, in his testimony.[40]

According to the report, white reporters, on average, were promoted to the position of special reporter within 59 months, compared to 113 months for blacks. The study also showed that between 1979 to 1981, the average white reporter received $118 a year in cash bonuses, compared to $50 a year for black reporters. None of the forty-seven people hired or promoted into management between 1979 and 1981 were black. According to the Commission, the pattern "in all likelihood could not have been obtained by chance. On no measure did black or Hispanic salaries equal or pass those of whites." The report found "substantial" disparities in pay, assignments, and promotions between black and white journalists. Mark Robert Killingsworth, a Rutgers University economics analyst, testified that there was "substantial evidence" that blacks were discriminated against "relative to non-blacks who are similar in terms of all the factors considered in the analysis."

Noting significant discrepancies in salaries of whites and blacks in comparable positions, he said that changing the racial designation of blacks to whites, without changing other variables such as experience and educational background, would proportionately increase the number of blacks expecting promotions from the actual number of ten to seventeen. In other words, whites were paid more by virtue of being white. "It appears fairly clear that blacks are less likely than otherwise identical whites to be in high-paying positions, more likely to be in low-paying positions," he said.

The *News* might have also benefited from the testimony of Benjamin Bradlee and Tom Litman, editors at the *Post*, and Alan Finder, a former *Newsday* reporter who wrote a story that contradicted Hardy's Abscam story. The three had planned to corroborate the *News's* contention that Hardy's work did not merit raises or promotions, but the judge excluded them because their testimony fell outside of the scope of the lawsuit. Also on the witness list was Thomas Winship, the former *Boston Globe* editor, who backed out for unknown reasons. Alterman recounted his heated confrontation with Winship during a pre-trial deposition.

"I deposed him for three days," said Alterman. "I told him I would destroy his reputation because he was supporting a racist organization," he said, noting he had dug up speeches by Winship calling for newspaper diversity. "He would have been devastating to us," said Alterman.[41]

In his summation, Morrison called the plaintiffs' case one of "distortion, innuendo and misstatement of facts. . . . They have hurt the *Daily News*, hurt it badly." Speaking of his star witnesses, James Wieghart and Michael O'Neill, he said: "Their honesty was attacked, their integrity was attacked, beyond the legitimacy of cross-examination." Countered Alterman in his four-and-a-half-hour summation: "This is a simple case. The news broke the law and when the plaintiffs complained about it, they were retaliated against. We have neither the money nor the staff, but we have the truth."[42]

He told the jurors that they could make history, like the Supreme Court did in *Brown vs. the Board of Education*, and challenged them to bring the *News* "kicking and screaming into the twentieth century." In a flash of either confidence or prescience, he said, while the plaintiffs were victims, "they are going to be heroes when you return with a verdict. . . . These are people of courage, idealism and hope, people who still believe in the system, still believe that civil rights laws mean something."

Sue Singer, who handled statistics for the case, told jurors: "I've heard some incredible things in this courtroom over the past couple of months, but one of the high points was hearing the *Daily News* lawyers tell you that the *Daily News* was a pioneer in moving people up the career ladder in the editorial department." She added: "The statistics you have heard are complicated and sometimes boring, but I do know that there is one simple statistic. . . . It's the number zero. The number of blacks who were promoted into management at the *Daily News* until this lawsuit was filed was zero."

The jury deliberated for twenty three hours over four days before delivering its verdict, which was reported on the front page of practically every major newspaper. Joseph W. Foley Jr., the jury foreman, said the jury found the plaintiffs to be "credible professional journalists" in spite of the assault by *News* editors. He added: "I don't think the *Daily News* was any better or worse than society in general." So while the *Daily News* alone had been guilty of discrimination, many news executives around the country were forced to consider how their own newsrooms would fare if they were held up to the same level of scrutiny. In 1987, blacks were still woefully underrepresented in the industry, and their number in news management was virtually nil.

In its front-page account on April 16, the *New York Times* presented a balanced account, which included reactions from both sides. Jack Dunleavy, a *News* spokesman indicated that the paper would appeal, saying the organization "remains convinced that it did not discriminate against four of its black staff members in the late 1970s and early 1980s." Black journalists hailed the decision as a landmark case. "It will trigger a more serious look at operations in newsrooms across the country," predicted Albert E. Fitzpatrick, the president of the National Association of Black Journalists and assistant vice president for minority affairs at Knight-Ridder.

But one line in the article grossly understated the impact of the decision. Alluding to the fact that twelve of twenty three charges of discrimination had been proven, Alex Jones wrote: "Though the verdict was mixed, the plaintiffs took it as a great victory." Despite the technical accuracy of a split decision, the verdict could only be viewed as an astounding victory, particularly given the uphill nature of the battle, which had pitted the plaintiffs not only against the *Daily News*—the nation's largest daily general interest paper and the crown jewel of the Tribune Company—but also against an entire industry. Riding on the outcome of the verdict was whether news organizations would be allowed to defend the uniformly inferior assignments and salaries accorded black journalists by chipping away at their reputations. But in spite of the imperfections of the plaintiffs, a jury had found that they were no less deserving of promotion and raises than their equally imperfect white peers. the

Daily News could not prove to a jury that, in the history of the paper, no blacks, prior to the lawsuit, were competent enough to be promoted to prominent positions.

Wrote *Time* magazine in a brief item on April 27: "The *New York Daily News* tried to bury the story on page 23 last week, but it didn't work. On the same day, the *New York Times* played it on page one—and with good reason. For the first time a major news organization had been found guilty of racial discrimination by a jury. . . . The case was messy: one of the *News*'s white editors was accused of repeatedly using racist epithets in the newsroom; one of the black plaintiffs was apparently denied promotion in part because he arranged for the congressman he was covering to cosign a bank note for him—a clear impropriety. Still, the verdict highlighted the absence of blacks from top management positions in the nation's newsrooms."

In June, the second phase of the trial began, with U.S. District Court judge Miriam Goldman Cederbaum reconvening the same six jurors to determine the amount in damages to be paid to the plaintiffs. The plaintiffs had reportedly asked for $12 million during court hearings, an amount *News* lawyers said would spell financial ruin for the paper. Vaughan "choked back tears," according to the *New York Times* account, as he described his feelings after being suspended and then demoted in 1981. "I felt suicidal, I really did," Vaughan said. "They destroyed my career through the implication that I had shaken down a Congressman." Hardy testified that he had headaches and couldn't sleep as a result of his diminished role in the Abscam coverage. "I didn't have a career anymore," said Hardy. "I was busted, humiliated."

And Shepard testified that, after being passed over for a promotion, she would go home and put the covers over her head. "I just looked down at these hands and I said, 'Why is this color so bad?'" Duncan said he had reached a dead end after he was passed over for a job in 1979, a situation he found "demeaning."

Days before the jury was scheduled to reconvene to decide damages, the *News*, on June 10, agreed to pay $3.1 million in damages and also to implement an affirmative action program that would increase the number of blacks reporters and managers.

As part of the settlement, Duncan opted to take early retirement, Vaughan was to be reassigned to a better position, Hardy and Shepard were to remain in their current posts. As part of the settlement, the EEOC agreed to drop its class-action suit on behalf of black *News* employees. But the plaintiffs' victory was overshadowed by the damage done to their reputations. The money they would receive in compensation could not begin to repair their shattered reputations and wounded spirits. "The plaintiffs felt their careers were over," said Alterman.

Given the character assassination they sustained throughout the trial and its aftermath, there was little reason for them to expect otherwise. In a troubling and steady refrain, white journalists continued to attack the competence of the black reporters as if the overwhelming evidence of systemic racial discrimination at the *News* was less important than the plaintiffs' individual foibles. The coverage assumed that the black journalists were inferior to white reporters who were deemed competent by virtue of their ability to advance. White journalists seemed resistant to the notion that their inherent biases, and those of their news organizations, required scrutiny.

A lengthy article published in the July-August 1987 issue of the *Columbia Journalism Review*, one of the bibles of the industry, perhaps best reflected how subjectively the case was covered by the mainstream press. The article, written by Jan Alpert, portrayed the plaintiffs as mediocre journalists and the *Daily News* as the victim of its efforts to diversify the newsroom. "Would the plaintiffs have been hired if they had been averagely talented white reporters?" Alpert asked. "It would seem fair to say that they were hired more because the *Daily News* was going all out to get black staffers on board than because of any particular promise they showed. Once hired, they were judged and expected to succeed on the merit system, just like anyone else." This assessment negated the plaintiffs' years of reporting experience at other major news organizations before going to the *News*, and suggested that the white men and women working at the *News* were all superstars.

Alpert's article went on: "In court, the adjectives their peers used most commonly to describe the plaintiffs' work were 'weak,' 'unimaginative,' and 'average.' 'Average' became almost an epithet." The fact that that assessment was made by the very white editors whom the plaintiffs were accusing of racial discrimination was not even raised as cause to question the validity of their claims.

Alpert continued: "Although, ultimately, the case was not about how good the plaintiffs' copy was but about whether promotion decisions were racially biased, the two points seemed inextricably connected because of the defense's contention that, as journalists, the plaintiffs were just average and average was just not good enough to get ahead at the *News*." That skewed conclusion, of course, ignored their demonstrated talent and wealth of experience, which, despite barriers, had, for example, resulted in Hardy's nomination for a Pulitzer Prize and Vaughan's ability to work in a top editing position without benefit of the titles. Alpert's contention also assumed that the white men and women working at the *News* were all major talents whose rise and fall were simply a result of their efforts, rather than a network of support. That support included ignoring the transgressions of the newsroom's favored sons and daughters.

Alpert's premise of the plaintiff's inferiority seemed particularly disingenuous given the reams of evidence that disproved this characterization, particularly in Hardy's case. While it could be argued that Hardy was arrogant, egotistical, and even that he had character flaws, it was impossible to argue after a careful review of the evidence that he lacked talent. In addition to the suggestion by a top editor that he be nominated for a Pulitzer Prize, Hardy had twice been recommended by a *News* editor for a prestigious Nieman Fellowship. Alpert was also privy to the letter by a *News* editor that had noted his talent and the racial glass ceiling that made the promotion of blacks all but unattainable. And Hardy had been hired not once, but twice by the *Daily News*.

Alpert also ignored the evidence showing that no blacks had been promoted to management positions prior to the lawsuit, but apparently chose to believe that it was because none were capable.

"If race was a factor, it was only in their favor," he quoted Sam Roberts, the former *Daily News* editor and urban affairs columnist at the *Times* who had testified against the plaintiffs. Jimmy Breslin, in a more measured slap at the plaintiffs, said: "This case was a loser from the start. . . . They [the lawyers] went all out to prove [the plaintiffs] weren't so good. All of us, including Breslin, aren't so good. The people who get promoted weren't so hot. Black people have every right to be as poor at their jobs as white people and get promoted."

Breslin applauded both sides for their courage and the *News* for hiring gutsy black reporters. "I think it says a lot that the *Daily News* had the only blacks with spines enough to deal with this head-on. At least it shows [management] wanted minority writers who were alive. That's more than you can say for any other paper in this town. . . . It was a neighborhood fight to the finish and at least both sides had the guts to do it."

Alpert based an entire article on a portrayal of the plaintiffs crafted by editors who had nothing to gain, and everything to lose, by fairly assessing the work of the four journalists. Not once did Alpert even hint at the inherent self-interest of those editors who freely impugned the reputations of the plaintiffs. The *News*, and the industry at large, was left to write its own epitaph, one that stained the characters and reputations of four African Americans who risked everything to bring the issue of racial discrimination in the news media out of the closet. So, while the plaintiffs would win the court battle, they would, in the end, lose the war.

Of the four plaintiffs, Duncan, perhaps, emerged most unscathed. He was sixty three years old, and the settlement allowed him to retire. Twelve years after the lawsuit, he lived in a New Jersey suburb with his wife and was more philosophical than haunted or bitter about the experience. But as a sign of the toll the ordeal had placed on him, he enrolled in Drew Seminary for a master's degree in theology and became an ordained minister following what he called "a life-altering experience."

He said while the three younger plaintiffs had difficulty sleeping and eating during the heat of battle, "Just before the trial, I made up my mind, 'God's work will be done,'" Duncan said. "I knew I was right. That's why I went on. I had had it." With the ordeal far behind him, Duncan and his wife edited *The Relay*, a newspaper published by the Methodist Church, and taught Sunday school.

Meanwhile, Causewell Vaughan, who had taken a buy-out from the *News* in 1993, was still living in Brooklyn and producing his own cable show, which provided news on the Caribbean community in the United States. The lawsuit effectively ended his career.

He knew his career in the mainstream newsmedia was over from the first day of opening arguments.

"What we were accused of doing was reported everywhere," he said.

"They cast us as wild revolutionaries. . . . I never dreamed that this would develop into what it did."

Vaughan applied for numerous positions following the trial. He briefly worked as city editor of *Her New York*, a short-lived daily newspaper dedicated to women that was published for several weeks by an eccentric New York millionaire before folding. Quiet and courtly, he nonetheless bristled with bitterness over the experience and its aftermath. He was critical of black organizations, his black colleagues, especially at the *News*. "We're supposed to be newsmen," he said. "None of them ever set foot in the courtroom."

But he was most enraged over the way his name and reputation had been irreparably sullied, while many of the people responsible for the *News'* guilty verdict continued to enjoy their reputations and careers. "I'm not struggling, but the thing that bothers me is that I'm dead in the water because they ruined my reputation," he said, still emotional twelve years after the trial ended. "We all had to struggle because our name was mud. Nobody would hire us," he said. Hardy, who had returned to the *News* following the trial, was one of the eight black reporters laid off when Mort Zuckerman purchased the newspaper in 1993. A group of twenty two employees—sixteen blacks, four Latinos and two Asian Americans—filed federal discrimination charges in the New York District office of the Equal Employment Opportunity Commission in July 1993. "There was a history of racism at the *Daily News* which was brought to [Zuckerman's] attention and he deliberately listened to people who were part of that policy before," charged Renee Steinhagen, their attorney.[43]

The *Daily News* responded through its highest-ranking black, Delbert Spurlock, an associate publisher and executive vice president, that twenty seven of ninety six new hires had been minority. Spurlock's role defending the *Daily News* against the dismissal of minority reporters had to be a bitter pill for Hardy, whose epic battle contributed to Spurlock's lofty position at the paper.

In 1999, the case was still pending, as was a lawsuit filed by Angela Dodson, a black former *New York Times* editor whose case threatened to rival the *News's* in hostility, character assassination, and in the attention it would generate in the media. Like the *News* plaintiffs, Dodson, who in 1991 became the *Times's* first minority female hired to a coveted editorial position, alleged her firing was the result of racial discrimination. Like the *News* editors, *Times* brass raised the issue of her competence. Long before the case would land in court, Dodson's reputation was already taking a thrashing in press reports. An article on her lawsuit in the *American Lawyer* quoted white editors and colleagues assailing her credentials, her preparation for the job, and the paper's affirmative action program.

"It was a question of competence," said Bryan Miller, a former *Times* restaurant critic. "I'm just tired of hearing 'race, race, race.' What happens to merit, merit, merit?"[44]

In his response to her complaint, Vernon Byrd Jr., the *Times* counsel, characterized her charges of discrimination based on race, gender, and disability "a complete sham . . . filed for the sole purpose of trying to embarrass the *Times* into a settlement."

In 1999, Hardy said he was looking forward to his day in court and still harbored resentment over his first court battle. He lashed out at the media's character assassination; at the lawyers, particularly Raymond Brown, who he claimed "abandoned" the plaintiffs; and at Alterman, whom he accused of attempting to settle the case for $500,000 on the eve of the trial and again following the verdict, when the *News* offered the plaintiffs $1.7 million. Alterman countered that he and Sue Singer had a legal responsibility to present the settlement offers to the plaintiffs and said he did not recall recommending $500,000.

And Hardy was still seething over the *Columbia Journalism Review* article, which he rendered "the ultimate lie" by putting forward the notion that the case was won "by a group of flawed black journalists who lucked out by hiring a smart white lawyer. . . . [S]he chose not to interview the white jurors who readily stated their verdict was based entirely on the credibility of the plaintiffs."[45] Hardy confined his comments to two e-mail responses and refused to grant a telephone or personal interview. He also declined to reveal where he worked, saying only that he mentored young reporters at a small New Jersey newspaper. He did, however, have kind words for Judge Cedarbaum, whom he credited for forcing the *News* to agree to an affirmative action package, and the heroism "by very decent white and black people who saw the injustice we were fighting."

Joan Shepard spent her final years attempting to find meaningful work. Following the trial, she worked for a brief period at the *City Sun,* the black newspaper which had aggressively covered the trial. She spent her final year trying to launch her own restaurant industry newsletter. In April 1998, she died quietly at her Manhattan home at age fifty six. Those close to her said she was battling asthma, loneliness, and depression, and that her body was discovered several days after her death.

A brief obituary in the *Daily News* said: "At the *News,* Shepard covered a variety of beats with verve and a brash style. Before leaving the paper in 1991, she was the Manhattan cultural affairs editor, winning a Victorian Society award for her coverage of historic preservation issues."[46] It also noted her role in the lawsuit, saying, "It was the first time a discrimination case against a major news organization went to a jury." Her death otherwise received scant notice in the press, which filed the details of her courageous battle in its newspaper morgues, where back issues are placed.

Meanwhile, more than a decade later, many of the editors who had been implicated for discriminatory behavior or who had tried to defend the paper against the lawsuit enjoyed prominent roles in the industry. Richard Blood, who had years earlier left the *News* to join the journalism faculty at Columbia University, was in 1999 teaching journalism at New York University. Richard Oliver was a prominent television personality on New York's Fox network. Sam Roberts was still a highly respected columnist at the *New York Times,* and hosted a news talk show on New York One, a popular local news cable station. Bob Herbert, who was initially on the *News*'s witness list but never testified, continued to shine as the first black regularly featured columnist at the *New York Times.* Prior to joining the *Times,* Herbert had been national correspondent for NBC News.

Meanwhile, blacks, many of whom were unaware of the bias lawsuit and the affirmative action package that may have contributed to their hiring, today serve at every level of the *Daily News.* Still, the percentage of minority journalists at the paper in 1999 was 13.9 percent, in a city where blacks and Latinos comprise half of the population. (*The New York Times* was slightly better, with 15 percent minority employment.) Between 1987 and 1999, the percentage of minority journalists nationally has increased from 6.56 percent to 11.55 percent. In real numbers, they increased from 3,600 to 6,400.

Besides Spurlock, whose job largely keeps him removed from editorial decisions, few blacks are in high-level, decision-making positions at the *Daily News*. An exception was Leon Carter, the paper's first black sports editor. The paper has seemed to prefer black personalities over black power. In addition to putting a black public face on the paper with the hiring of Spurlock and Adrienne Rhodes as the paper's press spokesperson, it hired E. R. Shipp, a former *New York Times* reporter who in 1997 won a Pulitzer Prize for commentary, and Stanley Crouch, a cerebral and iconoclastic writer well known in literary circles. Near the close of the century, the paper also appeared more inclined to cater, at least superficially, to African American interests. In 1999, the paper won another Pulitzer Prize, this time for its coverage of the campaign to save Harlem's fabled Apollo Theater. However, it is still haunted by decisions it has made on more critical stories. In 1995, for example, News columnist Juan Gonzalez challenged the paper's decision to exclude blacks and other minorities from the coverage of the O. J. Simpson trial, a story that had major racial ramifications.

"Our coverage," wrote Gonzalez in an open letter dated October 4, 1995, "dares to openly question whether a jury three-quarters black can produce an impartial O.J. decision but not whether newspaper coverage 95 percent white can do the same." He pointed out that not a single black male or female had gotten a major Simpson assignment. Six years after the monumental legal challenge, the struggle for racial parity in the *Daily News* newsroom continued.

Perhaps the contribution of the quartet to the cause of newsroom diversity and parity cannot be measured in terms of jobs accorded blacks at the *News*, but rather in terms of the triumph of right over might. For them, like so many who challenge powerful institutions, there would be no Hollywood ending. For the plaintiffs, there have been no book or movie deals, and many younger journalists are not even aware of their historic fight, which is rarely mentioned in the press. Several black reporters interviewed at the *News* were unaware of the drama that had unfolded in the newsroom a mere twelve years earlier.

But despite a near white-out of the case in the media, the historic battle is one of the imperfect acts of courage by blacks against a newspaper—and an industry—that has, unfortunately, been left to appraise its merits. It is akin to allowing a convicted felon to mete out his own punishment and write his own story. Unfortunately, many would not learn of the many legal struggles that would continue to prod the media further down the road to diversity. While most of the legal conflicts would continue to be settled behind closed doors, the *Daily News* trial would, at the end of century, remain in a league of its own for taking racial discrimination in the newsroom out of the closet.

What it revealed was that the plaintiffs, while flawed, were human, and, in the end, their foibles were no more assailable than those of their white colleagues. Their transgressions could not be used to explain, or defend, the *News'* failure to promote blacks or pay them comparable wages. The verdict told editors that it was not enough simply to hire minorities. They would also have to be valued. While the lesson would prove a hard one for many editors to accept, the verdict would at least serve as a gut check for the industry and a needed inspirational lift for minority journalists.

"It's very easy to talk about this and much harder to do anything about it," said Alterman. "The people who did that deserve the credit for having the ability to stand up and say, in a meaningful way, 'Enough.'"

But many may ask if the heroic battle waged by the plaintiffs was worth the irreparable damage done to their careers, their reputations, and their spirits. Like many of the nameless and faceless civil rights warriors who sustained deep emotional, psychological, and physical wounds in the heat of battle, the four plaintiffs were all but destroyed by a struggle that was both necessary and historically significant to improve newsroom diversity. While many would never know their names, their efforts did not go unnoticed by an industry that saw the consequences of hiring people without regard to their advancement.

The uphill nature of newsroom diversity raises a host of troubling questions for black journalists in the mainstream media. What, for African American journalists, is success in news organizations that find it difficult to value and embrace the ideas and aspirations of people who must, to make a difference, constantly swim upstream? Is it enough for blacks merely to be hired by the most elite news organizations even as their efforts to contribute in a meaningful way to news coverage are constricted? Why should veterans encourage young blacks to enter the field given the strife they are certain to endure?

The battle by the *Daily News* plaintiffs mattered not because it ushered in sweeping, systemic changes. It did not. In the end, the awarding of assignments and coveted positions is still, by and large, in the purview of men whose values, whose worldviews, conflict with those of many blacks. The changes are incremental, and, one could argue, symbolic—such as in the hiring of a black press person and of high-profile columnists while decisions are still made almost entirely by white men. But even the symbolic gestures and spotty improvements in coverage are significant, however agonizingly and frustratingly glacial they may be.

That is not to say that African American journalists don't have reason to be impatient with the slow rate of change. Journalism should continue to be more than a career, as it was for the pioneers in the black press. For them, it was a powerful vehicle for change. What blacks did not make in salary and prestige, they earned in the psychic rewards that accompanied being full players in the movement to uplift an oppressed people. In the mainstream media, many black journalists have had to trade in many of the psychic rewards for the prestige of well-paying jobs with fancy perks. The superficial trappings are often needed as bandages for the emotional wounds they sustain in the battlefield that is the newsroom. Some argue that their suffering is in vain, and they should simply give up the fight and return to the days of segregated media.

In a postmortem on the trial, Utrice Leid, an editor at the *City Sun*, expressed ambivalence over her support of the plaintiffs, behind whom the *Sun* had aggressively rallied throughout their ordeal. She suggested that their emotional scars were not worth the cost.

"The illusion of power, the empty promise of 'advancement,' the lure of big money, of travel, of starring in the three-ring circus were hard to resist," wrote Leid, describing the allure of the mainstream media for many black journalists. "I just wish they'd really understand that, like E.T., they're extra-terrestrials in a world that does not, cannot and will not understand them and, like E.T., they'd do the logical thing and phone home. Or better yet, come home."[47]

As tempting as it is to quit, as justifiable as it would be for African Americans to abandon the notion of news diversity, such a position would surely spell defeat for black journalists. The consequences for blacks and whites alike are too great. Every morsel of progress by African Americans in the United States, in and out of the media, has resulted from the painful conflict typified by the *Daily News* lawsuit. Just as blacks risked their personal comfort and, indeed, their lives to have their say in the early black press, they would have to fight to contribute in a meaningful way to the public discourse of which the mainstream media is a significant part.

While the kind of advocacy journalism exemplified by the *City Sun* is needed still, so too are the contributions of a David Hardy or a Steve Duncan to the mainstream media. For as long as we look to the media to define and analyze the problems plaguing our schools, our workplaces, and our public spaces, we will need the men and women in the newsrooms to reflect the full range of ideas that just may add up to a solution, or, at the very least, a heightened understanding of what ails us. So, while veteran black journalists would feel conflicted luring young African Americans into the field knowing the strife that certainly awaits them, they can do so knowing that the kind of progress that is necessary happens over generations. They would bring them along knowing that they are part of a struggle greater than their individual defeats and successes; and that the consequences of alienation and misrepresentation are too great to ignore.

FIVE

Private Dilemmas, Public Strife

> One ever feels his twoness—an American, a Negro; two souls,
> two thoughts, two unreconciled strivings; two warring ideals
> in one dark body, whose dogged strength alone keeps it from
> being torn asunder.
>
> —W. E. B. Du Bois, *The Souls of Black Folk*, 1903

Dorothy Gaiter was at her desk in the *Miami Herald* newsroom, read-ing, as she did each week, the city's black weekly newspaper when she spotted her name in a column. The director of the Urban League of Greater Miami wrote in his weekly *Miami Times* column that he had cre-ated the "Nigger of the Year Award" and that Gaiter was one of his five nominees.

Gaiter, a columnist and member of the *Herald's* editorial board, was stunned. The nomination stemmed from a column she had written crit-icizing City Commissioner Miller Dawkins, the city's lone black on the city commission who was seeking reelection. In the column dated Sep-tember 4, 1993, Gaiter had quoted T. Willard Fair, long a prominent fix-ture in Miami's black community, saying that Dawkins's seat was a "black seat" and that the Miami electorate "has always played fair in assisting us in retaining our seat."

Gaiter pointed out that since blacks comprised only a quarter of Miami's population, they needed to build bridges with whites and His-panics. But, she said, "the words 'playing fair' and 'giving us victory' convey a disturbing sense of dependency. They imply a sense of selfless-ness by Hispanics and 'Anglos' to vote with us, to do us a favor. While that selflessness may be a necessary component in community building, it cannot be expected always to carry the day for a black candidate. I'm not sure that it should."

Gaiter noted that Dawkins had made it difficult to win white or Hispanic support, and reminded readers that he had refused to allow a white representative of the NAACP to address the city commission, insisting on a black member. She noted that he had also threatened to burn down a Hispanic-run AIDS referral center planned for a black neighborhood. "And how about the time that he traded his vote for better Orange Bowl seats? Will performances like these hurt him? Probably, particularly because they can't be balanced against a record of good or strong leadership."

In nominating Gaiter for his dubious award, Fair said that Gaiter had acted against the interests of Miami's black community by publicly criticizing the commission's lone black incumbent. Over the weeks to come, Gaiter was, like the other four nominees, skewered in a series of devastating profiles in the *Miami Times*. For Gaiter, the attention the award generated was brutally humiliating.

"I would run into well-respected black people in the supermarket and they would say, 'We're just so sorry about what happened,'" she said. Finally, after weeks of public ridicule, a reporter from *Emerge*, a national news magazine, called to inform her that she had indeed been named "Nigger of the Year."

"It was a really ugly thing," Gaiter recalled. "What really hurt me, and it was painful, was I was disappointed in all of the good people who were whispering what a shame it was instead of speaking out against it. But you get tough."[1]

Gaiter's experience is not an uncommon one for black journalists in the mainstream media who write critically of black people. Rather, the ostracizing of black journalists by prominent members of their own race is an unavoidable consequence of working in the mainstream news media, which African Americans have historically viewed as tools of oppression and degradation. The latitude given blacks who write in the black press—which has resulted in a large body of critical writing on blacks by such luminaries as W. E. B. Du Bois—is not automatically accorded even to crusading blacks in the mainstream media. Their motives and loyalties are immediately suspect given their ties to an institution that has historically denigrated them.

Had Gaiter written her column in a black newspaper, it would not have been viewed as airing dirty laundry, a touchy affair for blacks long sensitive to exposing aspects of their lives that may provoke harsh condemnation from a society that is already insensitive to their plight. *Emerge*, a monthly news magazine, regularly publishes critical pieces on black public figures. But Gaiter's remarks about blacks in the *Miami Herald* were not aired in a friendly environment that would incite healthy self-reflection, but in one that many blacks consider hostile to them. Black journalists must often settle for the tentative embrace of editors who lavish them with praise when they write critically of African American people, since their ability to write harshly about blacks is seen as a barometer of their objectivity.

After *Washington Post* reporter Janet Cooke's September 28, 1980, cover story on an eight-year-old black heroin addict was condemned by black District of Columbia residents as racist and implausible, *Post* publisher Don Graham penned her a reassuring letter that spoke to his perception of the black reporter's dilemma. "The *Post* has no more important and tougher job than explaining life in the black community in Washington. A special burden gets put on black reporters doing that job, and a double-special burden on black reporters who try to see life through their own eyes instead of seeing it the way they're told they should. The *Post* seems to have many such reporters. You belong very high up among them."[2] Of course the story, which was awarded a Pulitzer Prize, was later found to be a fabrication and the paper returned the prize.

But it is the kind of reporting by blacks on blacks—reporting that too often freeze-frames pathology—that most often wins high praise in the newsroom. To pass an objectivity litmus test, black journalists, then, must show they can freely criticize, or even sully the character of, other blacks in order to win the acceptance and trust of white editors. This is not to say that that message is explicitly conveyed to black or white journalists. As discussed in chapter 1, the newsroom environment fosters dynamics of belonging and is supported by a system of rewards and punishments, including prominent story "play" in the paper and coveted assignments. So, many black journalists find themselves torn between their quest to portray blacks fairly—which means exposing their roses as well as their thorns—and the desire shared by all journalists to appear on page 1, which critical or controversial stories best insure.

In turn, the black public, not surprisingly, makes little distinction between black and white journalists given the dominance of negative portrayals of them in the news media. And where blacks have low expectations of most members of the mainstream media, the black journalist who is party to negative portrayals is seen as the ultimate turncoat, even in those instances when the negative coverage is warranted. For many blacks, the exposure of wrongdoing by a black person is seen as more sinful than the wrongdoing that was exposed. And at times, even legitimate targets of negative coverage use it as a convenient cover for their own misdeeds, citing the coverage as yet another example of media racism.

This approach appeared to be the strategy of supporters for the Reverend Henry Lyons, head of the National Baptists Convention USA. In 1997 Lyons was the target of state and federal investigations into allegations that he misused church funds. It was revealed that Lyons, who was married, lived a lavish life in a $700,000 waterfront home he reportedly shared with a female church employee. In a news conference, Lyons accused the "racist" media of misrepresenting his financial dealings and the alleged extramarital relations with a woman he described as a "business partner." Then, in a thinly veiled attempt at racial subterfuge, he added: "I'm proud I've enjoyed some financial success. What are you trying to imply? That blacks in this country cannot be successful and live well?"[3]

In spite of the appearance of financial and marital impropriety, board members—despite objections of a smattering of ministers including the Reverend Calvin Butts of Harlem's famed Abyssinian Baptist Church—voted to keep him in his post and to drop a church investigation into the charges. A newspaper circulated during the national meeting said: "Those elements that are testing Rev. Lyons, principally the white media—the puppet of the white establishment—believe Rev. Lyons is in a vulnerable position. The white establishment's target today is Reverend Lyons. Their target tomorrow, who knows? Black America, however, is the ultimate victim."[4] Lyons, however, eventually admitted guilt in five crimes, including bank and tax fraud. In February 1999, he was convicted of defrauding the denomination of $4 million and was sentenced to five and a half years in prison. He was also ordered to repay $2.5 million. He admitted that the media had not discriminated against him. As for his part in stealing $250,000, which had been donated by a Jewish group to rebuild churches destroyed by arson, he said: "It stinks in God's nostrils. I know it stinks in the law's nostrils, and it stinks to me."[5]

It is because of the widespread skepticism by black Americans concerning the news media that such a transparent ploy resonated in the African American community. Evidence of this mistrust can be traced as far back as 1827, the first copy of *Freedom's Journal*, the nation's first black newspaper.

"Too long has the public been deceived by misrepresentations, in things which concern us dearly," read the newspaper's first editorial. "From the press and the pulpit we have suffered much by being incorrectly represented. . . . Our vices and our degradation are ever arrayed against us, but our virtues are passed by unnoticed."

Contrast this, a full century and a half later, with the Kerner Commission report: "Our evidence shows that the so-called 'white press' is at best mistrusted and at worst held in contempt by many black Americans." One of the Kerner Commission interviewers reported: "Most black people see the newspapers as mouthpieces of the 'power structure.'" Indeed, much of the coverage reflects the perspectives of leaders in business, politics, and the criminal justice system who traditionally have been white males.

The infusion of thousands of blacks in the news media since the Kerner report has not resulted in an appreciable difference in the widespread suspicion by blacks. That is in part because black journalists have not, by and large, been integrated into positions of power from which they can considerably influence news coverage. A 1994 USA Today/ CNN/Gallup Poll found that blacks are twice as likely as Hispanics, Asians, or whites to believe the media worsens race relations, as it has done with its skewed reporting on a series of racially charged stories. It also found that 62 percent of blacks are angry at least once a week over how the media covers racial issues, and that half of blacks and a third of Hispanics believe their local crime coverage is unfair to them. One only has to look at the hysterical coverage of the O. J. Simpson trial, or at the daily barrage of stories on black pathology, contrasted with the paucity of stories on black achievement and white pathology, to understand this sentiment.

"One thing that's strange about newsrooms is that there are a lot of people who don't know black people," offered Felicia Lee, a *New York Times* reporter. "We cover the black pathology but not middle-class people. There are things that I understand that other people will not just because we live in very separate societies."[6]

Lee recalled reporting on racial unrest in Crown Heights, a Brooklyn community inhabited by Hasidic Jews and blacks. The community had a long history of racial tensions stemming from perceptions by blacks that the Hasidic community received a disproportionate share of government funding. For the first few days of racial clashes stemming from a fatal car accident involving a Hasidic driver and a black child, much of the coverage centered around the rage of blacks, while the Hasidic community was portrayed as a peaceful, religious group in mourning. Very little attention was given to the scenes, witnessed by black and white reporters, of Hasidim throwing rocks and bottles and hurling racial epithets at blacks. And none of the stories distinguished between the young, angry black rioters, and the mostly middle-class community of black residents.

The stories did little to explain the underlying reasons for the rage. For years, blacks in Crown Heights had complained of preferential treatment showered on Hasidim by police and other city agencies. The Hasidim, who comprised roughly 10 percent of the population, and whose sect leader was routinely given round-the-clock police protection and a weekly police escort to the cemetery where his wife was buried, seemed to receive a disproportionate share of city and state dollars for housing, police, sanitation, and other government services.

But, by and large, the reporting was focused on the angry young blacks on the street throwing bottles and turning over cars, but very little on the reasons for the rage.

"There were so many layers to that whole thing," noted Lee. "It was incredibly complicated. The first night I was there, I told my editor it wasn't a one-sided clash. There were Jews with bottles and pipes. Some of these [black] kids were very angry and hostile and just didn't trust white reporters."

As coverage in all of the city dailies revolved around the disaffected young blacks in the street, the neighborhood's black middle class was virtually ignored. "They're the people who are aware of the power of the press and how things can be distorted. They're more wary," Lee said, delineating between the reckless quotes of the young blacks in the street, and the more measured remarks that would come from the area's black homeowners. Once the latter were interviewed, they were able to articulate and provide context for the anger of the young blacks, which they shared.

Lee said the portrayals of Crown Heights's black residents was distorted, then, because of its overreliance on the least articulate and responsible people in the community. She added: "Some white reporters quote people using ungrammatical language that fits their preconceived notions. They don't do the same things when they go in poor white communities. What's the purpose except to stigmatize people and make them look uneducated. People in this city have all kinds of dialects." These distortions further erode the trust by blacks and worsen race relations by fueling white anger toward and misunderstanding of blacks.

These stories also serve to inflame relations between black journalists and their white employers. At *New York Newsday*, the final straw for black reporters was an August 22 story highlighting how reporters were injured during the riots.[7] The story focused on seven journalists who were injured, including Jimmy Breslin, the prominent Pulitzer Prize–winning columnist. He was mugged and stripped of his clothing while covering the story, and Curtis Rist, a *Newsday* reporter, was knocked unconscious. Both of the journalists were white, their attackers black. The story ignored the injuries sustained by black journalists, some of whom were beaten by overzealous police officers or by Crown Heights blacks mistrustful of black reporters. Among the injured African American reporters was Curtis Taylor, a *New York Newsday* reporter who was also attacked by blacks angered over the media coverage and presence.

The black and Latino members of the Brooklyn reporting staff called a meeting with editors to outline their grievances over the coverage. The editors responded by assigning a comprehensive article on the perceptions of preferential treatment. After weeks of reporting, a 3,500-word cover story concluded that the area's Hasidic community had indeed been shown favoritism. "The often profound sense of grievance voiced by black Crown Heights residents is not without foundation or tangible symbol," said the article. It substantiated claims by black Crown Heights residents that the Lubavitch community had, for a least ten years, been given round-the-clock police protection, which for blacks epitomized preferential treatment.[8] The article, which grew out of the activism of black and Latino staffers, stood in stark relief from much of the coverage of the unrest.

Thus, while the hiring of black journalists in the wake of the Kerner Commission was intended to bridge a knowledge and communication gap between whites and a community that was widely viewed as alien, the arrangement has had lopsided benefits. The media has gained its own reservoir of intelligence on black life, and, in some instances, black journalists have brought greater depth to the coverage of the inner cities and the emerging black middle class.

But black journalists often complain that their grasp of black life is more often than not exploited to expose the underbelly, rather than the upside, of the African American experience. Each critical story of blacks in the mainstream press serves to validate society's pervasive disparagement of blacks. The exposure of wrongdoing by an African American is rarely seen as an isolated transgression of an individual who happens to be black. And the black reporters who play a role in this negative reporting are seen by members of their own race as pawns of their oppressors.

The dilemma for black reporters in the mainstream media is a unique one. While white reporters are sometimes singled out for dishonor because of a critical report, they are not equally burdened by an implicit debt of racial loyalty spawned by centuries of slavery during which time blacks were routinely pitted against one another by their white masters. One of the lasting legacies of slavery is that many blacks to this day view one another through a lens of their long-deceased ancestors, implicitly assigning the loyalty of an African American to either the white oppressor or to the race. Inasmuch as journalism is a field that requires its participants to be outsiders, black journalists working in the mainstream media are the ultimate outsiders, embraced neither by members of their race nor by the industry in which they work. It has been the exceptional individual who has had the ability to serve white interests without compromising those of blacks.

Nearly a full century ago, W. E. B. Du Bois, in *The Souls of Black Folk*, poignantly described the schizophrenia within blacks, whose loyalties are so often divided between a nation which enslaved them, and their race. "It is a peculiar sensation, this double-consciousness, this sense of always looking at one's self through the eyes of others, of measuring one's soul by the tape of a world that looks on in amused contempt and pity," he wrote.

His depiction of warring ideals can be readily applied to black journalists. The black journalist is often torn between a devotion to the ideal of journalism to uncover truth, and to the knowledge that uncovering some truths in the black community will have devastating consequences given the already routine negative portrayals of blacks in the media. So the dilemma for black journalists is to determine to what end they are practicing their craft. If they became journalists, as many did, to address and expose injustice, then whose interests are served by perpetuating a demeaning or damaging stereotype of members of their race? Is it more important to uncover a particular truth, even when that truth affects not only the individual subject but is taken as further evidence of the race's propensity for a litany of ills? Or does the journalists' overarching commitment to the betterment of black people supersede a commitment to journalism?

For many whites, such questions are perplexingly irrelevant since, as members of the dominant group, racial allegiance—or even racial awareness—is not a matter worthy of conscious consideration. White Americans do not, as a group, have to overcome a stigma of inferiority, nor did they have to break free from shackles of servitude and the resulting implications of that status. They are judged on their individual merits, so they do not carry the weight of another white person's vices. A white corporate executive is not grouped together with a rapist, so a white reporter has no reason to feel a sense of disloyalty for reporting on a white sociopath. While news executives may be more inclined to report on a black sociopath than a white one, that decision likely springs more from a sense that black crime looms larger than white crime than it does from racial allegiance.

But as members of a subordinate racial group, racial identity is a constant consideration, because a black doctor, for example, knows that once he is out of his doctor's garb, and even while in it, he is viewed not as an individual, but as a black man with all the negative connotations. Black individuals thus find it difficult to shed their group identity.

That said, only the most unsophisticated black reporter operates without regard for the racial implications of his or her work. Most black reporters realize that a critical story about a black subject will have lasting consequences, the primary one being that it will help foment negative stereotypes of black people. To play a role in that coverage insures the black reporter short-term alienation in at least some segments of the black community.

More than one hundred years after the abolition of slavery, many blacks still judge one another as their enslaved ancestors had, condemning those seen as accommodationists. They are labeled Aunt Jemima, Uncle Tom, house slave, or, as Dorothy Gaiter was, "Nigger of the Year." Given the expectation of all journalists to write critically of their subjects, black journalists who write about the plight of blacks are in an unenviable position. Those who write compassionately about members of their race risk the mistrust of their white superiors, who deem them unable to be objective. Many black reporters say they feel their credibility is at stake in the newsroom unless they write negatively about black people. It may be one of the reasons why one-third of NABJ members surveyed said they feared reporting on race. Another reason, of course, could be the public censure by prominent blacks whenever they write critically about blacks.

Michael Cottman, while a reporter at *New York Newsday*, said he was instructed by his white editor to write a negative story about David Dinkins, New York's first black mayor, to prove he could be objective. Cottman said the challenge came early in the tenure of Dinkins, who was elected in 1989. He recalls that city editor Richard Esposito summoned him to his office, saying: "We want you to dig up some dirt on Dinkins. We want you to show us you can bust his balls."[9]

Cottman, at the time the paper's only African American covering City Hall, said he was stunned and offended by the bluntness of the directive, and responded: "If I don't, is my career in the toilet?" He said he then assured Esposito that he would cover Dinkins objectively, balancing positive stories with negative ones.

"We're expected to be the hit men for whites so they don't appear racist. They can always say 'It's fair. A black reporter wrote it.'"[10] Cottman left *Newsday* to write books, but in 1999 he became a political writer for the *Washington Post.*

The case that came to symbolize the kind of public censure that befalls African American journalists who write critically of members of their own race emanated from the publication of a *Washington Post* article in 1984. That article revealed that the Reverend Jesse Jackson had, in a private conversation with black reporters, referred to Jews as "Hymie" and New York as "Hymie-town."

For months, Milton Coleman, the black *Post* reporter who disclosed Jackson's comments, was vilified by blacks across the country, who accused him of betraying the nation's most prominent black leader to appease his white editors. Few blacks ever stopped to consider Coleman's responsibility as a journalist, or whether Jackson was at fault for placing a journalist in such a compromising position. Is it the responsibility of a journalist to cover up the indiscretions of a black presidential candidate? But given the racial climate in this country and the reluctance of whites to forgive blacks for their transgressions, many black journalists said they would have warned Jackson that his choice of words was offensive and given him a chance to redeem himself. They reason that their white colleagues have surely witnessed similar misdeeds by white politicians that have gone unreported.

Many of the same blacks who condemned Coleman said they would praise a white reporter who disclosed that a white presidential candidate had made an offensive remark about blacks in private conversations with reporters. And few of the same black reporters would have given a white politician who had uttered racially offensive remarks an opportunity to redeem himself. But given the racial paradox, Coleman was held to a different standard.

For Coleman, who says Jackson made the remarks on January 25, 1984, while discussing the Middle East at Washington National Airport, the dilemma over whether to disclose them was short lived. He said while he did not think Jackson's conduct warranted an immediate story, he did believe his remarks deserved inclusion in a story that could place them in context, given Jackson's public stance on civil rights. As such, he passed his notes concerning the conversation to Rick Atkinson, a white colleague who was writing a story on Jackson's relations with Jews.[11]

On February 13, the day the story broke, Coleman braced himself for a public outcry, which did not materialize. But five days later, after the *Washington Post* demanded an explanation from Jackson in an editorial headlined "Mr. Jackson's Choice of Words," Coleman became the target of a vitriolic backlash. For more than a week, Jackson denied making the disparaging remarks and Coleman was assailed by blacks across the country as a sell-out who, for career advancement, was attempting to derail Jackson's historic campaign. As the pressure mounted, Coleman and the *Post* stuck by their story, even after a black reporter who Coleman said was present when Jackson made the remarks said he had no such recollection.

Nearly two weeks later, following a string of denials, Jackson finally acknowledged he had made the derogatory remarks and apologized. But for Jackson, and for Coleman, the damage seemed irreparable.

In a March 11 nationally broadcast radio address, Nation of Islam leader Louis Farrakhan vowed to "make an example" of Coleman for betraying the black community. He denounced Coleman as "a no-good, filthy traitor" and said: "At this point, no physical harm. . . . We're going to keep on going until we make it so that he cannot enter in among black people."[12]

Jackson disavowed any form of "threats or intimidation" and said Coleman was merely doing his job, but nothing he could say could restore Coleman's reputation in much of black America, or Jackson's among Jews.[13] Years later, many Jewish leaders continued to characterize Jackson as anti-Semitic, in spite of his repeated apologies. Where white leaders, most notably Alabama's governor, George Wallace, a once staunch segregationist, have been able to overcome much more incendiary language and behavior toward blacks—Wallace was reelected governor with black support—Jackson has faced a stubborn refusal by many Jews to forgive and forget. It is precisely because of this troubling double standard that many African Americans find Coleman's actions so unforgivable.

Jackson and Coleman have both been frozen in a web of intractable racial psychodramas propelled by an unfair and irreversible branding of blacks by whites, and a demand for unconditional loyalty by blacks placed on other blacks in a racialized society. In such a scenario, blacks should not expose wrongdoing by other blacks because of the severe sanctions by whites. For the black journalist, it is a no-win situation since such high standards of blind racial loyalty would render him or her unfit for the profession.

The Hymie-town episode will long be remembered by African American journalists as it underscored their vexing dilemma: what do they do when their ambition and responsibilities as journalists appears at odds with racial progress? In the wake of the Coleman case, many began to question whether black journalists were journalists first or African Americans first, and whites—disturbed by black journalists' widespread criticism of Coleman—privately and publicly questioned whether black journalists could "objectively" cover black subjects. While the floodlights were fixed on black journalists, few bothered to question what white journalists would do, and indeed have done, in similar situations. Have they ignored similar behavior by white public officials, particularly those with whom they enjoyed close relations? Is it only the black journalists' credibility that is in doubt? Because questions such as these went unasked, the scrutiny was placed solely on black journalists, a situation that continues to date.

The kind of judgment call made by Coleman is made daily, on an individual basis, and black and white reporters are equally inclined to report or not to report indiscretions by those they report on regularly. For years, reporters ignored philandering by the politicians they closely covered. We will never know how many journalists ignore racially offensive or sexist remarks uttered in private by public officials.

Many black journalists critical of Coleman were most troubled by his decision to disclose off-the-record remarks. In a 3,200-word essay in the *Washington Post* on April 8, Coleman detailed the pain the ordeal had caused him and his family but insisted "I am convinced that I did the right thing and that I acted on principles and stuck to them firmly." Explaining how a black reporter could "do this to another black man. . . .

on a historic and inspiring presidential bid," he said, "in post–civil rights, post–voting rights, post–affirmative action America," the dilemma, for him at least, was not centered around race. His racial kinship with Jackson aside, he said, "this is about how a reporter covers a candidate for president of the United States."

A man who fashioned himself as a moral standard bearer, he maintained, should have known better than to utter such remarks, especially in the presence of a reporter. In August of that year, during a raucous session with some four hundred journalists attending the National Association of Black Journalists' annual convention, Coleman affirmed that as a presidential candidate, Jackson was necessarily held to a higher standard. "His remarks suggested to me he believed such statements were appropriate," he argued.

Coleman insisted that the character of a man running for the nation's highest office took precedence over confidentiality, especially since Jackson had made the disparaging remarks on a number of occasions in the presence of several reporters. He said Jackson should have been sophisticated enough to know his comments would eventually be exposed. Indeed, another black reporter, who asked to remain anonymous so as not to embarrass his editors, said he too had told his editors during the fall of 1984 that Jackson had used the word "Hymie" on a number of occasions, but they elected not to pursue the story.

Coleman, who has since the controversy moved from a reporting to an editing position, continued to be haunted by the episode. In the late 1990s Coleman was an assistant managing editor at the *Post*—the highest position held by a black staff member—and he had resigned himself to the fact that many African Americans will continue to view any future promotions as his reward because "I did in a brother. . . . Nothing I am ever going to do is going to erase that," he conceded.[14] Cathy Hughes, a popular Washington, D.C., talk-show host, agreed. Coleman, she said, "got rewarded for lynching the black community."[15]

It is widely accepted among African Americans that blacks, in and out of the media, are rewarded for condemning black people and there is evidence to support instances of this. Booker T. Washington became the most celebrated black person of his generation in the late 1800s and early 1900s—and moved freely in elite white circles—largely because of his conservative appeal to African Americans to be patient in their quest for full citizenship. While he was criticized by prominent blacks, most notably by Du Bois and William Monroe Trotter, the progressive editor of the *Guardian* in Boston, his message was widely hailed by whites in the mainstream press and by those blacks who benefited from his largesse.

Supreme Court Justice Clarence Thomas and Ward Connelly, the University of California regent who in the 1990s led the fight against affirmative action in higher education, are similarly viewed by many black intellectuals as modern-day counterparts to Washington. Both have attacked affirmative action and social programs that redress centuries of racial oppression. Many blacks believe that they, like Washington before them, have been rewarded for their conservative positions on racial issues, views considered anathema to many blacks.

To be a journalist in the mainstream press, and to succeed, thus often requires the surrendering of racial loyalty—which for African Americans has been an obliged kinship in a hostile environment—because of the ways in which it restricts the reporter's ability to report critically about an already downtrodden group. The challenge for the black journalist, then, is to maintain the high ideals of journalism while maintaining a semblance of credibility with black people; or, as Du Bois said, to merge being black and American "without being cursed and spit upon by his fellows, [and] without having the doors of Opportunity closed roughly in his face."[16]

Thus, while for public consumption, most black reporters would say their commitment is to truth, regardless of the consequences, privately they realize that truth is a deeply subjective concept, since every truth does not find its way into a newspaper or newscast. Much of what is true—for instance, the fact that most blacks are law abiding, or that most crimes are intra-racial—is not considered newsworthy by news managers, based on the paucity of stories supporting those realities. So much of what is true about daily occurrences in general, and about blacks in particular, does not find its way into the daily newspaper or television newscast. How, then, does one write critically of blacks for a white audience without further contributing to the degradation of black people?

Many of the stories that are considered newsworthy conform to a wide range of stereotypes that play into an established system of beliefs. The media makes major news out of a white teenager who kills her baby because it is viewed as being at odds with the stereotype of pathology-free white teenage girls. Black teenagers who commit similar crimes are not accorded prominent coverage because it would neither surprise nor arouse as much interest given their image as the embodiment of pathology. Because of the routine way in which white men are projected as symbols of authority and responsibility, the portrait of a violent white criminal, for instance, is viewed as exceptional. Since the media is a reflection of generally held stereotypes, most people are either cast as stereotypes or exceptions to stereotypes.

In reporting on members of their race, black journalists know their work is being closely scrutinized by black people—who sometimes hold them to an unrealistic standard—as well as by their white editors, who expect them to get from their own communities what white reporters often cannot.

Not surprisingly, black reporters are resentful of the pressure they work under. They are upset over the unfair expectations placed on them by their racial cohorts who expect them only to portray blacks in glowing terms to make up for the barrage of negative portrayals. For many African Americans, each story on black people, no matter how credible, is weighed against a history of negative and stereotypical reporting on blacks. So Gaiter's column criticizing a black political figure is not viewed in isolation, but in the context of a pattern of negative reporting on blacks. And African American reporters are angered over perceived expectations by white editors for them to churn out negative portrayals of blacks to prove their objectivity, or to confirm a false perception of blacks.

As they gingerly walk the tightrope, they see below them a pool of sharks. Included are the black demagogues who are quick to blame the disclosure by black journalists of their transgressions as betrayal and "Uncle Tomism," knowing the tactic resonates in a community already mistrustful of the media. The black reporter is assailed from the pulpit and from black radio stations, his crime against his race considered far graver than the wrongdoing he exposed. The Reverend Jesse Jackson, addressing the National Association of Black Journalists during its 1984 convention, said black reporters "operate with a needle in their backside and scissor in their chest," noting that management mistrusts them and black communities scorn them.[17]

Even crusading black journalists have found their reputations sullied in black circles after they write critically of blacks. In 1988, Les Payne, an assistant managing editor of *Newsday* on Long Island, became the target of black talk-radio venom after he wrote a story alleging that a black teenager's tale of abduction and rape by several white men—a story that for months fueled racial tensions throughout New York State—was a hoax.

Payne pursued the story himself after leads followed by a team of his reporters failed to uncover what had actually happened to Tawana Brawley. In November of 1987, Brawley was spotted in her upstate New York neighborhood in a garbage bag smeared with dog feces and the letters KKK and other racial epithets scrawled on her body.

Brawley, then fifteen, alleged she was abducted by up to six white men, one of whom she said flashed a badge, as she boarded a bus in Wappinger Falls, a predominantly white community near Poughkeepsie, New York. The Reverend Al Sharpton and activist lawyers C. Vernon Mason and Alton Maddox—riding a wave of favorable press for their role in securing a special prosecutor to investigate a fatal racial attack in Howard Beach, Queens—blamed local police for engaging in a state-sanctioned cover-up. For months, at circuslike rallies in New York City and Poughkeepsie, they demanded the governor's appointment of a special prosecutor. Governor Mario Cuomo complied by appointing State Attorney General Robert Abrams.

After a seven-month investigation, a 170-page report by a special grand jury in October 1988 concluded that Brawley had fabricated the tale of rape and abduction. The report was based on forensic and medical evidence and interviews with more than sixty witnesses. Brawley herself, acting on the advice of her advisers, refused to testify before the grand jury, insisting the panel was biased.

In the wake of the report, Brawley, flanked by Mason, Maddox, and Sharpton, stood by her story as the three activists blamed the criminal justice system for once again failing African Americans. The hordes of reporters from across the country who for months converged on the girl's small community quickly disbanded, accepting the report as the final word.

In New York's black community, however, questions remained. Why, many asked, would a teenager concoct such a tale and smear her own body with dog feces? Why did a local police officer commit suicide a week after her discovery? Was he, as the activists alleged, one of the attackers who was killed to keep quiet? Or had he committed suicide out of guilt? Many African Americans remained convinced that Brawley was the victim of an unspeakable racial and sexual assault which officials sought to cover up.

Six months after the grand jury report, on April 28, 1988, Payne's front-page story in *Newsday*, based primarily on an in-depth interview with Brawley's boyfriend Daryl Rodriguez, alleged that Brawley had fabricated the story to evoke sympathy from Ralph King, her mother's live-in boyfriend, and avoid further physical abuse for a late-night outing.

According to the 4,000-word story, Brawley told Rodriguez that King had slapped her around when she returned home late one evening, causing her to flee to avoid further abuse. According to Rodriguez, the girl and her mother concocted the scheme as a way to get her back in the house, and into King's good graces.

The plan backfired, he said, when a neighbor saw Brawley stepping into the plastic bag before her mother was to discover her. When Brawley's mother spotted the neighbor going to her daughter's aid, she left to file a missing person report, which she had not done in the four days since the girl had left home. Brawley was taken to a hospital, where she related her story of abduction and rape in a wooded area. Unaware that the story had been fabricated, Brawley's horrified aunt went to the media.

According to Payne's account, Brawley, when confronted by a *Newsday* reporter to verify Rodriguez's claim, denied the allegations and said she had not seen Rodriguez in months. However, the article noted that Brawley had been seen with Rodriguez on a number of occasions in the preceding weeks. The story also said that Rodriguez had relocated to Virginia to be with Brawley, and correctly directed *Newsday* to the library where she was found by a reporter.

The attacks on Payne's character began in the wee hours of the morning as the host of WLIB Radio read excerpts of the story, provoking a furious reaction from black callers and in-studio guests, including Sharpton.

"The story line is illogical," Sharpton told WLIB listeners that day. "You have to be an imbecile, an idiot or a fool, or a reasonable combination of all three, to believe that."[18] Maddox charged that the story was a "personal vendetta" by Payne against Sharpton, saying that Payne and *Newsday* had, since 1988, worked to discredit Sharpton with a series of stories alleging Sharpton's role as an FBI informant. Sharpton also sought to discredit Rodriguez, whom he described as "an ex-drug user and a lunatic," and threatened to subpoena him to appear in civil court.[19]

"They talked about me all day," said Payne. "Sharpton was saying things like 'he did this to please his white bosses.' I went on a show and the community beat up on me for two hours. It was the typical mob mentality."[20]

New York's black press joined the bandwagon, defending Brawley against *Newsday's* assault. A front-page headline in *Big Red*, a black, Brooklyn-based weekly newspaper, screamed "Just a Payne in the Butt." The verbal assaults continued unabated for months, threatening to diminish Payne's longtime reputation as a crusading advocate for African Americans, who, as one of the founders of the National Association of Black Journalists, had mentored many young black journalists. "A woman told me, 'White men have been raping black women for years in the South,'" Payne recalled. "I said, 'I'm aware that white men do that in the north too, but they didn't rape this one.'"[21]

One evening, at the invitation of Maddox, Payne went to face his critics at the Slave Theater in Brooklyn's Bedford-Stuyvesant section where Mason, Maddox, and Sharpton had for months held spirited rallies on Brawley's behalf. Payne said he had no choice but to go. "My view is, my responsibility to the community is to ferret out facts. What they do with those facts is their business."

For more than an hour, Payne fielded hostile questions. He told the audience he was clear about his responsibility as a journalist and as an African American when he wrote the story, and said the community had a right to know the truth. Payne said that while he respected the activists' wish to protect Brawley, "that little old lady giving part of her rent check to the Tawana Brawley Defense Fund, she should know this is a hoax." He said many of his critics believed that attacking Brawley and her prominent advisors was tantamount to attacking the black community.

"You have to be sure about your responsibility being to the community—not Al Sharpton or Jesse Jackson, but the total, abstract black community," maintained Payne. "Once you know that, there should be no conflict. There's going to be a hell of a lot of grief but you can't worry about that."

Payne's utilitarian outlook, in which the greater good for blacks to know overshadows the need to spare the reputations of a handful, is one way to withstand the turbulence inherent in reporting honestly on blacks. Gaiter says she simply strives for moral consistency and seeks to be constructive in her criticism. Either way, it takes courage for black journalists to report stories that are certain to provoke hostility in their own racial community.

"I don't think we have time to cut corners," says Gaiter, who, since 1991, has written about race for the *Wall Street Journal*. "When we have the opportunity to write in a way that moves us ahead in a healthy direction, you have to take it. When you try to be morally consistent, it enables you to write critically and lovingly of our problems. You have to tell the truth."[22]

At the *Journal,* Gaiter was the reporter who first exposed the financial and ideological problems within the National Association for the Advancement for Colored People, which eventually resulted in the ouster of Benjamin Chavis, then president of the NAACP.

Gaiter had learned from various sources that the group was sharply divided over Chavis's leadership and was troubled over an unprecedented deficit and the leader's controversial brand of politics and alliances with the Nation of Islam. With much of her reporting done, Gaiter finally contacted Chavis for an interview.

"He kept saying, 'Why are you doing this?'" recalls Gaiter. "He wanted to know who my sources were. I told him, 'They are people who love the NAACP and think it's going to go down in flames and by telling me their story, they think something can be done to turn it around.'"

Chavis, she says, subtly suggested that her story would hurt the organization's image and would ill serve black interests. She said Chavis implied that her allegiance should be to the NAACP and not to her professional calling. Gaiter asserted that by exposing the story, she was not only serving the interests of the NAACP, but also of blacks in general.

"I felt for me to be writing it, it was probably a good thing," Gaiter recalls telling him. "I'm forty-four and remember segregation. I went to segregated schools, and I don't think there's a black person in America who doesn't owe the NAACP a great debt of gratitude. If not me, who?" Gaiter asked Chavis. "It's important to have some perspective, and I think people talk to me because they knew I could be trusted and knew the importance of the organization continuing."

The page 1 article, published on June 10, 1994, painted a damning portrait of Chavis's leadership. It detailed how Chavis had, during his one-year tenure, presided over a $3 million deficit and divided the group by courting controversial African Americans, most notably Nation of Islam leader Louis Farrakhan.

"The hope was that Mr. Chavis, a baby boomer with a stream of 1960s activism, would rekindle the group's focus and build bridges to younger blacks while shoring up finances and membership," the article read. "But Mr. Chavis's first year on the job hasn't quite worked out that way. Instead the NAACP, the nation's oldest and largest civil rights organization, is engulfed in what longtime supporters say is the worst financial and philosophical crisis in its 85-year history. And much of it they lay at the feet of Mr. Chavis."[23] The article also quoted former NAACP director Benjamin Hooks, denying for the first time Chavis's allegations that he had inherited a deficit from Hooks.

Later that month, Gaiter went to Chicago to attend the NAACP's annual convention. She was among the hundreds of people assembled for Chavis's rambling address. Midway through, Chavis began criticizing the media. Then, according to Gaiter, he asked those assembled to "pray for the sister from the *Wall Street Journal*" to help her see the error of her ways. Gaiter was momentarily startled and attempted to avoid eye contact with anyone. By the next morning, Gaiter's sense of humor kicked in. "I saw the director of communications and introduced myself and said, 'Tell Reverend Chavis I really appreciated that.'" She said doctors had, a year earlier, mistakenly given her four months to live. "Now I had all these religious black people praying for me. It was great," Gaiter said.

But if black journalists are doubly-burdened by their responsibilities to their work—and to their race—are not white journalists also somehow burdened by race, or are they objective by virtue of not having conscious racial considerations? While their objectivity is often not questioned and they are somehow granted a presumption of impartiality, beneath the surface are racial biases that elude detection primarily because they ebb and flow with the tide of the news organization. The perspectives of blacks and other minorities more often go against the currents.

Caroline Brewer, an editorial writer at the *Bergen Record* in New Jersey, recalled an intense dispute with her white colleagues at the *Dayton Daily News* in Ohio. She had written an editorial expressing outrage over a judge's decision to release Rebecca Hopher, a white teenager from an affluent Ohio suburb, from jail as she appealed a murder conviction and a mandatory fifteen-year sentence. In the June 1995 editorial, Brewer said no such leniency would be accorded a poor black or Hispanic defendant. She said the decision smacked of race and class privilege and a double standard of justice.

But Brewer's boss, editorial-page editor Hap Cawood, and her colleague Martin Gottlieb said the editorial was too strong.

"They thought the family had been treated quite harshly, that they had to suffer through news coverage and seeing their pictures in the paper," recalled Brewer. "They said she had suffered through the trial and had not received favorable treatment."[24]

Brewer argued that the newspaper had handled the case with kid gloves by covering only the trial and bypassing routine reporting on the girl's background. "We never went to her school, her neighborhood to try to find out what kind of person she was. We would have turned rocks upside down for most people."

Brewer tried to show the men that many readers would see the court decision as a blatant double standard of justice and that the paper would be remiss not to expose it. In the end, her colleagues never wavered, and her editorial was killed. "I was incredulous," Brewer said. "I had to leave the office for a couple of hours because I was so angry." Brewer unleashed some of her ire in a column several weeks later in which she called the decision "a Dayton-area metaphor for much in the way the American criminal justice system generally conducts itself."

She said Ohio lawmakers did not have affluent young whites in mind when they passed a mandatory-sentence law for convicted murderers. "The raging anti-crime bulls had what they call 'predators' in mind. The young, black kind," Brewer wrote. "The legislators wouldn't be bothered with the 'what ifs' because they never imagined the 'what ifs' would pertain to 'people like them,' or people with whom they could sympathize. In the minds of most legislators, the criminal class is monolithic—poor and black—and deserving of no mercy."[25]

She ended the column by noting that Hopher, who had killed her newborn baby, was not the first young adult worthy of compassion, but no such compassion is typically shown young, inner-city defendants.

"Until the courts, legislators, and the general public come to that recognition," she said, "the notion of American justice will continue to have a hollow ring for those who know nothing of its kinder, gentler side."

Brewer left the newspaper to work for the *Bergen Record* in New Jersey shortly after her Hopher column. The incident was for her yet another example of the bias of white journalists that largely goes undetected—and unchallenged. In a white-centered nation, whites are not required to have the kind of double consciousness essential for the survival of blacks and other nonwhites. As a result, they have little need to concern themselves with the blind spot that members of any racial group are bound to have on issues of race.

"This was the kind of thing that happened often," said Brewer. "When I talk to people about journalism, I say don't talk to me about objectivity, talk to me about fairness because objectivity doesn't exist."[26] News objectivity requires a suspension of racial prejudice, a kind of blind justice, that should also inform the criminal justice system but often does not.

Meanwhile, many continue to question the ability of black journalists to be objective, at least until they prove their ability to condemn their own. For decades, news organizations, including the *Washington Post*, the *New York Times*, and the *Detroit Free Press*, restricted their black reporters from covering Africa, fearing their lack of objectivity.[27] No such dictate applied to white reporters covering Europe. Les Payne said that when he applied for a job at his paper's Africa bureau, he was bluntly told that blacks could not be fair covering Africa. White members of the media openly inferred that a Black Entertainment Television (BET) journalist preparing to conduct the first television interview with O. J. Simpson after acquittal in the murder of his wife and her friend Ronald Goldman would not be objective. In newspapers and on television, speculation was rife that the interview by Ed Gordon would be a public relations coup for Simpson.

Reuters News Service, on January 20, reported: "As word of the interview spread, doubts surfaced about whether it would be the kind of no-holds-barred session that he has refused to grant to any other TV news outlet."

Gordon found himself defending the selection of BET, and his own credibility. "Those who are skeptical should afford me the same grace that we would afford a white journalist interviewing a white newsmaker," he told reporters. "Nobody asks, 'Did they pick you because you're white?'"[28]

Although Simpson predictably maintained his innocence throughout the hour-long interview and refused to discuss specifics regarding his whereabouts the night of the murders, Gordon peppered him with questions about his abusive relationship with wife Nicole, his public golfing outings that many had criticized in the wake of the murders, and whether he had, over the years, turned his back on blacks by living in an almost exclusively white world.

In the end, white media critics appeared divided on the effectiveness of the interview, which was lauded by some, including a *New York Times* writer, and panned by others. And black reporters continued their high-wire act across a pool of sharks.

"We must acknowledge that as a people—E Pluribus Unum—we are on a slippery slope toward economic strife, social turmoil, and cultural chaos," wrote Cornel West. "If we go down, we go down together. . . . The paradox of race in America is that our common destiny is more pronounced and imperiled precisely when our divisions are deeper. The Civil War and its legacy speak loudly here. And our divisions are growing deeper."[29]

The news industry can do more to close this breach than any other institution in America, but it has largely chosen to be a mirror of white entitlement rather than a guide for racial enlightenment. But as America, with lightning speed, becomes a distinctively multiracial place with no dominant racial identity, it will increasingly become essential for whites in the news industry to develop the kind of double consciousness that has historically been required of other Americans. Blacks and other people of color can no longer be viewed as "the other," "the alien," if the news media are to survive the economic realities of the not-too-distant future. Given the sordid history of the media's reporting on African Americans in particular, the news media should require its reporters, black and white, to tread ever more carefully in black affairs, mindful both of current events and the pattern of past injustices. While it is unreasonable to expect journalists to appease blacks by revealing only their virtues, it is also wholly unethical to have them primarily delve into their vices. Both defy the ideals of fairness and objectivity. Since much of this clamoring for the negative, sensational, and stereotypical in news today occurs subconsciously or in accordance with generally accepted news values, it will take a determinedly conscious investigation of the preponderance of this negative coverage to get the media on the road to building good faith with blacks.

Among the questions media executives need to investigate is why so many of the stories about welfare on television and in print are accompanied by pictures of black women, even though the majority of welfare recipients are white women. And for each story on pathology in communities like Harlem, they must ask if similar stories on pathology in white communities are being ignored. For instance, little attention is paid to the fact that roughly 70 percent of the Orthodox Jewish families in Brooklyn's Borough Park community receive some form of public assistance.

Without this kind of serious soul searching by news executives, black reporters will never enjoy the trust of the communities from which they are increasingly becoming as alienated as their white counterparts. It is not uncommon for black reporters reporting on sensitive issues in a black community to be physically assaulted, vilified as contributors to media misrepresentation of their race. Without a discernible difference in portrayals, black journalists will be seen as little more than enemy spies, and will be no more valuable to their news organizations covering black people than whites.

Unless there is a major overhaul in race coverage—a conscious attempt to eradicate the negative and pervasive stereotyping of black people—the contributions of black journalists will continue to be made in environs considered hostile to most black people. So the black journalists in the trenches will continue to feel the pressure of double jeopardy, a situation that has contributed to a turnover rate that is double that of white journalists.

| SIX |

Double Standards and the
"Double-Special Burden"

The Post has no more important and tougher job than explaining life in the black community in Washington. A special
burden gets put on black reporters doing that job, and a double-special burden on black reporters who try to see life
through their own eyes, instead of seeing it the way they're
told they should.

— *Washington Post* publisher Don Graham
in a letter to Janet Cooke, 1981

On September 28, 1980, the *Washington Post* led the front page with a
chilling story entitled "Jimmy's World," which chronicled the tragic
life of an eight-year old, third-generation drug addict born into a life
of spiraling dysfunction. According to the article, written by Janet
Cooke, an ambitious twenty-five-year-old African American reporter,
Jimmy—"a precocious little boy with sandy hair, velvety brown eyes
and needle marks freckling the baby-smooth skin of his thin brown
arms"—is the product of the rape of a teenage girl by her mother's
boyfriend. So despondent was she after his birth that she didn't bother
to name him. "My sister liked the name Jimmy and I said 'OK, call
him that, who gives a fu—?'"

Jimmy is said to live in an apartment—where addicts drift in and out,
some jittery in their withdrawal, others in a drug haze—with his mother
and Ron, her "live-in lover," who is a drug dealer.

It was Ron who first turned Jimmy, at age five, on to heroin. "I let him
snort a little and, damn, the little dude really did get off," Ron is quoted
saying. Six months later, Jimmy was hooked. Cooke quoted Jimmy as

saying: "I felt like I was part of what was goin' down." Added Ron: "I don't really like to see him fire up. But you know, I think he would have got into it one day, anyway. Everybody does. When you live in the ghetto, it's all a matter of survival. . . . Drugs and black folk been together for a long time." The story ends with Ron injecting the boy with heroin, and Jimmy climbing into a chair where he goes into a drug-induced nod.

In 2,256 words, Cooke had written the ultimate black dysfunction story, replete with broken English, teenage pregnancy, immorality, hopelessness, and a sweeping indictment of every law-abiding African American in the "ghetto." Rather than challenge the shallow portraits of inner-city life, which adjoins poor, working- and middle-class people of varying aspirations and inclinations, or offer a way out of mind-numbing despair, "Jimmy's World" cemented in many minds the worst stereotypes of urban blacks. "Jimmy's World" was not simply Jimmy's, but that of the black urban poor. It was a dramatic story naturally destined for the front page of one of America's greatest papers. The story was picked up by another three hundred papers across the country and throughout the world.

"Jimmy's World" turned out to be a fabrication that would forever haunt Cooke, the *Post*, and all of American journalism. But "Jimmy's World" is not merely the story of a woman, journalism ethics, and an institution; it also helps illuminate a pervasive double standard that determines the disparate rewards and sanctions for black verses white journalists in the American news media. It is a persistent and stark double standard that places greater pressure on blacks to write negative stories on African Americans. "Jimmy's World" also provides a window onto a routinely employed double standard that allows whites, but not African Americans, to overcome egregious journalistic transgressions.

In all of the postmortems on "Jimmy's World"—and there were many, including the *Post*'s candid ombudsman's report published in its own paper—little attention has been paid to the role of race in the story's creation, prominent display, awards, or in Cooke's quick ascension at the *Post*. And in an industry in which the contributions of blacks have always been viewed skeptically, the rise and fall of Cooke reveals how indelibly etched in our psyches are the flagrant transgressions of black journalists, and how some are quick to translate them into an indictment of all black journalists.

The Sunday that "Jimmy's World" was published on the front page of the *Washington Post*, it immediately provoked suspicion in Washington's overwhelmingly black community. Many district blacks, already mistrustful of the *Post*'s coverage of African Americans, contended that the story was not only racist, but also criminal, since the paper appeared unconcerned about the boy's welfare. Indeed, the story noted that medical experts said Jimmy's risk of death from an overdose was "extremely high." Dr. Dorynne Czechowicz, of the National Institute on Drug Abuse, was quoted as saying: "He might already be close to getting a lethal dose." She added: "It probably isn't too late to help him."

The Sunday the story ran, Washington's police chief Burtell Jefferson called on his youth division to find the boy. By Monday morning, he and Mayor Marion Barry, both African Americans, launched a task force of hundreds of police officers and social workers to fan the city to find the boy. The *Post* was inundated with phone calls and letters from outraged readers who insisted that Jimmy's identity be revealed so he could get help.

Cooke told her editors that "Ron" threatened to kill her if his identity was revealed, and the editors continued to insist that the family's anonymity, and Cooke's safety, be protected. When asked by police to identify the boy, the *Post* invoked First Amendment protection of confidential sources. The *Post*, however, launched its own investigation, with six reporters assigned to find another Jimmy to show the prevalence of the problem. One reporter, Courtland Milloy, was sent out with Cooke to find another "Jimmy," but Milloy was privately determined to find the actual Jimmy in order to get him help. A red flag was raised when, while out in the area where Jimmy was said to live, Cooke did not seem familiar with the neighborhood. Milloy told his editor that they combed the neighborhood for seven hours, but Cooke was unable to point out where the boy lived.[1]

By October 15, some two weeks after the story broke, Mayor Barry suspended his search while assailing the story's credibility. "I've been told the story is part myth, part reality," he said, adding that no one believes the mother or her boyfriend would "allow a reporter to see them shoot up."[2] The *Post* stuck by its story, and Cooke quickly became a newsroom star. The day after the story ran, she was promoted from the weekly section to the metropolitan staff. And a week later, on October 7, came a letter from publisher Don Graham to Cooke: "With all the turmoil of the last week, it's important that one say the basic thing: not only was that a very fine story in Sunday's paper a week ago, it was only one of many you've done in the last year."[3]

He added: "The *Post* has no more important and tougher job than explaining life in the black community in Washington. A special burden gets put on black reporters doing that job, and a double-special burden on black reporters who try to see life through their own eyes, instead of seeing it the way they're told they should. The *Post* seems to have many such reporters. You belong very high up among them."

For Graham, Cooke had passed an unspoken litmus test by demonstrating her willingness to expose the warts in the black community while ignoring the pressure exerted on black reporters by other blacks to write uplifting stories. He seemed to suggest that while it may be more difficult for black reporters to "see life through their own eyes," given the pressure from African Americans, the rewards in the newsroom were greater for those who did. Thus, while white reporters are judged by their ability to write well and break stories that are compelling and important, blacks have "a double-special burden" also to expose ills in their own community. The implicit message is problematic.

While black reporters, to be credible, should not, as Graham suggests, bow to external pressures to write stories favorable to blacks, neither should they feel compelled to bow to internal pressures to write negatively of them. Bowing to either side tarnishes that reporter's credibility since the search for truth should not be driven by a preference for either positive or negative stories. If many African American reporters believe the rewards are greater for stories that confirm stereotypes, they could easily slant the news in a certain direction while undermining the benefits of racial diversity in the newsroom. If the role of black reporters is primarily to uncover warts in the black community, then many people— particularly African Americans—have ample reason to question their value in the news industry.

Of course, the pressure on all journalists to turn up negative or controversial stories are great, since scandal and controversy are highly regarded news values, but the double-special burden Graham describes specifically relates to African Americans and other members of minority groups who are implicitly asked to transfer their group identity and loyalty from their racial group to the news organization. And the significance of a black reporter writing "Jimmy's World" is great. The same story by a white reporter would not have allowed the *Post* to diffuse, as well or for as long, charges of racism by the black community. This shield enhanced Cooke's value to her employer.

It took three weeks before *Post* editors publicly acknowledged the hit-and-run nature of the story, which, like so many stories on black dysfunction, failed to address solutions. Wasn't it irresponsible for the *Post* to leave a youngster in such a perilous situation, many asked? Others questioned if a white boy would be shown such disregard. With criticism mounting, *Post* editors asked Cooke to find Jimmy to get help for him. Milton Coleman, the district editor for the daily staff, to whom Cooke reported on "Jimmy's World," said he would accompany her; but Cooke told him that she had gone by the apartment and the family had relocated to Baltimore. Bradlee would later concede that *Post* editors were irresponsible. "Worse, none of us editors thought about the life and safety of the child," Bradlee wrote. "If we had insisted that a *Post* doctor examine Jimmy, we would have escaped disaster."[4] On November 17, 1980, in spite of mounting suspicions and community outrage, "Jimmy's World" was nominated by *Post* editors for a Pulitzer Prize, an act that would forever stain the legacy of Cooke, the *Post*, and American journalism.

On April 3, members of the Pulitzer Prize advisory committee informed Bradlee that "Jimmy's World" won the Pulitzer, with the formal announcement scheduled for April 13. *Post* editors were elated. Bradlee personally congratulated Cooke, who was on assignment in New Haven working on another plum assignment: the assassination attempt on President Reagan by John Hinckley Jr. Soon after, she was working on another story on black pathology. This time, she planned to write about a fourteen-year-old prostitute and her twenty-year-old pimp.

"Hooray," wrote Graham in his second letter to Cooke. "I've never heard a prize announcement make people so happy. People here like you. They think you're the kind of journalist the *Post* needs for its future because you understand people and you get a part of their nature into your stories." He added: "Your prize seems to me to say that we're on the right track in writing about this city and it's strong encouragement to do even better."[5] The letter would have chilled the blood of the district's black residents, who already felt besieged by negative coverage. And only later would it be shown how far off the mark Graham was. Not only was Cooke the last person who could enter a world of the kind of dysfunction she described, but she had also distanced herself from her black colleagues. She would later reveal in an interview that she had never had a black girlfriend or boyfriend.

That a study of black pathology—and one branded as racist by so many blacks—would be awarded journalism's highest honor was disturbing, but more troubling is what little effort it required for Cooke to concoct such a tale simply by drawing on the worst portrayals of urban blacks already prevalent in the popular press. The story, which required a major suspension of skepticism, and the Pulitzer, the first awarded singularly to an African American woman, were emblematic of the resounding embrace of negative black portraits in the news media. Despite all of the bells that sounded in the days after the story broke—the inability for the city's agencies to locate "Jimmy"; the doubts raised by the mayor, other prominent people, and those in the *Post* newsroom; the improbability of a drug dealer injecting a child with heroin in the presence of a reporter (or even relating his culpability in the boy's addiction); Cooke's inability to locate the house—none of Cooke's editors saw through her deceit. They were too enthralled by a story that embodied the best of a well-defined newspaper genre: poetic prose on black pathology.

Admittedly, Cooke's story was created in a fertile and devious mind, but so ingrained are the stereotypes she presented of poor blacks that the story was embraced by the most discerning editors, among them the legendary Bradlee and Bob Woodward of Watergate fame. Bradlee was still executive editor, and Woodward had, since 1979, been Metro editor. For them, and for Milton Coleman, the black editor to whom Cooke reported, the black dialect and the stunning dysfunction were immediately plausible, as was, it seemed, the belief that a criminal would commit crimes in the presence of an attractive, clean-cut, and decidedly middle-class young reporter.

In his extensive ombudsman report published in the *Post* on April 19, 1981, Bill Green concluded that the story reflected a total systems failure, beginning with Bradlee and the managing editor, Simons, who should have asked tougher questions. Green did not explore why they didn't, but it is difficult to imagine a similar story on a young white boy being greeted with so little skepticism. A white Jimmy would not, to most white editors, have been as plausible; he would not have so easily evaded detection in a newspaper that rarely exposed white pathology. Even if the story had gone past Coleman, it would have invited greater scrutiny by his superiors. So exceptional are the stories of white pathology that the very notion of it would automatically raise eyebrows. That is not to say that Cooke's deceit was instantly detectable (even though many in the newsroom did, early on, find her story implausible), but it is to suggest the images she created already resonate with enough people to render them credible. The fascination with black pathology pervades the news industry, and reporters quickly learn that stories like "Jimmy's World" are a quick ticket to page 1. "In a way, both she and the story were almost too good to be true," Woodward told the ombudsman after the hoax was revealed.[6] White editors would do well to ask themselves why such a depiction of black pathology is "too good to be true."

Wrote Bradlee of the episode: "White reporters, much less white editors, don't circulate much in Jimmy's World. I had smoked marijuana maybe a dozen times in all of the 60s and 70s. And I have never used cocaine or heroin. To me, the story reeked of the sights and sounds and smells that editors love to give their readers. The possibility that the story was not true never entered my head."[7] Unspoken was Bradlee's assumption that black reporters were familiar with Jimmy's World, a distorted perception of African Americans that ignores the fact that many of the black reporters who advance in the news industry are as middle class and law abiding as their white counterparts. They are no more familiar with the world created by Cooke than Bradlee.

The willingness to embrace the worst stereotypes of blacks has, throughout history, enabled a host of criminals, black and white, to impugn innocent or fictitious African Americans. Scores of black men were lynched at the turn of the century, many falsely accused of raping white women. Near the end of the twentieth century, a number of high-profile stories had whites inventing fictitious black suspects to hide their own heinous acts. In 1994, a white woman in Union, South Carolina, for days riveted the nation's attention after accusing a black male of forcing her from her car and driving away with her two small children. Scores of black men were detained by police for questioning, and an entire community was paralyzed by fear until it was learned that Susan Smith had killed her own children. Five years earlier, Charles Stuart, a white Boston man, had claimed he and his wife were attacked by a black man in a robbery. His wife was fatally shot, and Boston police arrested a black man who, in news reports, was identified as the lead suspect. It was not until Stuart committed suicide that evidence showed he had shot his wife and then himself, and fabricated the story of the black perpetrator in a scheme to cash in on insurance money.

Like Cooke, the perpetrators of these hoaxes knew their negative portrayals of innocent blacks would be instantly believable, and that the victims—African Americans—would have little recourse. Indeed, in the aftermath of the Cooke debacle, the National News Council upheld a complaint by Howard University, saying the *Post* "failed to react in any constructive manner to questions from the community and its staff" over the truthfulness of the story.[8] Similarly, once Stuart's hoax was brought to light, some thought the black community was overly sensitive and was not owed an apology. The *Globe's* Mike Barnicle, Boston's most famous columnist, defended the police department's handling of the investigation and dismissed what he called the "wail of a black community demanding apologies for the fact that a black man was arrested."[9]

On April 13, 1981, when the Pulitzer Prizes were announced, "Jimmy's World" came crashing down. In the story that moved on the Associated Press news wire, Cooke's biography noted that she had graduated from Vassar, held a master's degree from the University of Toledo, and that she had studied at the Sorbonne. *Post* editors were not only hiring a black reporter, but, in their minds, a super black, one who could gain entry into the black world but who, in other ways, shared the values, privileges, and worldview of her Ivy-leagued editors. Editors at the *Toledo Blade*, where Cooke had worked prior to going to the *Post*, called the AP to point out the discrepancies in their own records and the information in the wire story. Michael Holmes, an AP correspondent in Toledo, checked and confirmed that Cooke had not graduated from Vassar, and that she held a bachelor's degree, not a master's, from the University of Toledo. AP also checked with the Sorbonne and discovered she had not studied there. The biography released by the Pulitzer committee came from the *Post* biographical form that Cooke had filled out. This biography clashed with her resumé on file with the *Post*. The new biography said she spoke or read French, Spanish, Portuguese, and Italian, while her resumé filed with the *Post* said she spoke only French and Spanish. While her resumé had claimed she graduated magna cum laude from Vassar, it did not indicate, as the new biography did, that she attended the Sorbonne in 1975.

Coleman called Vassar personally, where his fears were confirmed. He was told by a registrar's clerk, and her supervisor, that Cooke had attended Vassar for one year, but had not graduated. Cooke initially insisted she had, but eventually admitted she did not. But, during an inquisition by Bradlee and Woodward, she continued to insist that Jimmy was real. She said she would prove it and got in a car with Coleman to drive to the house where she said he had lived.

Back at the *Post*, editors, including Woodward, inspected 145 pages of her handwritten notes, which had been kept in a safe but were never reviewed by editors. They found no evidence that she had interviewed a young heroin addict.

Cooke and Coleman returned to the *Post*, where they met with Woodward and David Maraniss, the deputy Metro editor, in a *Post* conference room.

"It's all over," Woodward told Cooke. "You've got to come clean. The notes show us the story is wrong. We know it. We can show you point by point how you concocted it."[10]

Cooke held firm, but at one point said: "This is getting too cruel. . . . All I have left is my story." Cooke was eventually left alone with Maraniss, where both held hands and wept.

They talked for one hour, during which she confessed she had fabricated the story, and shared her fears about being nominated for the Pulitzer. "You can recover and you will," Maraniss told her.

"The only thing I can do is write," Cooke said.

"That's not true," Maraniss replied.

Finally, she told Maraniss he could tell the others: "There is no Jimmy and no family. It was a fabrication. I did so much work on it, but it's a composite. I want to give the prize back."

Once the editors were told, they hugged and kissed Cooke. She asked Maraniss: "What will happen to me? Will I be able to write again?"

Maraniss assured her he would stand by her and would try to get her another job.

The next day, Cooke wrote her letter of resignation. 'Jimmy's World' was in essence a fabrication. I never encountered or interviewed an 8-year-old heroin addict. The September 28, 1980, article in the *Washington Post* was a serious misrepresentation which I deeply regret. I apologize to my newspaper, my profession, the Pulitzer board and all seekers of truth. Today, in facing up to the truth, I have submitted my resignation. Janet Cooke."

Her apology did little to heal the wounds of resentment in the District of Columbia's black community or in the journalism community, which found itself under intense scrutiny. But no group was more publicly scrutinized than black journalists, who found themselves somehow implicated in Cooke's fabrication. A cover story in the *Wall Street Journal* openly questioned if the Cooke affair stemmed from affirmative action. "To what extent do the pressures facing big city papers to recruit and promote promising minorities cloud the initial hiring procedures—as well as the decisions as to which of their stories should be published," the front page article posed.[11] It suggested that the resumes of all black reporters should be double-checked. Pulitzer Prize–winning author James A. Michener suggested that Cooke's transgression impugned all black journalists.

"The damage Miss Cooke has done to black and women reporters is incalculable, and she should have anticipated this when she wrote her fake story and allowed it to be nominated for a Pulitzer," he said in an article in *U.S. News & World Report*. "Recent requirement that a company must have a balanced staff should not be interpreted as meaning that it must have an incompetent one or one ignorant of the great traditions."[12]

It was as if Cooke—and blacks—had alone brought down the industry by breaching the ethical codes of journalism. The many transgressions by white journalists were instantly forgotten as the credentials of many black journalists were suddenly called into question, and their references and past employment were verified. Just as an individual black criminal was seen as representative of all blacks, so did Cooke's crime brand all black journalists.

Bill Green, the *Post* ombudsman, in his 18,000-word report, touched on the issue of race in Cooke's tenure at the *Post*. Among the fifteen conclusions, in his report was number 11, which posed the question: "Did race have anything to do with Cooke's ascendancy? Did she get choice assignments and move up because she was handsome and black? Was she employed for the same reason?"

Green concluded: "There's some yes, some I-don't-know in any honest answer. If there's an employer who says he wouldn't have hired her, he hasn't seen Cooke either in person or at work. There are white editors on this paper who want to report news on the black community but who know they can't get at some of it in the same way blacks can." He concluded: "Race may have played some role, but professional pride and human decency were deeply involved in this story and that has not a diddle to do with race."[13]

It is difficult to argue that human decency was a factor in the story given the *Post*'s reluctance to reach out to the child to safeguard his life. But, more importantly, Green's conclusion altogether ignored a nagging perception by African Americans: that black reporters who master black dysfunction are placed on a fast track and on page A1, while those who write more complex stories that examine black life, but without dramatic, stereotypical flourishes, are not accorded the same trust and respect. Cooke, like most African American reporters, had reason to believe that advancement would come more quickly if she wrote unflinchingly about the underside of black life. Following "Jimmy's World," she became a newsroom celebrity and was in the process of writing more stories that would highlight black dysfunction. However, while Cooke managed to scheme her way into her editors' hearts, their loyalty to her was fragile. She would not be able to overcome her transgressions the way many of her white peers had done and would continue to do. She would, years later, still wear her misdeeds like a scarlet letter.

In 1996, a full fifteen years after Cooke returned the Pulitzer, a story in *GQ*, written by Michael Sager, a former colleague and intimate friend, detailed Cooke's life since her dramatic descent into journalism's hall of infamy. The talented writer was, he reported, earning $6.15 an hour as a clerk in a department store in Kalamazoo, Michigan.

"I'm in a situation where cereal has become a viable dinner," Cooke, by then divorced, revealed to Sager. "What I did was horrible. But I don't think that in this particular case the punishment has fit the crime."[14]

After publication, Sager struck a deal to do a movie on Cooke. The movie, tentatively titled "Janet's World," was in development for Columbia Pictures in mid-1999.

In stark contrast, Michael Daly, a *New York Daily News* columnist who in 1981 had also been exposed for fabricating characters in columns filed out of Northern Ireland, was back at work as a *Daily News* columnist. More amazing was that, unlike Cooke, Daly paid little penance for his transgression. Following his resignation from the *Daily News* after admitting to fabricating characters, Daly was quickly hired by *New York* magazine, where he worked for years before returning to the *Daily News*. Daly is in good company. Ruth Shalit, who penned a damning *New Republic* article attacking diversity efforts at the *Washington Post*, was promoted at the *New Republic* and landed a writing contract at *Esquire* after admitting to several instances of plagiarism. For African Americans, however, because of prevailing suspicions about their competence (suspicions fueled by articles such as Shalit's) and their small numbers in the industry, their every transgression stands in stark relief, leaving an indelible stain that many fail to overcome.

That is not to say that either black or white journalists who intentionally defraud their readers *should* retain their positions in the industry. Ironically, African Americans seem to come down even harder than their white peers on black offenders, perhaps because they realize the transgression of one black journalist unfairly reflects on all black journalists. African Americans tend to be more conservative, in general, on issues of sanctions, with a greater percentage favoring, for example, the death penalty. So African Americans are often among the harshest critics when one of their own commits a journalistic felony.

However, the awarding of second chances is, and perhaps should be, subjective, with the offense weighed against industry standards and against the damage done to the organization's credibility. The problem is that for African Americans, that standard shifts, depending on the offender's race and social standing. It makes Cooke's burning at the stake all the more hypocritical, even for those who believe her punishment fit the crime. If African Americans, in the interest of fairness, severely deplore African American offenders, why do whites in the news industry find the offenses of those like Daly or Shalit less worthy of rebuke? They are allowed to survive transgressions that would irreversibly doom a darker colleague.

During the summer of 1998, the contrasting applications of justice applied to another pair of journalists also served to expose the double standards based on the race and influence—two factors that are often inextricably linked—of the journalist. Patricia Smith, who is black, and Michael Barnicle, who is white, both resigned from the Boston Globe within six weeks of each other after they were found to have fabricated portions of their columns. Barnicle was also found to have plagiarized the work of others.

First came the revelations that Smith, an award-winning columnist had fabricated a column. Smith, a renowned poet who in 1993 became the first black woman to be given a column at the *Globe*, had faced similar allegations in the past. While she was a young staffer at the *Chicago Sun-Times*, editors suspected that she reviewed a concert she hadn't attended. And then in 1995, after a reader challenged the veracity of one of her columns, a database search by Walter Robinson, the assistant managing editor, failed to turn up the quoted person's name. The editor then examined ninety of Smith's columns written in 1995 and was unable to verify that twenty-seven people named in them existed. Matthew Storin, the *Globe* editor relating the story to a *Washington Post* reporter, said he sat down with Smith and told her of the findings, and how such behavior "just can't be tolerated."[15]

In press accounts, Storin said he did not confront her about the disputed account reported in her column. "I thought we would have a racially divisive situation," he told the *Washington Post*. "I thought if Barnicle was guilty of the same thing, he'd be much more clever in covering it up and we'd have a hard time getting at it, so we'd better start from ground zero and document what they were both doing."

But that excuse ignored Barnicle's history of transgressions at the paper, transgressions which he had not managed to cover up. In 1981, Barnicle was sued, accused of falsely attributing a racial slur to a white merchant in the heat of the racially heated Boston bus crisis. According to an article by Harvard Law professor Alan Dershowitz, the court found that the statements attributed to the merchant were not true, and that Barnicle had doctored his notes to lend credibility to his story. Barnicle was convicted of libel, and the *Globe* paid $40,000 for damages. In 1990, Dershowitz accused Barnicle of fabricating a quote attributed to him, in which Dershowitz was said to have uttered a sexually and racially offensive remark. The *Globe* paid Dershowitz a reported $75,000 to settle the case. As part of the settlement, Dershowitz was not allowed to disclose the settlement amount. Barnicle reportedly apologized to Dershowitz on a radio program, saying he had a "legitimate beef." That same year, according to Dershowitz, another threatened libel suit was settled for an undisclosed amount.[16] In "Alibi Mike," published in the October 1991 issue of *GQ*, Barnicle was accused by *Chicago Tribune* columnist Mike Royko of lifting passages or ideas from his column. He said a satirical column about President Reagan selling arms and legs to Iran "either was lifted or it was a peculiar coincidence."

In a follow-up, *Boston* magazine began what became an ongoing feature, first called "Unbelievably Barnicle," but later called "Barnicle Watch." In the first installment, the reporter, Lamar B. Graham, reported that a Barnicle column, "On Cold Street, A Glow of Life," published in the *Globe* on December 22, 1991, contained material remarkably similar to Royko's column originally published in the *Chicago Tribune* in 1966. Both columnists wrote about a homeless couple who were beaten and robbed and given $20 for pizza by police officers. More amazing was that in both, the subjects are named Mary and Joe. In Barnicle's column, Mary is pregnant, but in Royko's, she finally gives birth.

Royko had included "Mary and Joe, Chicago-Style" in his 1968 anthology, *I May Be Wrong, but I Doubt It*. So popular was the piece that he re-ran it every Christmas for more than twenty years.

Graham noted that Barnicle's story line, "On Cold Street, A Glow of Life," bore a striking resemblance to Royko's column. Wrote Royko: "They went to a cheap hotel. But the clerk jerked his thumb at the door when they couldn't show a day's rent in advance." Wrote Barnicle: "They were looking for a rooming house to spend the night. . . . 'No rooming houses around here,' the man told them."

Royko: "Joe said he was good at working with wood." Barnicle, quoting Joey: "I mean, I'm good with my hands. I'm a good carpenter."

Royko: "The stranger hit Joe on the head and took his over-coat." Barnicle: "Suddenly, he [Joey] was hit from behind by a guy who lunged after the cash in his palm."

"What a coincidence," wrote Graham. "The whole thing reminds us of Christmas 1984, when the Bigfoot of Morrissey Boulevard [Barnicle] got a lump of coal in his stocking for a column that seemed a little too much like 'Loser's Christmas,' a 1954 piece by the late, great Jimmy Cannon." Graham compared Barnicle's line "It's for . . . the trumpet player who has lost his lip," with Cannon's "Put music back in the horns of musicians with broken lips."

Subsequent installments, which were still running in 1999, had reporters attempting to substantiate information contained in Barnicle's columns, or to find people who were quoted. The magazine went so far as to hire a private detective to find people he had quoted, without success. So notorious was Barnicle's transgression that Dershowitz dubbed him a "serial fabricator and recidivistic plagiarizer."[17]

Wrote Dershowitz in 1998: "*The Globe* has been Barnicle's enabler for almost two decades. It has paid huge sums of money to keep his victims quiet. It has changed the rules to keep Barnicle employed, and it has lowered its journalistic standards to Barnicle's level."[18]

But so afraid were *Globe* editors of doing anything that would draw attention to the popular Barnicle's misdeeds that they were apparently willing to let a known black fabricator skate. Barnicle served, in essence, as Smith's human shield. As long as he remained at the paper, her job appeared safe. So in 1995, after Smith was confronted with evidence of ethical lapses, rather than being punished, both she and Barnicle were warned that their columns would be closely scrutinized for their veracity. In June 1998, with Smith a finalist for a Pulitzer Prize and recipient of the American Society of Newspaper Editors' Distinguished Writing Award, came fresh suspicions that Smith had fabricated characters in her columns. *Globe* editors found some of her quotes too eloquent to be believed. When several people she quoted could not be found, Smith was confronted, and she admitted she had incorporated fictional characters in four columns. Smith was asked to resign, and *Globe* editors revealed that an extensive investigation into her columns had turned up fifty two instances of fraud.[19]

In a final column, Smith apologized to readers. "From time to time in my metro column to create the desired impact or slam home a salient point, I attributed quotes to people who didn't exist." She acknowledged committing "one of the cardinal sins of journalism: Thou shall not fabricate. No exceptions. No excuses."[20]

She added: "I will write as long as I breathe, despite the dire predictions that this indiscretion spells the end of my career." She added: "To those colleagues and readers who salivated daily at the thought of my head on a platter, congrats."

Storin called the revelation a "tragic development" but said it was their job "to deal with these errors forthrightly." Finally, in an eerie similarity to Cooke's case a decade and a half earlier, Smith's writing award, at the *Globe*'s request, was withdrawn.

While public reaction to her ouster, and the paper's detailed coverage of it, was immense, any sympathy for Smith was overshadowed by harsh condemnation by many of her colleagues, black and white. Much of the criticism suggested that her race was somehow related to her predicament. Said Eileen McNamara, a prize-winning white *Globe* columnist, of Smith's demise: "Her fall had nothing to do with race; her rise had everything to do with it."[21] Chimed in Viola Osgood, an African American and retired *Globe* editorial writer: "I don't think the *Globe* should have asked for Patricia Smith's resignation. I think the *Globe* should have fired her."[22]

Osgood, who was interviewed by Thomas and quoted in his ombudsman report published on June 22, also related Smith's travails to the plight of black journalists, as if her offense somehow implicated them. "I was one of the first black women to work at the *Globe* full time. I was 'the girl,' and 'honey' and 'dear.' And I was given 'soft' stories along with two other black women, Carmen Fields and Gayle Pollard, until we rebelled and got to do the same stories as everybody else," she said.

"We came in as black women and walked out as respected journalists who did the job as well as anyone else, black or white, male or female. We worked hard to leave a legacy where black women like Patricia Smith would be trusted to do the job without regard to sex or color. Well, Patricia Smith has prostituted that, and I'm angry. What she did is unforgivable. I worked 24 years at the *Globe*, and it never occurred to me that anybody would make up quotes. And Patricia Smith's column of so-called apology was an insult to blacks in journalism who worked so that she would have the status."

Smith's sin was thus not only an affront to journalism, but some black journalists had internalized society's view that the sins of one black reflected on all, particularly given the tenuous status of blacks in the news industry. Compounding matters for Smith was that her support in Boston's black community was, at best, ambivalent. While she had won writing awards and was seen as a strident advocate whose angry columns chafed white readers, others were wary, as they are of many black journalists working for mainstream news organizations. In some of her columns, Smith targeted black leaders, thereby alienating large sectors of Boston's black community. "She never really garnered the deep and loyal support in the African American community," said Margaret Burnham, an MIT professor.[23] Burnham was, nonetheless, among twenty-two women who wrote a letter to the *Globe* protesting what they believed to be insensitive coverage of her resignation. The letter objected to "the ugly, vindictive campaign the paper is now waging to obliterate the columnist's otherwise stellar record of achievement as a journalist."[24]

Many, like Peter Bhatia, executive editor of the *Portland Oregonian,* agreed that Smith had committed an unpardonable sin. "There are basically two things in journalism that cause immediate capital punishment: plagiarism and fabrication," he told *Editor and Publisher.*[25]

But some African Americans demanded to know how Barnicle had managed to escape similar punishment given the trail of transgressions that had plagued his storied career. In response, *Globe* editors said they would again scrutinize Barnicle's columns. After a review of 364 columns dating back to January 1996, Barnicle was cleared by his editors, even after critics, including those at *Boston* magazine, insisted they go back to 1995, where citations of his abuses appeared unassailable. Nonetheless, Barnicle appeared to have survived, at least for the next six weeks. But on August 2, Barnicle's column included eight one-liners that were found to have been taken, practically verbatim, from *Brain Droppings,* a book by comedian George Carlin. None of the jokes were attributed. The apparent plagiarism was revealed on August 4 by the *Boston Herald.* A day later, Barnicle insisted he had never read the book and had gotten the jokes from a bartender friend. He was slapped with a one-month suspension, despite the improbability of anyone repeating, practically verbatim, eight distinct musings.

Hours later, his bartender alibi—and his twenty-five-year career at the *Globe*—seemed shattered when WCVB-TV, where Barnicle did a weekly show, rebroadcast a television segment from June in which Barnicle was seen holding up *Brain Droppings* and recommending it to viewers. On August 5, Storin asked for Barnicle's resignation. "It is clear that he misrepresented himself either to his television audience or his editors," said Storin at the time. "This contradiction is unacceptable." But, unlike Smith, Barnicle went on the defensive and refused to resign. Instead, he embarked on a national media campaign to save his job, enlisting a slew of powerful friends, including radio host Don Imus, NBC newsmen Tim Russert and Tom Brokaw, and *Washington Post* columnists Mary McGrory and Richard Cohen.

A day after he was asked to resign, Barnicle appeared on ABC's *Good Morning America*, where he made the case that he was being unfairly penalized because the paper was trying to appear fair after forcing out a black woman. That night, on *ABC World News Tonight*, he again denied being guilty of plagiarism. "What I did was foolishly accept some funny lines, a series of jokes, from a friend of mine who unfortunately had taken them from George Carlin unbeknownst to me. . . . I'm guilty probably of stupidity and maybe even laziness."

He then mocked a well-established journalistic expectation to present original work or attribute material to its original source. "Do I call Henny Youngman at home and say, 'Henny, what's the source of this joke?'" And Barnicle continued to characterize *Globe* management as unfair. "The story arrives, I'm asked for my resignation, all within the space of 24 hours, after 25 years of employment."

Lending credence to Barnicle's plea for sympathy, Charles Gibson followed up by asking: "So is this a situation, given the Patricia Smith case, other famous cases recently, where leaders of the press, editors of your paper are trying to be more pure than Caesar's wife?"[26]

Later that evening on *Larry King Live*, on CNN, Tim Russert, host of NBC's *Meet the Press*, came to Barnicle's defense while also disclosing he was a close friend and the godfather of Barnicle's son. "The fact is,

Mike Barnicle deserves a second chance," he said. "After 25 years, and to say that because you didn't give full credit for a joke; give it up."

"If you owned the paper, would you hire him?" King asked, even after it was clear that Russert was not objective. "Barnicle, tonight . . . I'd put his column on the front page."[27] On August 11 came a *Washington Post* column by Richard Cohen that ran in numerous other newspapers. In the column, Cohen downplayed the seriousness of Barnicle's offense, saying he too had once plagiarized a line from a column: his own. "I loved it and was just about to send the lovely column and its even lovelier line to my editor when, as it happened, I looked on the wall. There, pinned up and a bit faded, was an old newspaper ad promoting my column. It quoted that lovely line."[28]

Columnists, he argued, are "literary kleptomaniacs." That he could compare his experience nearly reusing a line from a previous column to Barnicle's plagiarism of someone else's published work was incredible enough, but Cohen went so far as to impugn the character of all newspaper columnists. "Half the things we find in our pockets—notes and jottings on scraps of napkins, matchbook covers with mysterious references—come from someone else, but after one rewrite they are—to a moral and polygraphical certainty—our own," he wrote. "This is how I came to write what I had already written. This could be how Barnicle came to write jokes that came from Carlin's book."

Just as implausible—and racially inflammatory—was Cohen's suggestion that Barnicle's major offense was to err less than two months after a black woman, who he noted was "exposed as a liar." "The moment he did anything wrong, he would have to suffer the same fate as Smith," he wrote. "It didn't seem to matter that she concocted characters in her columns, while he at worst lifted some jokes. She is both a woman and black. He is a man and white. For the *Globe* to appear fair, it was necessary to be unfair." Tom Brokaw, a network news anchorman, also jumped to his defense, telling *Newsweek*: "Good grief, there is some proportion in all of this."[29]

Suddenly, plagiarism, and an attempt to cover it up by lying, was reduced to a minor offense, one that would not severely damage the credibility of the journalist and his news organization. One line from the writer's own past column was as harmless as seven lines from someone else's work. Barnicle was being punished for the offenses of a black woman, and not for his own. A trail of transgressions could be ignored to lend support to an argument that Barnicle deserved a *second* chance. The other chances apparently didn't count.

Barnicle repeated this argument in a series of interviews. "The *Globe* chose to put me on the rack to appear even-handed within the politically correct, agenda-driven journalism of the age," he said.[30]

But his most remarkable pitch came on Don Imus's nationally broadcast radio program, when a pitiable Barnicle appealed to listeners for their support. "I'd like to tell you a story," he began. "It's a story about sleepless nights. It's a story about TV crews in the driveway at midnight and coming back at 5:30 in the morning, and ringing your doorbell at 20 minutes of six, and waking up a five-year-old. It's a story about me, it's a story about 1998, it's a story that I would write in a column if I still had a column."[31]

Imus, blasting Barnicle's removal as political correctness gone amok, instructed listeners to demand Barnicle's reinstatement and gave listeners the publisher's phone number.

Support for Barnicle could be found everywhere. David Warsh, the *Globe*'s business writer, in a column prominently featured on page 1 of the "Economy" section, fired back at Dershowitz and other critics of Barnicle, whom he called "the second-best pure newsman in Boston, after Eileen McNamara (the paper's other Metro columnist), not counting Will McDonough, who covers sports." Of Smith, he wrote: "Her orientation to news was too weak; her orientation to Boston nonexistent. She was a Chicago woman through and through. And she came to her newspaper column 20 years after Barnicle, in more demanding, less forgiving times."[32]

The pressure on *Globe* management was not limited to powerful journalists and thousands of readers who called and wrote letters. (Given the national campaign, many of the calls could have likely come from people outside of Boston.) Thomas Stemberg, the chief executive of Staples, in a thinly veiled threat wrote a letter to *Globe* brass saying Barnicle's departure would effect circulation, and therefore the company's $1 million ad account with the paper. "The diminished editorial content of the *Globe* that would result from Mike Barnicle's departure would render the *Globe* a less attractive advertising vehicle," he wrote.[33]

On August 11, six days after demanding Barnicle's resignation, *Globe* editor Matthew Storin reversed his position and instead suspended Barnicle for two months without pay. "Frankly, I'm persuaded by the argument that the punishment didn't fit the crime," he said at a news conference with Barnicle. Said Barnicle: "I apologized to Matt, I apologized to the publisher for putting the newspaper in this terribly awkward position due to my own personal sloppiness."[34]

He added: "You can accuse me of sloppiness, and I plead guilty. You can accuse me of intellectual laziness, and I plead guilty. But plagiarism, no."[35] Barnicle's denial of plagiarism evidently carried more weight than evidence of it.

The reversal prompted a meeting of the Globe's minority staff, and the next day a protest letter signed by about fifty black and white staff members was presented to management. "The reversal by *Globe* management not only cripples the paper's integrity, but undermines the efforts of staff members who work daily to produce a newspaper that is beyond reproach," read the letter, dated August 12. "Barnicle's reprieve gives the appearance of a double standard that allows one individual to ignore journalistic principles other reporters must follow."

It added: "*Globe* management did the right thing by demanding Patricia Smith's resignation and publicly airing management's decision-making process in the newspaper. . . . It erred by not firing Barnicle and keeping information about his case a private matter.

"The whole debacle is a national embarrassment and an outrage to the staff and our readers."[36]

Many, far and wide, weighed in, with NABJ President Vanessa Williams calling the hair splitting about whose offense was worse "intellectually dishonest." In a contentious debate among Williams, a *Washington Post* staff writer, and syndicated columnist Robert Novak on CNN's *Crossfire*, Novak said NABJ's role in the debate was racist. "Let's be honest," said Novak. "You feel that a black woman was bounced off the paper and a white man was kept on and that's why you're in that, and that sounds like racism to me."[37]

Marvin Kalb, director of Harvard University's Shorenstein Center on the Press, Politics and Public Policy, agreed with Novak that Barnicle's was not a dismissable offense, but was merely "sloppy," "bad," and "admittedly stupid" journalism. Once again, Barnicle's past actions were ignored. Kalb said it wasn't obvious that he had plagiarized the jokes, and said the public humiliation stemming from the ordeal might make him a better columnist. He argued that tribalism was not behind Barnicle's national support network. "There's very little tribalism in any newsroom," he said.[38]

Williams, who had already gone on record supporting Smith's forced resignation, appeared incredulous. She wondered aloud how Barnicle's supporters could defend him on such weak grounds. "[H]ow any journalist of any color can defend someone who admits to even sloppiness and laziness at a time like this when, over the last couple of months, this profession has been hammered by a series of professional and ethical lapses. Right now journalists should be rallying around the flag, reassuring the public that we are honest, we work hard, we play straight with them [by] not asking for forgiveness and trying to split hairs over whether fabricating a story or making up a story is worse than stealing other authors' work."[39]

In the strongest, and most public, rebuke of the *Globe's* actions, Howell Raines, editorial page editor for the *New York Times*, which owns the *Globe*, flatly rejected arguments that Smith's lapse was more serious than Barnicle's. "Life is full of gray areas," he wrote, "but the intellectual contrast that makes mainstream newspapering possible is stark and clear. Editors have to be able to trust what reporters and columnists write and say. Journalists do not make things up or present others' writing and thoughts as their own."[40] He said the *Globe's* flip-flop was due to Barnicle's immense popularity, and "a vigorous public-relations campaign among the profession's old-boy network."

Barnicle, he said, "like this writer, is a product of a male-dominated, mostly white tribal culture that takes care of its own. A great deal of effort has been expended throughout journalism over the past 20 years to make sure the newsroom tribe includes every color, gender and sexual orientation. Long after Mr. Barnicle settles back into his column, the historical bottom line of this event will be that a white guy with the right connections got pardoned for offenses that would have taken down a minority or female journalist."

The column in the *Times* had to send shock waves through the *Globe's* management ranks. *Globe* publisher Benjamin B. Taylor fired back the next day with a terse, 191-word response published in his paper. "First," Taylor wrote, "Mr. Raines never mentioned that Mr. Barnicle, rather than being pardoned, received a two-month suspension without pay, agreed to apologize for his actions and to cut back on his outside activities.

"Second, Mr. Raines never mentioned that Patricia Smith, the *Globe* columnist who was recently dismissed for fabrications in her column, was given a second chance by Matthew V. Storin, the paper's editor, when he put her on notice in 1995." He added: "Mr. Storin's decision on Mr. Barnicle was not based on 'loyalty, public relations and readership' as Mr. Raines suggests. It was based on determining the appropriate punishment given the severity of the crime."[41]

But Taylor neglected to mention that Barnicle was also issued a warning in 1995; nor did he cite the string of other transgressions that resulted in out-of-court settlements on Barnicle's behalf. The defense, based on half-truths that glossed over compelling context, only served to widen a gulf between seekers of truth—particularly African American readers—and an institution that was trying, at whatever cost, to preserve what was left of its credibility.

Storin continued to insist his decision was unrelated to public pressure or a racial double standard. "I'd have a lot harder time living with myself if I ended a guy's 25-year career just to be consistent," he told an interviewer. "The two cases were very different. I gave Patricia Smith, perhaps to my everlasting regret, a second chance."[42]

Boston's blacks were stunned. "This is a sad day for Boston and a particularly sad day for Boston's minority citizens," said Margaret Burnham, a prominent lawyer and former judge. "It will take a long time for the minority community to regain confidence in the *Globe*."

Leonard Alkins, president of the Boston branch of the NAACP, also issued a statement in protest: "It is clear to the NAACP that the *Globe*'s editor and publisher are turning their backs on a portion of its readership that enjoy both columnists (Barnicle and Smith), but expected equal punishment for . . . both."[43]

On the other hand, Barnicle's supporters were jubilant in victory. Wrote Cohen in his column: "Matthew V. Storin is a great newspaper editor. He runs an excellent paper, the *Boston Globe*, which covers the world, the country and its region with distinction, but that is not exactly what makes Storin great. Instead, it is in his willingness to admit a mistake. Last week, he tried to fire his star columnist, Mike Barnicle. This week, he merely suspended him for two months. Storin, bless him, decided the punishment ought to fit the crime."

He added: "Barnicle was sloppy and he himself admitted as much. But after 25 years at the *Globe*, he had earned some clemency from the governor."[44]

Mary McGrory, in her syndicated column featured in *The Washington Post*, crowed: "He's OK now, because he's good—his copy is the freshest and funniest in the paper. And he was right about the gravity of his offense. Stealing other people's jokes is a transgression more common than adultery."[45]

Barnicle's supporters simply glossed over his history, neglecting to note all of the chances accorded Barnicle. However, the paper's ombudsman, Jack Thomas, in his report published on August 17 concluded, as would most who closely observed the public spectacle, that the decision smacked of a double standard.

"The *Globe* maintains that the lighter punishment for Barnicle is appropriate because having been exposed, warned, and then found again to be making up quotations, Smith was given a second chance, and now Barnicle deserves the same.

"But the warning two years ago was given to Barnicle as well as to Smith, and it represented a second chance for him as well as for her. And where is it written anyway that journalists are entitled to be dishonest even once without more severe punishment?"[46]

Thomas also dismissed editors' arguments that Smith's transgression was far worse than Barnicle's. "The Globe insists that there is a difference in degree of dishonesty. But both Smith and Barnicle are guilty of having compromised the ethics of the newspaper to an egregious extent, and who can say which of them has done greater damage to the credibility of the *Globe*?"

Thomas would not have the last word on Barnicle's fate at the paper. The same day his report was published, Kenneth Y. Tomlinson, a retired editor in chief of *Reader's Digest*, faxed Storin a note saying that the magazine, in 1995, had discovered that Barnicle had fabricated a column that the magazine had planned to make its lead article in the January issue. Tomlinson was preparing to write about the episode for the *Weekly Standard* and sought Storin's help in confronting Barnicle.

According to Tomlinson, the column, published in the *Globe* on October 8, 1995, "was a magazine editor's dream." In it, Barnicle related the story of two boys, one black, one white, who were patients in the Children's Hospital cancer unit in Boston and formed a bond based on their mutual love of baseball. For Tomlinson, the column took on special meaning because his son, as a child, had been stricken with cancer. Tomlinson said he wept as he read the exquisitely scribed column.[47]

In one passage, Barnicle had written: "And on those dreamy summer nights when the Olde Town Team was home, the two of them would sit by a window on an upper floor in a hospital ward and listen to games on the radio as they looked at the lights of the ballpark off in the distance, washing across the July sky like some brilliant Milky Way all their own."

According to the column, the black father lost his job, and then his son "died on a crisp fall day when his favorite game had long fallen silent from a strike. The combination of hospitalization and unemployment had nearly bankrupted the family, yet they had to fight on for their three surviving children."

In the depths of their despair, the black family received a letter from the white family, along with a check for $10,000. Barnicle said the black mother "lifted her head toward the perfect sky and, for a moment, she could hear her son singing his favorite song." After she told her husband he was initially silent before saying, "There really is a God."

As is the practice at most magazines, Tomlinson assigned a researcher to check basic facts in the story. According to Tomlinson, Barnicle maintained that the quotes were accurate, and that he had interviewed both parents. But he refused to provide their names and numbers to allow the fact-checker to verify their quotes. So eager was Tomlinson to run the story that he assigned a research supervisor to confirm the facts through Children's Hospital employees. While the staff was cooperative, no one there could recall any patients who matched the description outlined in Barnicle's moving column. All of the nurses were consulted, as were doctors. A similar search at the American Cancer Society in Connecticut and Massachusetts—the two states where the families were said to have resided—also failed to turn them up. By then Tomlinson was convinced the column was fabricated, and he killed the article.

Presented with this latest allegation, Storin assigned Walter Robinson, an assistant managing editor who had turned up fabrications in Smith's columns, to investigate Barnicle's. Robinson confronted Barnicle, who first said he couldn't remember the column and then claimed that he heard the story from a nurse. He admitted that the parents, who were quoted throughout his column, were not interviewed. Instead he said he got the details from the nurse while in a South Boston bar. Not surprisingly, he said he could not remember the nurse's name. Like Cooke, Barnicle had fabricated, at the very least, large portions of the article and all of the quotes.

Barnicle was also confronted with a memo written in 1995 by Deirdre Casper, a *Reader's Digest* researcher, in which she wrote: "Barnicle did call me back but explained in no uncertain terms that he would not reveal the names of those involved." She added: "I asked him if he's spoken to both sets of parents—he said he had. I asked if all details of the story were accurately depicted, or had he changed some/all to protect identities. All real, he said."

This time, Barnicle agreed to resign, which he did on August 19. Said Storin: "In light of his failure to follow the most basic reporting requirements as well as the duplicitous way in which the story was written, it's clear that Mike Barnicle can no longer write for the *Boston Globe*."[48]

In a parting statement, Barnicle still insisted the story was basically true, and implied, as he had in the past, that *Globe* management was being unfair. "I was asked to explain circumstances and columns written in 1973, 1981, 1986 and 1995, and was given 24 hours . . . to rebut all the allegations at once. Frankly, this is not what I want to do with my life."[49]

His resignation generated national attention, with stories reported on the network news and prominently featured in newspapers. At the end of the episode, the paper was left with egg on its face, and Barnicle's many prominent supporters were rendered silent. Some questioned Storin's fitness to continue as editor. When asked why Smith was not fired in 1995 when serious problems were detected in her columns, Storin was quoted in the June 21 *Globe* as saying: "I knew going way back that people said Barnicle made things up. To the best of my knowledge, the paper had not addressed the Barnicle questions head-on. I had this very talented black woman. How then can I take action against this woman under this circumstance."

But his explanation begged the question: Why hadn't the paper more closely investigated the veracity of Barnicle's columns in light of the pervasive credibility problems surrounding them? It was easier, it appeared, to protect a known fabricator than to fire the paper's marquee journalist. A day after Barnicle's resignation a task force of one hundred blacks demanded Storin's resignation. But in time the frenzy died down, even though Barnicle's career, and the media hypocrisy, was far from over. Barnicle was quickly dismissed from PBS's *News Hour*, where he was a regular contributor, because, according to a station spokesperson all of its regional contributors had columns; but Barnicle requested, and was granted, a ninety-day leave of absence from WCVB and the WSNBC cable television network. A statement from WCVB said the leave would give Barnicle time "to address the issues raised about his work at the *Globe.*"

As inconceivable as it seemed, on January 11 AP moved a story which said Barnicle would return to his job as a contributor to WCVB-TV's *Chronicle.* "Mike's distinctive voice and style have been missed," Paul LaCamera, the general manager, said in a statement. "In a spring 1998 episode, Mike recommended for summer reading a book of humor which he later acknowledged he had not read. Mike has expressed his regret for this lapse, an apology which we have accepted," the statement said. Barnicle would resume his role on the magazine show, providing stories and hosting half-hour specials called "Barnicle's Boston."

Said Barnicle: "Last summer I found myself caught up in one of those messy media frenzies and left the *Boston Globe* after 25 years. . . . My mistake was one of laziness. I failed to be factually accurate in a column written three years ago, one of 4,000 I wrote over a quarter century. It was flawed and incorrect and I am sorry to have disappointed anyone."

Thus he reduced the fabricating of quotes and, most probably of people—since the subjects of his column were never found—to "laziness" and failing to be "factually accurate," when in fact his offense was no different than Cooke's or Smith's. The difference is that he continued to put his spin on what he had done, refused to confess, and was supported by people in high places. And many incorporated his spin on his resignation from the *Globe* into their reporting on his return. Unlike his noisy exit, his return generated little attention. On January 12, 1999, the *New*

York Times ran a six-paragraph, 216-word wire story at the bottom of page 15 in the C section that noted his return to his television job. That same week, Howard Kurtz, the media writer for the *Washington Post*, who had provided detailed coverage of the Smith and Barnicle episodes over the summer, tagged a small item announcing Barnicle's return to television near the end of his column. He also minimized his offenses, as he did again on a January 16 segment of CNN's *Reliable Sources*, when he said the *Globe* had "let him go for sloppy journalism." On January 2, Kurtz, in a segment on media credibility, merely reported that "serious flaws" had been discovered in Barnicle's work. It should be noted that *Boston* magazine, which had for years chronicled Barnicle's abuses, reported in its February 1999 issue that the columnist had also misrepresented his military record. But given his track record, it would take far more to undermine his ability to secure employment in the media. On March 16, 1999, the *New York Daily News* announced that Barnicle would write a weekly column. The news was greeted with barely a whimper with the exception of a fairly lengthy article in the *New York Times*, which prominently noted his transgressions.[50]

Lamar Graham, the *Boston Magazine* reporter who first began seriously trailing Barnicle's transgressions, was stunned. "I just never thought he could go this far," he said.[51]

Few believe that the return to the news industry of Smith or Cooke would command so little attention or scrutiny. The mere prospect of Cooke receiving a second chance provoked angry reaction by journalists, black and white. In 1996 following publication of the *GQ* article, Cooke was shown little sympathy in interviews with ABC's Ted Koppel or NBC's Bryant Gumbel. Noted Gumbel: "Your reputation is that of one who is a certifiable liar. Why should anybody believe you now? . . . Why not pursue a career in fiction?"[52] And Arthur Fennell, then president of the National Association of Black Journalists, angrily countered a suggestion by *USA Today's* Al Neuharth that she deserved a second chance. "Making up the news has long been considered the worst crime in journalism," he said. "In Cooke's case, she damaged not only her own credibility, but unfortunately also that of an untold number of black journalists. If she deserves a second chance, let her write fiction."[53]

Chimed in Donna Britt, an African American columnist at the *Washington Post*: "People of every color lie, some egregiously. So why does the Cooke scandal still smart? Because her hoax made me and other black writers feel as awful as a stranger's act finally could. When we first heard that she'd won the Pulitzer for feature writing—saw her face beaming from photos in the newspapers for which we worked—many of us felt pride and kinship."

But, she added, when the hoax was revealed, "Black journalists—for whom the stakes feel as high as their numbers are low, found it excruciating."[54]

The quiet perseverance of Barnicle and Daly makes the contrasting fates of Cooke and Smith all the more glaring.

Viewed in isolation, it is difficult to argue that either Smith or Cooke deserved second chances in the news industry. A news organization's covenant with the reader or viewer is based on trust, the kind of trust that their actions erode. But how can one place trust in organizations whose duplicitous actions suggest that standards are not fixed, but are based on factors like race or influence? How vigorously should African Americans condemn black offenders given the lighter sanctions meted out to white offenders? And while it is true that the transgressions of blacks stand in stark relief due to their smaller numbers in the industry and the very mark of their blackness, African Americans should neither suggest, nor accept the suggestion by others, that the transgression of one reflects on all. The sins of Cooke and Smith have no relation to the credibility of black journalists as a group, just as those of Daly and Barnicle do not implicate Irish journalists. Daly and Barnicle—and the litany of other white offenders—are viewed as individuals; so too must Smith and Cooke. Of course, many will continue to view African Americans as monolithic, with the transgressors among them viewed as the rule, and the achievers, the exceptions. However, black journalists must stop fighting a phantom that has been unfairly placed before them.

The kind of troubling double standards applied in these cases should concern not only African Americans, but anyone who cares about fairness or media trustworthiness. Such partiality practiced by news industry decision makers compromises the integrity of the individual news organization and the industry as a whole. When an overlay of race renders news standards flexible, the credibility of the journalism profession is irreparably tarnished. These cases are less about race than they are about fairness and consistency, and it is fairness that cuts to the heart of news

media credibility. A news organization that harbors fabricators and pla-
giarizers because of their popularity, talent or connections cannot be
trusted. Neither can a news industry that is silent as lenient penalties are
meted out to white journalists, while others are banished from the field.

SEVEN

The Kerner Legacy

Race matters.
—Cornel West, 1996

If, at the beginning of the twenty-first century, one were to judge the news industry's racial progress by the impressive titles held by African Americans, then it would score high marks indeed. In 1998, Mark Whitaker, a veteran *Newsweek* writer and editor and member of the National Association of Black Journalists, was named its editor, becoming the first African American at the helm of a major weekly news magazine. He joined a long line of firsts who broke the color barrier near the close of the century, including Bob Herbert, who in 1993 became the *New York Times*'s first African American columnist; and Robert McGruder, who in 1996 became the first African American executive editor at the *Detroit Free Press*. Around the country, African Americans were similarly poised to occupy top executive positions at major news organizations.

The racial symbolism aside, few could argue that the hiring of someone like Whitaker was merely a case of affirmative action tokenism. Whitaker, for example, had been groomed all his professional life to take the reins of one of the nation's most significant news magazines. He began as a *Newsweek* intern in 1977, while a student at Harvard. He graduated from Harvard summa cum laude in 1979, received a Marshall scholarship to Oxford, and was a *Newsweek* stringer in San Francisco, Boston, Washington, London, and Paris before he was hired for the international section in 1981.

He continued to ascend at *Newsweek,* and for three years he was a managing editor and the first deputy to the magazine's legendary editor, Maynard Parker. When Parker took a one-year sick leave, it was Whitaker who ran the magazine, leaving him perfectly poised to succeed Parker when he succumbed to cancer in 1998. But in years past, Whitaker, like a long list of well-educated African Americans, would not, despite his qualifications, have been considered for such a post.

Whitaker's hiring also seemed to portend the nation's multiracial future. As the product of a black father and white mother, both academics, he embodied the balance the news industry most needed. He effortlessly straddled two worlds: he played golf, was passionate about jazz, and had friends across the racial spectrum. And Whitaker was adamant about not being the "black" editor, placing his emphasis on technology and business coverage and appealing to younger audiences.

"I have no plans of pushing an agenda, racial or otherwise," Whitaker maintained in early 1999. "Obviously what Newsweek is about is covering the great issues of the day. A lot do have a racial dimension."[1]

Early in his tenure, Whitaker, who as a correspondent had written a cover story titled "The Hidden Rage of Successful Blacks" had successfully pushed for the cover story "Black Like Who?" which examined the gap between the civil rights and hip hop generations. He also took credit for the hiring of a cadre of young African American writers and planned to continue placing an emphasis on minority hiring, but not for its own sake. "It enriches the content of the magazine," he insisted. "To me it's how you get smart stories."[2]

In another significant barometer of change, the Federal Communications Commission, which once had to be ordered by a court to integrate the airwaves, was, beginning in November 1997, led by William Kennard, the agency's first African American director who was at the forefront of the effort to diversify the broadcast media. Kennard had angered many on Capitol Hill for pushing a wide range of social policies, including free airtime for political candidates and adding a fee to telephone bills to finance public school wiring to the Internet. Senate appropriations chairman Ted Stevens, a Republican from Alaska, even suggested abolishing the agency because of Kennard's policy positions. Kennard's tenure nonetheless indicated the changing racial attitudes over three decades.

In the newspaper industry minorities who near the close of the century comprised roughly 27 percent of the population, held 11.4 percent of newsroom jobs. This was a significant if disappointing increase from 30 years earlier when blacks held less than one percent of jobs, and other minorities were practically nonexistent in the industry. "The Newspaper Journalists of the '90s," a 1997 report published by the American Society of Newspaper Editors, provided a graphic snapshot of change. It noted that the under-thirty age group in the newsroom was 50 percent female and 15 percent minority, compared to the over-50 group, which was 78 percent male and 99 percent white. In broadcasting minorities comprised about 20 percent of newsroom jobs, nearly double the number held in 1971 three years after federal regulations first required broadcasters to consider minorities in hiring.

A study released in 1999 showed that women and minorities were more visible on television than ever. According to the survey, the percentage of minority reporters on the evening news doubled since 1991. In 1998 racial minorities comprised 20 percent of the broadcasting corps, compared to 10 percent in 1991. (Women comprised 33 percent of correspondents, up from 17 percent in 1991.) Journalists of color also filed about twice as many stories as they did eight years earlier. Of minorities, African Americans fared best, while Hispanics and Asian Americans fared worst.

Of 6,230 stories aired, African Americans delivered 11 percent, compared to 2 percent for Hispanics and one percent for Asians. NBC had three of the five most visible African American reporters. They were Gwen Ifill on Capitol Hill; Byron Pitts in Miami; and Dan Lothian in Los Angeles. The survey, "TV Network News Correspondent," was conducted by Joe S. Foote, the dean of Southern Illinois University's College of Mass Communication and Media Arts. Foote has tracked correspondent visibility on ABC, CBS, and NBC since 1983.

On the surface, all of these gains spoke to a will to embrace something approaching racial parity in the news industry. Minorities were finally gaining a foothold in one of the last bastions of white male privilege. While minorities had a long way to go before securing true power in the industry—with media ownership remaining the real measure of control—significant progress in the media had been achieved due to the sheer will of some government leaders and news executives to improve hiring and news coverage.

But despite the undeniable progress that had been made—much of it the result of massive urban rioting in the mid- to late 1960s—there was, by the end of the twentieth century, a prevailing sense in white America that racial equality had been achieved. Behind the obvious numerical gains, a wide and deep racial and cultural chasm still divides the industry. African Americans and their minority counterparts are still woefully underrepresented in the industry and are far from integrated into the newsroom culture. They are resented by many of their white colleagues who believe the increased diversity, particularly of blacks and Latinos, is due to unfair affirmative action policies that have compromised the industry's standards.

This prevailing view was documented in a polemic against diversity efforts at the *Washington Post* in the October 2, 1995, issue of the *New Republic*. Using unnamed sources, the writer, Ruth Shalit, quoted white journalists charging that many of the new African American and Latino hires were either unqualified or incompetent and had tarnished the paper's reputation. Shalit went on to impugn, by name, numerous black journalists in key positions, saying that more qualified whites were bypassed to hire people solely because they were black. Then, providing a glimpse into her own bias, she asserted that it was necessary for editors to adjust their hiring standards, otherwise "they will end up with a nearly all-white staff."[3] Although the *Post*'s executive editor fired off a three-page, single spaced letter denying it had lowered its standards to hire minorities and cited numerous factual errors in Shalit's story, the damage was already done. Shalit's story had brought to the fore the long-held notion of black and Latino inferiority that was deeply imbedded in the psyches of many white journalists. It had been fostered by insensitive newsroom managers who have confided to staff that a certain job is being reserved for a minority, which many whites translate to mean that the person need not be qualified, and that a qualified white would be overlooked. Few interpret it to mean what it does to most black journalists: once the "reserved" slot is filled, no other qualified black or Latino candidates need apply for other jobs.

The cloud of perceived inferiority hangs like a cloud over most black journalists throughout their careers. Exacerbating racial tensions is the view by many black journalists that they must be better than their white peers to succeed. "Muted Voices," a 1995 survey of members of the National Association of Black Journalists, revealed that 28 percent of the members polled believed the standards for promotion were the same for blacks and non-blacks, while 59 percent said the standards for promotion were higher for blacks. Seventy-three percent said blacks were less likely to be considered for career opportunities, and 67 percent said black reporters spend more time in entry-level positions than their white peers. The low percentage of blacks and other minorities in management positions—particularly in newsroom positions such as city editors, managing editors, news directors, and publishers—seems to support the widespread perception of a glass ceiling.

"I wanted to be treated the way they'd have treated a white person who came there, as I did, with advanced degrees in journalism and law," wrote E. R. Shipp in her parting shot to the *New York Times* in January 1993. "There was no compelling reason for this self-respecting black woman to stay."[4]

But these continuing expressions of impotence and frustration by black journalists has been met with either indifference or hostility by white journalists who dismiss the incessant criticism by their black colleagues as ungrateful belly-aching or excuses for their personal shortcomings. Since many white journalists believe their black colleagues are already faring better than they deserve to, they are annoyed by their legitimate impatience over the slow rate of progress and their inability to adequately convey the travails, aspirations, and contributions of African Americans.

Instead, there is in and outside the news industry a growing impatience with discussions of racial redress. It is an impatience fueled by the high-profile promotions of people like Whitaker, which serves to support a notion that racial equality has been achieved. Ignored by those in the news industry was the fact that there were still relatively few blacks in positions of influence, and that negative images of blacks still pervaded the media. An ASNE survey released in 1997 reported that where most white journalists considered their paper's commitment to ethnic diversity "appropriate," 75 percent of African Americans, 66 percent of Hispanics, and 65 percent of Asian Americans found it "inadequate."[5]

A fierce backlash against many of the measures implemented in the 1960s at the Kerner Commission's urging was far ranging: passage by Congress of a welfare reform measure removed hundreds of thousands of women and children from the welfare rolls; a landmark court decision outlawed the Federal Communication Commission's thirty-year-old affirmative action program which had doubled minority employment in the television industry; the American Society of Newspaper Editors proposed scaling back its diversity hiring goals; and affirmative action was nullified in California and Washington, with similar measures under consideration in thirty other states.

In fact, an initiative to repeal affirmative action in Washington State threatened to scuttle unity between the nation's minority journalism associations, which had planned a joint convention in Seattle during the summer of 1999. The NABJ president, Vanessa Williams, cast the sole vote on the Unity Board in favor of canceling the joint convention of the black, Latino, Asian and Native American journalism associations if the measure passed. Williams argued that the groups should not spend a projected $40 million in a state that was inhospitable to people of color, a position that sparked a vigorous debate within NABJ, whose members were sharply divided. Some NABJ members reminded fellow members that not all blacks supported affirmative action. In the end, the groups proceeded with plans for a joint convention in Seattle, a decision that riled some NABJ members.

Nurturing the emerging view that America had done enough to repay blacks—who were characterized as squandering a benevolent nation's charity at the expense of whites—were a wave of books published near the end of the century. Among them were Jim Sleeper's *Liberal Racism*, Dinesh D'Souza's *The End of Racism*, and Stephen and Abigail Thernstrom's *America in Black and White: One Nation Indivisible*, all of which purported that racism was no longer a significant issue in America. Blacks were widely depicted as whining loafers who'd rather cast themselves as victims and accept handouts than take responsibility for their plight. Disregarded were the ways in which unconscious racism was still responsible for the persistent racial disparities in income and other social measures. And in the newsroom, many complained of advantages given to black reporters, despite their still small numbers and low visibility.

The closing days of the twentieth century—an era of retrenchment fed by white anger and resentment—were reminiscent of the period following Reconstruction, when gains by blacks in politics and employment were followed by a furious backlash, with black political disenfranchisement followed by legally sanctioned Jim Crow laws. Of course, that period was also marked by the widespread lynching of African Americans.

The nation's growing conservatism sent tremors through the minority journalism community, with association leaders fearful that industry executives had finally found a climate in which they could, with ease, rest on their laurels. Their fears were fueled by a proposal in March 1998 by the American Society of Newspaper Editors to renege on a 1978 pledge to achieve newsrooms that reflected the percentage of minorities in the population by the year 2000. When the goal was set in 1978, minorities comprised 4 percent of daily newspaper staffs and 15 percent of the nation's population. At that meeting in 1978, the pledge for parity by the year 2000 was unanimously endorsed by ASNE's board as "fair and obtainable." That same year, a Dow Jones Newspaper Fund survey revealed that minority journalism school graduates seeking newsroom jobs experienced unemployment rates almost three times greater than their white counterparts, and a study by the University of Michigan, "Kerner Plus Ten," concluded that the industry's efforts to hire, train, and promote blacks slowed to a trickle following the decline of urban violence.

The ASNE committee's proposal to scale back minority hiring goals, which some members said had been unrealistic to begin with, was viewed not only as an acknowledgment that the industry would not reach the parity goal, but also as a willful sign of rescission.

"The industry has not just lost interest in diversity, but there seems to be outright hostility," said Williams, the NABJ president and *Washington Post* reporter in reaction to ASNE's proposal.[6] The 11.4 percent minority representation in the newsrooms fell far short of ASNE's parity goal. But rather than call for heightened urgency in the face of this failure, the news industry was proposing to scale back the goal to 20 percent by the year 2010, by which time minorities were expected to account for more than 30 percent of the population.

Just as Congress, the courts, and state legislatures seemed to have forgotten the chronic alienation of blacks caused by centuries of slavery followed by systemic racism that brought hiring goals and policies into being, so too, it appeared, had the news industry. Forgotten, too, were the prevailing racial attitudes that continued to necessitate them. Twenty years after the parity goal was set by ASNE, reports continued to show that minorities were not only underrepresented in rank-and-file reporting jobs, but more pronouncedly, in news management. According to

ASNE's 1998 newsroom work-force census, whites held 91 percent of supervisory jobs. The percentage of minorities holding supervisory positions had barely changed from 8.9 percent in 1996, to 9 percent in 1997 and 1998.

Also, a 1998 University of Georgia survey conducted by Professor Lee Becker noted a widening gap in employment between whites and minorities hired out of journalism school. According to his 1997 survey of journalism graduates six months after graduating, 66 percent of minorities seeking daily newspaper jobs were hired, compared to 84 percent of non-minorities. On the whole, minorities were 18 percent less likely than whites to find newspaper jobs in the first six months after graduating.[7]

A month after the ASNE proposal came a federal appeals court decision which declared that the Federal Communications Commission's equal employment opportunity regulations were unconstitutional. Under the thirty-year regulations, stations were required to consider minorities for jobs. The agency argued that the policy promoted a diversified work force. Prior to the policy, stations like WLBT in Jackson, Mississippi, not only refused to hire black journalists, but also refused to give black candidates equal air time. But thirty three years after the court overturned the FCC's granting of a license to WLBT, the courts once again sided against the FCC. This time, however, it was an agency that was staunchly behind policies that encouraged minority hiring. Ironically, while deriding hiring preferences based on race, the ruling upheld a Lutheran church-owned television station's right to hiring preferences based on religious grounds—even if the preferences excluded minorities.

The decision resulted from a 1989 challenge of the license renewals of two stations in Clayton, Missouri, owned by the Lutheran Church–Missouri Synod. The National Association for the Advancement of Colored People argued that the stations did not sufficiently employ minorities. The church argued that the job requirements—knowledge of Lutheran doctrine and classical music training – precluded many blacks. The FCC required the station to submit reports every six months outlining its hiring activities and recruitment efforts, and fined the church $25,000 for misrepresenting the importance of classical music training. The church appealed the ruling, saying that as a religious institution, it should have the right to hiring preferences based on religious affiliation.

The 1998 court ruling held that the policies placed undue pressure on employers and served no compelling public interest, such as the eradication of discrimination. According to the ruling, the FCC's thirty-year-old equal employment provisions appeared to be intended "as a permanent justification for policies seeking racial proportionality in all walks of life." Centuries of legalized slavery followed by decades of official and de facto discrimination were presumably insufficient grounds on which—at the very least—to warrant policies seeking "racial proportionality in all walks of life." The decision virtually ended a program that has more than doubled the number of minorities working in broadcasting and came three years after a conservative-led Congress eliminated a program that granted tax breaks to companies that sold radio and television stations to minorities. In 1998, the National Telecommunications and Information Administration's Minority Commercial Broadcast Ownership Report showed that minorities owned 337—or 2.9 percent—of the 11,524 commercial broadcast stations nationwide. Of those, 157 were black owned. Minority ownership of television stations fell from thirty eight to thirty two stations, with the number of minority television station owners falling from twenty two to thirteen, the report said. There were still no minority owners in seventeen states.

Given the composition of the Supreme Court and the recurrent 5–4 split against policies intended to eradicate racial discrimination, there was little hope for a reversal of the FCC federal ruling, and the agency, in the end, decided against an appeal. Instead, it clung to the pledge by many of the leading media companies to abide by the FCC's equal opportunity principles whether they were required to or not. Among the companies were ABC, CBS, Cablevision, Time Warner, and Fox.

While progress over a thirty-year span had been impressive, it was, by every reasonable measure, too soon to throw in the towel on diversity efforts. In 1998, virtually all daily news organizations were still owned and operated by white men. And almost twenty years after Max Robinson left ABC News, no black or other minority had filled that void, leaving the major network weekday newscast the sole province of white men, except for occasional stand-ins by women, black and white. More significant, however, was how the tendency by whites to cling to notions of a color-blind industry conflicted with a deeply embedded notion of a racial caste system lurking beneath the surface. This notion, evident in both news coverage and in industry hiring patterns, is the barrier to progress that has remained steadfastly in place.

David Shipler's *A Country of Strangers* contains interviews of hundreds of Americans, and Shipler found the belief of black inferiority deeply ingrained in the white consciousness. "The notion that blacks are not as smart, not as competent, not as energetic as whites is woven so tightly into American culture that it cannot be untangled from everyday thought, even as it is largely repressed in polite company," Shipler wrote. He said the view is one of "the deep, abiding currents" in everyday life.[8] This view is responsible for the fact that books like D'Souza's 1995 *The End of Racism*—which argues that racism is a relic of the past while suggesting black inferiority, are on the best-seller lists, just as *The Negro, the Beast* and *The Negro: A Menace to Civilization* were a century earlier. It is a pernicious view that has remained at the heart of many of the animosities and misunderstandings between the races. It is the cancer that permeates so much of news coverage, but instead of addressing the tumor, we continually attack its symptoms.

The view that racial equality is a reality, coupled with a sweeping denial by whites of the ways in which actions in the past contribute to present-day social conditions, has made a sober and even-handed dialogue on race nearly impossible. The merits of affirmative action are debated in a climate in which D'Souza's hollow declaration that racial discrimination is dead glosses over the ways in which whites continue to benefit from the economic inequities of slavery, as well as the lingering effects of discriminatory laws and practices that still hold sway. We're all on the same playing field now, say those who reap the benefits of history and its legacy.

Meanwhile, alternatives to affirmative action, such as reparations to blacks for 250 years of slavery and decades of official and de facto discrimination—which could once and for all end the contentious affirmative action debate—are hardly explored in the media. When the specter of reparations is raised, it is roundly dismissed even in some of the more progressive circles. People like D'Souza are engaged by mainstream media outlets to debunk its merits. Ignored is the $69 billion Germany paid to Israel and another $15 billion to Holocaust survivors, and President Ronald Reagan's apology to Japanese Americans interned during World War II, after which nearly 60,000 survivors were eligible for $20,000 in reparations. But any attempt to engage such a debate is derided as unrealistic, even foolish, as the arguments for and against affirmative action drown out all other options. Instead of reparations, black Americans get an awkward apology for slavery from President Bill Clinton, which, while well meaning, is oddly inadequate in the face of a gaping income, infant mortality, and technology gap between blacks and whites.

Similarly, a raging debate over whether to add a biracial category to the census was prominently featured in the news media, with most of the coverage neglecting to mention the millions of existing biracial "blacks" already the result of miscegenation over the centuries. The widespread miscegenation during and since slavery, which is apparently impolite to discuss in the news media, had already rendered a new racial category absurd. But rather than delve into these matters, many in the public sphere swept America's dirty little secret under the rug. Perhaps the news coverage that best illustrated this persistent negation of the extent to which white America wishes to ignore the bloodlines shared by blacks and whites was the revelation in 1998 that Thomas Jefferson had, at age sixty five, fathered at least one of the children of his slave, Sally Hemings.

Disclosure of the DNA lab results put to rest a two-century-old debate which had some of the nation's leading historians insisting that a man of Jefferson's character would not bed his slave. Joseph J. Ellis won the National Book Award in 1997 for his book *American Sphinx: The Character of Thomas Jefferson*, in which he joined the chorus of Jefferson scholars who dismissed claims of a Jefferson-Hemings sexual relationship. Ellis said Jefferson was incapable of carrying on such an affair because he "was not that adroit at the kind of overt deviousness required to sustain an allegedly 38-year affair in the very center of his domestic haven."[9]

Said Merrill D. Peterson in his *Thomas Jefferson and the New Nation*, published in 1970: "Unless Jefferson was capable of slipping badly out of character in hidden moments at Monticello, it is difficult to imagine him caught up in a miscegenous relationship. Such a mixture of the races, such a ruthless exploitation of the master-slave relationship, revolted his whole being." Added Dumas Malone, an eminent Jefferson authority in his *Jefferson the President, First Term, 1801–1805*, also published in 1970: "It is virtually inconceivable that this fastidious gentleman whose devotion to his dead wife's memory and to the happiness of his daughters and grandchildren bordered on the excessive could have carried on through a period of years a vulgar liaison which his own family could not have failed to detect."[10]

Fawn Brodie's *Thomas Jefferson, an Intimate History*, which took aim at the idealization of Jefferson by scholars, was widely rebuked. So vehement was the rejection of Jefferson's paternity of Hemings's child, and so naïve the purported reasoning for rejecting it, that the debate at times took on bizarre forms that almost always disregarded the humanity of blacks. Garry Wills, in a *New York Review of Books* review of Brodie's book, said there was no evidence of a union between Hemings and Jefferson, and that even if the rumor were true, "There was less risk in continuing to enjoy her services than in experimenting around with others. She was like a healthy and obliging prostitute."[11]

Just as blacks and whites had reacted to the O. J. Simpson verdict in conflicting ways, so too did they receive the news of Jefferson's dalliance with his slave in ways that were both predictable and disturbing. Twenty-four years later, whereas many blacks saw the DNA test as further evidence of the hypocrisy of slavery and its proponents—many of whom publicly debased blacks while sexually exploiting slaves in private—many whites likened the relationship to an isolated "affair" between two consenting adults. Such a romanticized view angered many blacks, who saw it as an attempt to sanitize not only Jefferson, but slavery itself.

The extensive and awestruck coverage of this historic episode perhaps best revealed just how little whites and blacks had come in their mutual understanding of their shared history in the 133 years since the abolishment of slavery—or the thirty years since the Kerner Report highlighted the problems of race in the nation and in the media. Both races are locked in a past that both sides have failed to reconcile. In black America, Jefferson was not the hero he was in white America. His views on black inferiority and his stance supporting slavery were legendary. Also, many blacks had long accepted the claims that Jefferson had sexual relations with his slave, despite the heated refutations by some of the nation's preeminent historians. Blacks found the allegation no less difficult to grasp than the vile institution of slavery itself which placed men, women, and children in the service of whites. Instead of greeting the news as an isolated incident, many blacks were amazed by the persistent denial of white Americans of the sexual violation of black women and children. The varying skin shades, ranging from ebony to ivory, in many black families is testament enough to the pervasive miscegenation among blacks, whites, and Native Americans during (and since) slavery, and therefore DNA evidence of it held little meaning. For blacks, what was most newsworthy about the DNA revelation was the white reaction reflected in the media. So strong, it seemed, was the will to ignore the widespread miscegenation in America that few stories even intimated how prevalent it was during slavery. So intense is the denial of this historical fact that few stories reported that Hemings was herself the half-sister of Jefferson's late wife, whose father had impregnated his slave. Instead, the reaction of whites, as reflected in the mainstream media, was that the nation's third president had had an "affair" with Hemings, who was almost always described as beautiful. In a brief article in the *New York Times*, Hemings was described as Jefferson's "black and comely slave."[12] Said another *Times* article that day: "DNA tests matched a descendant of Thomas Jefferson with those of his beautiful slave, Sally Hemings."

Somehow, the sordidness of Jefferson—one of the most revered men in American history—bedding his slave, who was also his late wife's half-sister, was sanitized, and her attractiveness was used in part to excuse him. The slave became, in the minds of members of the media, his mistress and a willing partner in a mutually satisfying relationship. Nowhere was it even intimated that Hemings, as a slave, did not have free will and had no choice but to submit to her master's sexual desires. While it is true that no one will ever know Hemings's true wishes, for she may in fact have loved Jefferson, the media story line is a bit of romanticized fiction that served to decontaminate Jefferson's actions and that of his peers. Glossed over was the fact that Jefferson owned Hemings since she was one or two, and that he was nearly thirty years her senior. Some have suggested that women, black and white, of that era were treated as property, but no white woman of that era would have been accorded so little sympathy.

Little compassion was expressed for Hemings, a young woman trapped in a relationship with her much older master. Underlying the reporting was, it seemed, the prevailing view that Hemings's blackness rendered her unworthy of the basic human compassion that would be extended to young white women of that era. Hemings was, it seemed, just another black woman whose violation could somehow be explained away by attitudes and institutions of the era. In the major media, there was no attempt to personalize Hemings and explore how a young girl would feel in her unenviable situation. Hemings was, to many members of the media, no Anne Frank, whose story every young child is taught. Hemings was instead characterized as "a healthy and obliging prostitute."

While discussing the revelation concerning Jefferson on her show *The View*, ABC newswoman Barbara Walters went so far as to suggest that President Clinton's extramarital affair with Monica Lewinsky, his adult intern, was worse than Jefferson's sexual relations with a slave he had owned since she was a baby. Just as no one would consider an adult's seduction of an under-aged youth an "affair," it would seem that few could equate Jefferson's sexual relations with a girl—his property—anything less than a serious moral and ethical breach. But somehow, some of the leading members of the media did just that.

In what was yet another sign of the times, the United Paramount Network, in its fall 1998 lineup, debuted *The Diary of Desmond Pfeiffer*, a sitcom set in the Lincoln White House whose lead character was Lincoln's black butler. One of the episodes had Pfeiffer caught in Confederate territory, where an officer says that if he didn't know better, he'd mistake him for "a genuine, simple-minded Negro." In an early version of the pilot, which never aired, two men were shown after they had been hanged, their covered heads concealing their race. Another scene in which Pfeiffer was taken to the United States against his will, was also cut, but the mere idea of a sitcom about slavery was enough to provoke black outrage across the country. A coalition of African American groups organized a picket line in Los Angeles, and a number of major advertisers withdrew sponsorship.

Dean Valentine, president of the network that has the largest black viewership, was unapologetic in the face of protests, as he and other network officials defended the show as sophisticated satire. "We have nothing to feel bad about and we're not going to feel bad about it," he told the *Los Angeles Times*. "They can march up and down the street all they want to."[13] But the show, which was panned by the critics for poor writing and lack of humor, was ultimately doomed by poor ratings. Despite the controversial media coverage, the show ranked 133 out of 135 prime-time shows, and its audience dropped a combined 25 percent in its second and third weeks. The show was pulled before the November sweeps period.

In 1994, a joint report issued by Unity 94, a collaboration of the associations of black, Latino, Asian, and Native American journalists, said there was much that the industry could do to "fire up young people of color about journalism." The laundry list of suggestions included urging local news operations to adopt schools or school districts to help produce newspapers or broadcasts, and providing intensive training workshops such as the Dow Jones Newspaper Fund's High School Journalism Workshops for Minorities. The report also urged the industry to provide internship opportunities and hold job fairs, and to assign mentors to Latino, black, Asian, and Native Americans when they enter the newsroom "to help newcomers navigate these baffling, exhilarating first years as a professional journalist."[14]

Four years later, it was painfully apparent how out of step these initiatives were in a climate far less sensitive to multiculturalism, particularly multiculturalism that relied on the largesse of others. At the end of the century, with self-reliance serving as the nation's mantra, minority associations could no longer rely on the goodwill of news executives, even when the proposed initiatives seemed the right thing to do. The expectation seemed curiously unrealistic, for news leaders to care enough to "fire up" minorities about journalism careers, and it suggested an unfortunate level of dependency and paternalism. That minority journalists would view the increasingly conglomerized news industry as a paternal figure indicated how high expectations, fueled by the heady progress of the 1960s, had been raised. By 1998, however, a new reality was setting in, although it was unclear how minority groups would gear up for a diversity battle far more complex than the black and white one of years past. Not only would minority groups have to devise a more sophisticated strategy, but they would also have to reconcile their competing interests toward the goal of diversity. The term had been broadened to include gays and lesbians, women, the physically disabled, and anyone who ever felt disadvantaged. The unique history of African Americans, whose past experiences warranted some form of redress, was obfuscated by a larger, less-defined constituency whose issues were wide and varied. And while other groups were also underrepresented and misrepresented in the news media, the most virulent strains of bias have continued to be aimed at people of African descent.

It is clear that the changing demographics of the nation dictate coverage that will appeal to the nation's increasingly diverse population. This need was accentuated by a decade and a half of circulation declines in the newspaper industry, in which between 1984 and 1998, circulation dipped from a high of 63.4 million copies to 56.7 million. According to a 1997 Media Usage Study published by the Newspaper Association of America (NAA), daily readership had fallen to 59 percent, a number that was expected to dip to 50 percent by the year 2000 if the trend continued. The disparity between blacks and whites was wide, with whites comprising 54 percent of newspaper readers, compared to 37 percent of African Americans and Hispanics. Among households where the annual income was over $35,000, 59 percent of whites read the paper, compared to 44 and 42 percent, respectively, of African Americans and Hispanics.[15] Black readers had become an even smaller percentage of the news-reading public, dropping from 11 percent in 1995 to 10.3 percent in 1997, according to the Simmons Market Research Bureau. Of the ten largest U.S. dailies, six, including the *New York Times*, the *Los Angeles Times*, and the *Washington Post*, suffered circulation declines in weekday, Sunday, or both, according to Audit Bureau of Circulation reports during the six-month period ending September 30, 1998. The *New York Times* lost more than 8,000 weekday copies and an additional 31,000 Sunday copies compared to the same period the previous year.

Couple this with U.S. Census projections, which estimate that the non-Hispanic white population will drop from the current 72.9 percent to 52.8 percent by 2050, and it is clear that the industry, for its survival, will need to appeal to this growing non-white population. Already by 1988, there was a growing recognition that newspapers needed to appeal more aggressively to minorities due to the industry's economic interests more than any altruistic impulses. "Cornerstone for Growth," a report underwritten by major news organizations, argued that publishers needed to focus on the "dynamic segments of their local communities—minorities" in order to counteract declining newspaper readership. Another report, "Diversity, a Business Imperative," released in 1995 by the

Newspaper Association of America, the group representing newspaper publishers, argued that nearly one out of every two children under five will belong to an ethnic minority by 2010. "These young people," said the report, "are the ones the newspaper industry must learn to attract as readers and as employers."

However, competing with these spirited calls for diversity were creative ways of looking at the bottom line. A 1995 NAA report, "Circulation Facts, Figures and Logic," noted that "good business decisions" are not necessarily driven by high circulation. "One of the newspaper's most basic and fundamental principles is changing," said the report. "That is, more is not necessarily better." Gone, according to the report, are the incentives to drive up circulation by luring readers, including those in non-affluent communities, with discounts and coupons. Among the report's recommendation to publishers was to avoid "marginal subscribers" or those lured by discounts, eliminate "fringe circulation," and instead focus on the upscale readers preferred by advertisers. Many translated that to mean there was no longer a time-honored business imperative to appeal to the growing number of urban minorities.

Similar sentiments were apparently shared by broadcast industry executives. In an internal memorandum in May 1998 leaked to newspapers, Amcast, a division of the Katz Radio Group that sells national advertising to radio stations, advised its representatives to discourage clients from placing commercials on black and Hispanic stations. "When it comes to delivering prospects, not suspects, the urbans deliver the largest amount of listeners who turn out to be the least likely to purchase," the memo read. The memorandum confirmed long-standing suspicions by minority broadcasters that they were being shunned by advertisers. A survey of New York stations showed that even the top-rated stations did not yield comparable advertising revenue if they had large minority listeners. For example, WSKQ, the second highest rated station in terms of listeners in the New York area, ranked thirteenth in revenue, largely due to its Hispanic format. The number 1 station, WLTW, with 6.2 million listeners, netted $37.9 million in revenue, while WSKQ netted $21.5 million, nearly half the amount. Similarly, in Detroit, the number 1 station, WJLB-FM, a black station, was number 4 in billing.

A survey of one thousand stations in the top one hundred markets conducted by Kofi Ofori, counsel of the Telecommunications Civil

Rights Forum, a public interest law firm based in a Washington, D.C., showed wide disparity between ad revenues for minority and nonminority stations. He said white-owned stations, on average, take in $3.5 million annually, while minority-owned stations average $2.6 million, even when their audience is larger. White-owned broadcasters were shown to yield 30 percent more revenue than minority broadcasters when both were minority formatted. Robert L. Johnson, chief executive of BET Holdings Inc., the parent of Black Entertainment Television cable network, told the *Washington Post* that even though BET's household ratings were close to those of MTV, MTV commands advertising rates that are six to ten times higher than BET's.

The Katz memorandum merely shed light on a systemic problem in the industry in which black consumers were devalued by advertisers. Vice President Al Gore was among those who expressed outrage over the memorandum and vowed to promote measures to curtail racial bias by advertisers and media buyers. The National Association of Black Owned Broadcasters called for an investigation into the matter. While FCC chairman William Kennard obliged, saying the memorandum represented "just the tip of the iceberg," the limits of government in matters of discrimination were clear in the wake of the scuttled FCC equal employment policy and attacks on affirmative action across the nation. An agency that could no longer require broadcasters to consider minorities in their recruiting efforts would have little authority to require companies to advertise on minority-owned stations.

The Association of National Advertisers, which had already formed a committee on minority media and advertising in 1996, vowed to step up its efforts in light of the memo. At the same time, Stu Olds, the president of Katz—who had initially downplayed the memo—finally offered apologies while appealing publicly to companies to advertise on minority stations. He insisted that the memo was "not reflective of how we try to do business" and pledged to initiate a diversity training program to educate his representatives about the importance of the minority market and to recruit more minority employees.

The memorandum sparked a threat by the Reverend Al Sharpton, a New York activist, to boycott numerous advertisers accused of shunning big market minority stations. By December, one of the targeted advertisers, Macy's department store, announced that it would increase by 50 percent the amount of money it spends advertising on minority stations. The pledge meant it would increase its ads in thirty-one black and Latino media outlets in New York, Boston, Baltimore, Philadelphia, and Miami. Why, at the end of the twentieth century, company officials were still speaking of the need to educate advertisers about the $460 billion that African American consumers alone would spend and how the over-whelming majority of African Americans are not criminals, was evidence of the racial attitudes permeating society. The stereotypes embedded in the mass media have real effects that pervade every aspect of African American life, to the point that, even in a capitalist society, it mattered to companies whose money it vied for.

Mark H. Willes, the chief executive of Times Mirror, a bottom-line businessman who had spent most of his career at General Mills, was among the industry leaders who saw the growing minority population as reason enough to cover them more aggressively. In the spring of 1998, after assessing the bylines, sources, pictures, and quotes in the *Los Angeles Times*, he asked his editors to find ways to quantify and improve coverage of minorities and women. His preliminary assessment convinced him that the paper's coverage of those two groups did not reflect the diversity of the Los Angeles community. Many decried his dictate as the invasion of marketing into news decisions, but his actions could also be seen in keeping with the Kerner report, and the Hutchins Commission, both of which called on the news industry to reach out to a broader audience. It is obvious that Willes's actions had less to do with social responsibility than the bottom line, but regardless, underrepresented and underserved racial minorities can only benefit from such bottom-line considerations.

There were similar efforts to appeal to minorities elsewhere. The *Rockford Register Star* in Illinois instituted a corporate plan to aggressively court minority readers by sending direct mail featuring graphics and pictures reflecting the ethnic base. The paper also alternated circulation routes so drivers would deliver the papers during daylight hours to appease fearful drivers. The newspaper also sold the newspaper at half price to black churches, allowing the churches to profit from sales.

It is not surprising, given African Americans' deep dissatisfaction with the mainstream media, that readership levels, even among the educated, are significantly lower than that of whites. But given African Americans' growing economic muscle, they could, by taking a more proactive approach, do more to pressure companies to reflect their interests. A report released by the University of Georgia's Selig Center for Economic Growth projected that the buying power of African Americans nationwide would reach $532.7 billion in 1999, which would represent a 72.9 percent jump since 1990. The consumer buying power—which reflects personal income after taxes—for the nation as a whole would have increased 56.7 percent during the same period.

Economic boycotts and other progressive tactics defined civil rights activism from the 1940s through the 1960s, when segregation and more blatant forms of bigotry called for more drastic measures. But in the late 1990s, there was no discernible, sustained, and proactive movement aimed at media accountability. Perhaps in a more mainstreamed era, the idea of a boycott strikes many African Americans as radical, ineffective, or too much of an effort, despite their undeniable efficacy. So despite the pervasive disregard for their interests, exemplified by shows like *The Diary of Desmond Pfeiffer* and advertiser boycotts of black radio stations and black publications, many black organizations and individuals seem resigned to support institutions that, while far more racially representative than they were thirty years ago, still systemically present stereotypical and offensive portraits of them.

Where the United Church of Christ, the NAACP Legal Defense Fund, and other organizations once aggressively monitored media outlets and rallied public support around their efforts, many of these organizations now primarily rely on press releases and reports that are filed and dismissed almost as quickly as they are issued. Missing is the moral imperative that defined an earlier time. It was easier to organize against stations that blatantly debased blacks than it is the subtler stereotyping that pervades the news media now. The daily parade of black men in handcuffs on the nightly news numbs more than it enrages. It takes the most egregious offenses—the smoking gun of a leaked memo or a comedy about slavery—to spark media activism, and even that is not the kind of sustained activism that typified the United Church of Christ's efforts in the 1950s, which involved scores of field workers, black and white.

The last significant show of black media activism occurred in Washington, D.C., in 1986 when African Americans, angered over the negative portrayals of blacks in the premiere issue of the *Washington Post* magazine, formed a recall campaign. For thirteen weeks, the *Washington Post* Recall Committee, supported by a coalition of nearly fifty groups including area churches, the Washington Urban League, and the Archdiocese of Washington, dumped thousands of magazines at the *Post's* doorstep. The magazine's offending cover story, titled "Murder, Drugs and the Rap Star," was about a twenty-year-old rap singer accused of murdering a Washington, D.C., man, while an inside column by Richard Cohen, titled "Closing the Door on Crime," sympathized with store owners who feared young black men. The magazine highlighted what many blacks had long contended was unbalanced and overwhelmingly negative coverage by the *Washing Post*. African Americans comprised about 70 percent of the district's population. The protest triggered an apology from executive editor Benjamin Bradlee and prompted editors to produce an internal report on the stories the paper had done about blacks over a fifty-three-day period. Bradlee consulted a number of African Americans, including the Reverend Jesse Jackson, Mayor Marion Barry—both targets of devastating stories in the paper—and members of Congress on ways to overcome the crisis. In the heat of the recall campaign, more than six hundred people attended a forum called "Negative Media," where actor Ossie Davis spoke.

The protest ended when Graham appeared on a local black radio station and apologized. An April 1991 article in *Regardies*, a business magazine in Washington, D.C., cited the boycott as one of the reasons the *Post* had watered down its tough city coverage. "The word boycott has struck terror in the hearts of the paper's brass since 1986, when blacks threw bundles of the *Washington Post* Magazine on its doorsteps because it had printed what they'd viewed as racially insensitive stories," the story said. Similar efforts, such as Operation Push's 1985 boycott of WBBM-TV after the only black week-day anchor was demoted, also yielded results. One of the demands, that the station hire two male minority anchors for the weekday newscast, was met.

But with these sporadic spurts of activity aside, most of the African American discontentment over media coverage and hiring is aired in polls, or in the reams of reports and press releases issued by minority associations, media watchdog groups, the Freedom Forum's Media Studies Center, and civil rights organizations. Unfortunately, the reports no longer have the bite they once did, since media executives, and the public, have become desensitized to what they perceive as whining. Much of the heavy lifting to improve coverage is left to the journalists already working for the mainstream media. This has, as has been explored, only contributed to an even higher rate of burnout, and therefore the high turnover, of black journalists. A survey by the Newspaper Association of America revealed that four of ten black journalists left the industry in 1994, compared to 22 percent of whites and 37 percent of minorities overall. Many cite frustration over a perceived glass ceiling and the daily resistance to diversity of thought they encounter in the newsroom as reasons for their planned exodus. Sixty-seven percent of black reporters surveyed by the National Association of Black Journalists said they spent more time in entry-level positions than their white colleagues. In ASNE's 1996 report "Newspaper Journalists of the '90s," 54 percent of blacks surveyed predicted they would leave newspapers before age fifty, compared to 33 percent of others. Similarly, 54 percent of black journalists said people of color are treated unfairly in their newsrooms, compared to 12 percent of whites, 38 percent of Asian Americans, and 29 percent of Hispanics. In 1996, the number of blacks in the industry declined for the first time in twenty years.

E. R. Shipp, upon resigning from the *New York Times* in 1993 after thirteen years there as a writer and editor, had few kind words for the industry. In a parting shot in the *NABJ Journal*, she said: "There was no compelling reason for this self-respecting black woman to stay." She added: "I wanted to be treated the way they'd have treated a white person who came there, as I did, with advanced degrees in journalism and law." Shipp went on to win a Pulitzer Prize for her columns at the *Daily News*, became a journalism professor at Columbia University, and in 1998 became an ombudsman at the *Washington Post*.

Karen Howze, after twenty years of working as a journalist, culminating in a ten-year career at *USA Today*, left the business frustrated and weary in 1992. Years of battles with news executives over issues of fairness and balance had taken its toll, as did the rivalries among black colleagues due to a glass ceiling that would only allow a few to break through. Howze left the newsroom to start her own law practice in Washington, D.C. She said while she managed to make a difference during her tenure at *USA Today*, where she recruited scores of black journalists, she also had the battle scars to show for her efforts. Some, like Robin Stone, a life-styles editor at the *New York Times*, left the paper in 1997 to become an editor at *Essence* magazine, the black women's life-style magazine, where she felt she could have more meaningful input.

In what is, perhaps, the most searing indication of the racial divide in the media is that 166 years after the establishment of a black press in America, many African Americans still see the need for one. Part of the need is cultural. Black Entertainment Television continued to expand its holdings, with its purchase in 1998 of *Heart and Soul*, a black fitness magazine, adding it to its stable of BET Television and *Emerge* magazine. But sadly, the black press, once a viable alternative to the mainstream media, was fighting for relevancy and quality. Where the early black press had scores of highly educated men and women covering the arts, entertainment, foreign affairs, and local politics, some with correspondents in several cities and nations, many black newspapers are eking by with a bare-bones staff. While the black press still provides an important service in many markets by providing information the mainstream media deems irrelevant, it serves, at best, as a supplement rather than an alternative to the mainstream press.

In 1998, Donald L. Miller, a former Dow Jones executive, was still trying to get his *Our World News*, a national newspaper targeting middle-class African American readers, off the ground. Prospects for the paper had been promising. In 1995, Miller, former vice president of employee relations at Dow Jones & Co., publisher of the *Wall Street Journal*, resigned to launch the paper. Plans called for a four-color newspaper that would provide news and commentary while covering politics, sports, and entertainment. Miller announced he had struck a deal with the Gannett Company to print the weekly and with Dow Jones to distribute it. He said he had raised nearly $4.5 million in start-up money from private investors, including $1 million from the Freedom Forum, the nonprofit media foundation. He hired a staff of twelve, which included some of the most respected members of the mainstream media, including Joel Dreyfuss, an editor at *Fortune*, and Paul Delaney, a former *New York Times* correspondent, editor and recruiter. Dreyfuss was managing editor and Delaney the editorial page editor of the prototype issues.

But several launch dates were postponed as Miller tried to raise an additional $2 million in capital. By the end of 1998, hopes for the paper were dimming as Dreyfuss returned to his job at *Fortune* magazine and Delaney took a job at the *Baltimore Sun*. Even as he closed the Baltimore office, Miller insisted that the paper would indeed happen. While many black journalists were skeptical about the prospects of the venture, given the demonstrated reluctance by advertisers to support black media, many privately hoped it would succeed to provide an antidote to the mainstream press. The project, many hoped, would ultimately improve mainstream news coverage of African Americans by providing a viable alternative.

At the close of the twentieth century, many were looking to new media to close the entrepreneurial and information gap for African Americans and other groups disenchanted with the mainstream media. Kennard and others heralded new media as a most promising development for African Americans given that start-up of potentially lucrative companies required less capital than traditional media companies. Adam Clayton Powell III, the technology director at the Freedom Forum Media Studies Center, said the Internet would have a profound impact on the media. "For the first time in human history," he said in a 1995 speech on cyberspace, "every consumer, every reader and every viewer can be a global publisher, with free instantaneous worldwide distribution by the Internet." Indeed, the possibilities seemed limitless.

In 1995, two young African Americans, Malcolm CasSelle, a twenty-five-year-old computer science graduate of MIT and Stanford, and E. David Ellington, a thirty-five-year-old entertainment lawyer, launched NetNoir on America Online, the nation's largest Internet company. NetNoir, which provides news, entertainment, as well as job postings and chat rooms targeted to African Americans, was the first outside company supported by the America Online Greenhouse Program which helped finance "infopreneurs" who could provide unique content on the Net. NetNoir reports having about 250,000 visitors per month, and its advertisers and sponsors included IBM, Hewlett-Packard, and Wells Fargo Bank.

In April 1997, Barry Cooper, manager for the Tribune Company on-line news service, founded Black Voices to fill a void in coverage he did not find elsewhere. Owned by the Tribune Company, Black Voices' traffic quadrupled in less than a year, with up to 400,000 visitors and five million hits a month. The site has been used by Walt Disney and New Line Cinema to promote films. With the rise in PC penetration, advertisers were increasingly testing the ethnic market, particularly given its upscale base. In 1996, Timberland, the maker of expensive athletic boots, became the first sponsor of Unity First, a weekly direct e-mail news service that targets African Americans nationally. The service is an offshoot of Unity First News, a Boston weekly whose sponsors include T.J. Maxx and Sun Microsystems. Scores of other African American sites sprung up, as did those targeted to other ethnic groups, including LatinoLink, Chinese.Yahoo, and Chinese Cyber City. "Media's Global Future," a report released in 1998 by Forrester Research, predicted that online ad revenues in the United States would exceed $10.5 billion in 2003, up from $1.3 billion in 1998.

But while NetNoir, Black Voices, and a host of other similar ventures would fill an information void for African Americans, news did not play a primary role in their operations. NetNoir filtered news from the Associated Press by keying in words and phrases like African nations, black leaders, and the like.

"I'm not building a newspaper here," Ellington stated emphatically. "I don't see the community supporting it financially."

Ellington said that while many people insist vehicles like his and Black Entertainment Television should have more serious content, in-house tracking showed that more people are looking for entertainment. Seventy percent of his subscribers sign on for the chat rooms and programmed events. He said the comedian Sinbad draws more attention than public and elected officials. "I'm creating programming that the majority of my audience is telling me they want. There's a significant chunk of people who really like chat. What we have decided is we're not going to base programming on what people say is important." Instead, it will be based on audience conduct. However, NetNoir did provide some news and serious content, but it was not central to the service.

Ellington understood the criticism aimed at African American-owned companies like Black Entertainment Television, which is saturated with often explicit music videos, rather than the kind of serious programming African American critics say they should carry. "But at the end of the day, I understand why he has all those videos," Ellington offered, referring to BET president Robert Johnson. "It's cheaper and the masses are staring at it. Media is often an escape valve. Yes, I watch PBS but the overwhelming majority don't." So those African Americans who look to the Internet as an emerging alternative to the status quo press have little cause for optimism. Any successful business model, Ellington stressed, would rely on brand names, which have increasingly dominated the Internet. People tune in for news from the *New York Times*, CNN and the same reliable sources they've known. It will be more difficult than ever for African Americans to break through without a high-profile logo. Providing the kind of news and information so lacking in the mainstream press would require more than an economic incentive. Required is a public service incentive, which is so often lacking in the mainstream media where news and information are concerned.

Compounding the difficulty of establishing on-line opportunities for African American journalists is the widening disparity in computer ownership and access between upper and lower income people, black and white. While between 1994 and 1997 home ownership of personal computers had increased by more than 50 percent and the number of people using e-mail quadrupled, white households were twice as likely to own computers as black and Latino households, according to a federal study released in July 1998. The study, "Falling through the Net II: New Data on the Digital Divide," estimated that 40.8 percent of white households owned PCs, compared to 19.3 percent of African American homes, and 19.7 percent of Hispanic homes. For households earning $75,000 or more, the gap narrowed but was still significant. While 76.3 percent of whites had PCs, only 64 percent of African Americans did. The study also reported that households earning more than $75,000 a year were seven times more likely to own a computer than those earning $5,000 to $10,000 annually. It showed that people with college degrees were ten times more likely than those without a high school degree to own a computer. And as much as the Internet had been mainstreamed, with millions signing on to read the Starr Report outlining President Clinton's alleged sexual escapades with an intern, only about 36.6 percent of U.S. homes had personal computers, and about 18.4 percent had on-line access.

The report was an update of a 1995 study, "Falling through the Net: A Survey of the 'Have Nots' in Rural and Urban America," which had reported that 11.8 percent of urban black households had computers, compared with 30.3 percent of white households.

Equally disturbing is a 1998 Education Department survey that found that 63 percent of poor and minority schools nationwide had access to the Internet, compared to 78 percent of all schools in the nation. A Nielsen Media Research study of 5,813 people between December 1996 and January 1997 found that 72 percent of white high school and college students owned a computer, compared to 32 percent of black students. But as computer prices continued to drop, many were predicting big increases in first-time buyers in 1999. Clearly, business leaders, government, and the on-line services themselves have their work cut out for them if they plan to tap into this immense market.

And just how long small entrepreneurs would be able to partake in the new frontier was unclear as more and more small companies were consolidating to bolster their place in the market. America Online Inc. guarded its dominant position in the industry by acquiring Mirabilis, whose ICQ chat service had international appeal. It also was poised to acquire the Netscape Communications Corporation for its World Wide Web site. Meanwhile, Lycos, which in 1997 reached 14 percent of Internet users, a year later reached 47 percent as a result of the acquisition of five companies. In 1998, Yahoo, one of the top-rated search engines, was valued at $23 billion, rivaling the worth of CBS Inc. But the Internet still offered the best opportunities for news entrepreneurs to enter at the ground floor. It also presented the best alternatives for news diversity, although it appeared that without major government intervention, the economically disadvantaged could be totally shut out of the Information Superhighway.

How the news industry would respond to challenges posed in the new millennium was anybody's guess. What's clear is that the imperative for the news industry to better reflect the nation's changing demographics was great. But whether change would be gradual or whether it would happen in a surge, as it did in the 1960s, was not known. While many spoke of a need to reach out, the resistance to change was all around as there were few attempts to get at the root causes of the attitudes that drive policies and news coverage. In addition to progressive hiring policies and story quotas on ethnic coverage, a revolutionary way of looking at African Americans was needed. The media were in the best position to change the way African Americans were portrayed. But media executives would have to take the lead by first overcoming their own denial of deep-seated black inferiority beliefs. Denial would only prolong the process of change.

Also, until the nation, once and for all, addresses the ways in which the past contributes to present-day attitudes and conditions, there will be little progress in race relations. This is not to negate the need for greater self-reliance by all individuals. There would be resounding support for welfare reform and other conservative measures if African Americans truly believed equal opportunity in employment was a reality. So, along with the need for African Americans to see themselves less as victims than pilots of their own destiny is the need for whites to engage in less denial about the myriad ways that advancement continues to elude some of the most talented and hard-working blacks due to stubborn racial barriers of the past—and present.

One of the solutions is for African Americans to complain less about the things that are within their power to change. Greater self-reliance would include being more proactive as entrepreneurs and as consumers of news and information. If minorities continue to buy newspapers or support the sponsors of television shows that roundly devalue their humanity, they can never expect to win the respect of those media organizations. African Americans must use the power of praise and punishment to call attention to the ways in which they are portrayed. Of course, the lack of a strong alternative medium makes it more difficult for minorities to exercise their power as consumers, but to the extent they can, they must.

Meanwhile, whites should place a moratorium on telling blacks to pull themselves up by the bootstraps. The ascent of Mark Whitaker at *Newsweek* does not mean he was the first supremely talented minority able to run a magazine. It only means he was the first to have been given the opportunity. Without a convergence of increased activism by blacks, and fair-mindedness by whites, many of the same issues concerning news coverage and minority hiring will endure for years to come. Until and unless that occurs, African Americans and other minorities can find solace in the nation's steadily shifting racial dynamics, which, over time, will dictate a new arrangement if news organizations are to survive. The question is how long those in positions of influence will hold out before they begin to take seriously the task of diversity and of tackling distorted attitudes of not only the more than 34 million blacks in the United States, but millions more people of color around the world. To date, the most sweeping policies on race occurred as a result of national anarchy—in the 1860s and again in the 1960s. Given the nation's track record, there is little reason to believe change is around the corner, barring major racial upheaval.

So for now, progress will be defined by the spurt of activity that follows unusual incidents, such as race riots, successful lawsuits, and revelations of questionable actions by media executives that have racial overtones. But without renewed activism on both sides, the brunt of the responsibility for improved media coverage will continue to rest primarily with the African American men and women already in the newsroom who, with little outside agitation, endeavor to challenge distorted view of African Americans. The difference they make in coverage will, without an overhaul of our thinking patterns, continue to be overshadowed by the negative racial attitudes permeating the media and society.

Langston Hughes perhaps best conveyed the power of dreams. "Hold fast to your dreams, for when dreams die, life is a broken-winged bird that cannot fly," he wrote. While black journalists cannot adopt Hughes's words as a combat plan, they can find in them the spiritual renewal required to overcome a period of pessimism and despair. Many of the great victories of modern times, from the fall of apartheid in South Africa to the crumbling of Jim Crow and the advent of female suffrage in the United States, were dependent on reservoirs of optimism that gave warriors heart in the face of overwhelming odds.

While the problems confronting blacks in journalism hardly compare to apartheid, they are emblematic of larger problems facing black people worldwide. Retreating from the struggle is not an option. African Americans must continue to pry open the doors in the mainstream media while working to insure they have unfiltered vehicles through which to communicate effectively to African Americans. The mainstream media would be forced to be responsive to African Americans if strong black media posed a viable threat. Of course the difficulties that face black publishers loom large, especially given the resistance of advertisers to support serious black journals. Just as Trotter had difficulty publishing the *Guardian*, black publishers will have problems publishing a quality newspaper for African Americans. But great need is usually followed by even greater entrepreneurship or, in some cases, pure principle. BET president Bob Johnson is setting a notable example by continuing to publish a money-losing *Emerge*. Perhaps his example will be followed by other prominent African Americans who will put the progress of African Americans over profits.

Were African Americans only to measure progress by the statistics, or by the resistance to change, then they would find it difficult to celebrate, or even see, the progress made over the past few decades. So far and so fast have they come that few of the mainstream media pioneers could ever have imagined *Newsweek*'s appointment of Whitaker as they sought merely to pry the doors open to minorities a scant thirty years earlier. Neither could many have envisioned the soaring achievements of Bryant Gumbel in network television and William Kennard as FCC commissioner. The change from all-white newsrooms in the 1950s to newsrooms which, in some markets, mirror the community's racial composition is worthy of applause. But pride and observance of these gains cannot muffle the pain and injury of a dominant view of black inferiority that is both transmitted and adopted by much of the mainstream news media. Acknowledgment must be followed by action. The damage this pernicious and outmoded mindset has done to national unity is too great a price for the nation to pay.

APPENDIX

Table 1. Broadcast News Workforce

Race	Television	Radio
Caucasian	80%	84%
African American	10%	9%
Hispanic/Latino	6%	5%
Asian American	3%	2%
Native American	1%	>1%

Overall, minorities in television news slid from 21 percent in the 1998 year's survey to 20 percent in 1999. Minorities in radio news rose by 4 percent from 1998, with African Americans and Hispanic/Latinos each picking up 2 percent from the year before. Asian Americans rose slightly, and Native Americans slipped slightly.

Table 2. Broadcast News Directors

Race	Television	Radio
Caucasian	90%	89%
African American	3%	7%
Hispanic/Latino	5%	1%
Asian American	1%	1%
Native American	1%	2%

Minority news directors rose by 2 percent in television and 3 percent in radio news compared to 1997. In both cases, almost all of the gain went to African Americans (up to 2 percent in television and 3 percent in radio). In radio, Hispanic/Latinos slid slightly from 2 percent to 1 percent while Native Americans rose from 1 percent to 2 percent.

Table 3. Numbers and Percentage of Minorities by Race and Job Category, 1998

	Blacks		Hispanics		Asians		Native Americans	
	No.	%	No.	%	No.	%	No.	%
Supervisors	551	19	348	18	178	15	63	25
Copy/Layout Editors	481	16	320	17	240	20	43	17
Reporters	1,651	56	900	48	537	46	113	44
Photographers	263	9	321	17	223	19	37	14
Totals	2,946		1,889		1,178		256	

From the Radio-Television News Directors Association/Ball State University Women and Minorities Survey. (© *Communicator*, October 1998. Reprinted by permission.)

Table 4. Numbers and Percentages of Whites and Minorities by Job Category, 1998

		Minorities		Whites	
Work Force	Total	No.	%	No.	%
Supervisors	12,724	1,140	9.0	11,584	91.0
Copy/layout editors	10,656	1,083	10.2	9,572	89.8
Reporters	25,551	3,202	12.5	22,349	87.5
Photographers	5,790	844	14.6	4,946	85.4
Totals	54,721	6,269		48,451	

Appendix

Table 5. Minority Employment in Daily
Newspapers: Projections Based on Responses
to Annual Employment Census
(numbers rounded)

Year	Total Workforce	Minorities in Workforce	% Minorities in Workforce
1978	43,000	1,700	3.95
1989	45,000	1,900	4.22
1980	47,000	2,300	4.89
1981	45,500	2,400	5.27
1982	49,000	2,700	5.51
1983	50,000	2,800	5.60
1984	50,400	2,900	5.75
1985	53,800	3,100	5.76
1986	54,000	3,400	6.30
1987	54,700	3,600	6.56
1988	55,300	3,900	7.02
1989	56,200	4,200	7.54
1990	56,900	4,500	7.86
1991	55,700	4,900	8.72
1992	54,500	5,100	9.39
1993	53,600	5,500	10.25
1994	53,700	5,600	10.49
1995	53,800	5,900	10.91
1996	55,000	6,100	11.02
1997	54,000	6,100	11.35
1998	54,700	6,300	11.46
1999	55,100	6,400	11.55

- Racial/ethnic groups: In 1999 there were 2,946 black journalists (5.38 percent of the newsroom work force); 1,889 Hispanic journalists (3.45 percent); 1,178 Asian journalists (2.15 percent), and 256 Native American journalists (0.47 percent).
- More dailies have integrated newsrooms today than in 1978. In 1999, 58 percent of newspapers employed minority newsroom professionals, compared to one-third in 1978.
- The proportion of minorities working in all job categories in the newsroom has grown significantly in the past two decades. In 1999, 9 percent of newsroom supervisors were minorities, compared to only 1 percent in 1978. The representation of minority reporters and writers has doubled to 12.5 percent, from 6 percent in 1978. Minority copy and layout editors represented 10.2 percent of the newsroom in 1999, compared to 3 percent in 1978. The proportion of minority photographers and graphic artists has almost tripled, from 5 percent in 1978 to 14.6 percent.

Table 6. Regional Comparison of Minority Newsroom Employment, 1999

Region	Minority	White	Total	Minority %
East North Central Illinois, Indiana, Michigan, Ohio, and Wisconsin	791	8,391	9,182	8.61
East South Central Alabama, Kentucky, Mississippi, and Tennessee	272	2,302	2,575	10.58
Middle Atlantic New Jersey, New York, and Pennsylvania	1,040	8,174	9,215	11.29
Mountain Arizona, Colorado, Idaho, Montana, New Mexico, Nevada, Utah, and Wyoming	359	3,027	3,387	10.61
New England Connecticut, Massachusetts, Maine, New Hampshire, Rhode Island, and Vermont	225	3,373	3,599	6.26
Pacific Alaska, California, Hawaii, Oregon, and Washington	1,275	6,644	7,919	16.10
South Atlantic Delaware, District of Columbia, Florida, Georgia, Maryland, North Carolina, South Carolina, Virginia, and West Virginia	1,356	8,864	10,220	13.27
West North Central Iowa, Kansas, Minnesota, Missouri, Nebraska, North Dakota and South Dakota	244	3,727	3,971	6.13
West South Central Arkansas, Louisiana, Oklahoma, and Texas	743	4,267	5,010	14.83

Table 7. Numbers and Percentages of Men and Women by Race, 1999

	Blacks		Hispanics		Asians		Native Americans		Whites	
	No.	%	No.	%	No.	%	No.	%	No.	%
Men	1,533	52	1,141	60	630	50	143	59	31,335	64
Women	1,420	48	764	41	634	50	98	40	17,407	36
Totals	2,953		1,905		1,264		241		48,742	

From the Newsroom Employment Census conducted by the American Society of Newspaper Editors. (Copyright © 1999 ASNE. Reprinted by permission.)

NOTES

Notes to Chapter 1

1. Author interview with Sylvester Monroe, July 11, 1995

2. "Is Concept of Race a Relic?" *Los Angeles Times*, April 15, 1995.

3. Jannette L. Dates and William Barlow, *Split Image: African Americans in the Mass Media* (Howard University Press 1990).

4. Geoffrey Cowley, "Testing the Science of Intelligence," *Newsweek*, October 24, 1994, 56.

5. As an indication of its intolerance, the *New York Times* published a series of editorials condemning Jeffries, including "A Professor Flaunts His Bias," August 9, 1991; "Watching Dr. Jeffries Self-Destruct," August 25, 1991; "Why the Delay on Dr. Jeffries?" October 30, 1991; "Bigotry Punished," March 27, 1992; "Handling a Campus Demagogue," August 6, 1993; and "Bigotry on Display; Hate Speech and the University," April 6, 1995.

6. See Patrick Goldstein "Public Enemy and A Psychiatrist's Theory of Race," *Los Angeles Times*, April 29, 1990. Also see Richard Harrington, "PE and the 'Pigment Envy' Theory," *Washington Post*, May 2, 1990.

7. Figures from 1998 annual minority employment statistics prepared by the American Society of Newspaper Editors and the Radio and Television News Directors Association/Ball State University.

8. *Social Control in the Newsroom*" 2d ed. (Urbana: University of Illinois Press, May 1960).

9. Herbert Gans, *Deciding What's News*, (New York: Vintage Books, 1980), 39.

10. Ibid., 61.

11. "New Orleans' Newspapers Give White View of the City," the *Times-Picayune*, June 17, 1993.

12. Stacey Teicher, "When Journalists Wrestle with Race: A Case Study of the *New Orleans Times-Picayune* Series 'Together Apart: The Myth of Race,'" M.A. thesis, University of Missouri—Columbia, August 1998, 59.

13. Ibid., 61–62.

14. Ibid., 42.

15. Author interview with Jim Amoss, May 27, 1999.

16. Ibid.

17. Teicher, "When Journalists Wrestle with Race," 68.

18. Ibid., 67.

19. Author interview with Keith Woods, March 15, 1999.

20. Amoss interview.

21. Teicher, "When Journalists Wrestle with Race," 65.

22. "News Junkies, News Critics: How Americans Use the News and What They Think about It," February 1997, A Newseum Survey by the Roper Center for Public Opinion Research.

23. H. Himmelstein, *TV Myth and the American Mind* (New York Praeger, 1984), 206.

24. "Editing Reality: An Ethnographic and Analytical Study of Photographic Production at Four Major Newspapers," Dissertation Abstracts International, University at Austin, 1995, 239.

25. "Negative News and Little Else," *Los Angeles Times*, which was part of a Pulitzer-Prize-winning series on minorities in the media.

26. "Crime, Drugs and the Media: The Black Pathology Biz," *Nation*, November 20, 1989.

27. Author interview with Paula Walker, June 1995.

28. Ibid.

29. "The Big City: Once, Racism Meant Leaving Harlem Alone," *New York Times*, February 18, 1999, B1.

30. BBDO's 12th annual "Report on Black TV Viewing," February 21, 1997.

31. Open letter written by Juan Gonzalez, *New York Daily News*, October 4, 1995.

32. "Keyes Takes High Road, Hard Line," *Des Moines Register*, December 3, 1995.

33. "Why I'm Marching in Washington," *New York Times*, October 14, 1995, A19.

34. "Tensions over Racism and Anti-Semitism Have Surfaced in Georgia House Campaign," *New York Times*, October 16, 1996, A2. The article notes McKinney's 1994 House vote. Also see "Georgia Campaign '96: McKinney Opponent Urges Her to 'Renounce' All Bias," *Atlanta Journal and Constitution*, October 16, 1996.

35. "Two Standards About Words on Farrakhan," *New York Times*, B1, April 11, 1997.

36. Letter to author from *News* editor William Borders, July 18, 1995.

37. "Signal from Central Park," *Washington Times*, G1.

38. "Race in the News: Mainly about Whites," sec. 4, 27.

39. "Papers Reveal Bias in Central Park Case," *St. Louis Post-Dispatch*, May 22, 1989, 3B.

40. Author interview with Curtis Taylor, 1995.

41. "One Precinct, 2 Very Different Murder Cases," *New York Times*, March 15, 1999, A1.

42. *Today Show* transcript, November 13, 1992.

43. Sanford J. Ungar and David Gergen, "Africa and the American Media," November 1991.

44. Author interview with Bryant Gumbel, Occasional Paper 9, The freedom forum Media Studies Center, May 30, 1995.

45. Author interview with Gartner, June 1995.

46. Gumbel interview.

Notes to Chapter 2

1. Jannette L. Dates and William Barlow, *Split Image: African Americans in the Mass Media"* (Howard University Press: 1990).

2. "Shotgun Rule Defended by U.S. Senator Tillman," *New York Press*, February 27, 1900.

3. "*New York World*, September 1895.

4. The Niagara Movement Declaration of Principles.

5. John Edward Bruce Collection, Schomburg Library, Rare Books division, New York.

6. Ibid.

7. Lester Walton Papers, 1905–1977, Schomburg Center for Research in Black Culture, New York.

8. Dates and Barlow, *Split Image*, p. 354.

9. "New Orleans' Newspapers Give White View of the City," *Times-Picayune*, June 17, 1993, A18.

10. George Schuyler Papers, Schomburg Center for Research in Black Culture, New York.

11. Ibid.

12. Report of the Hutchins Commission on Freedom of the Press, p. 26.

13. Ben Bradlee, *A Good Life* (New York: Simon and Schuster, 1995), 280.

14. Author interview with Simeon Booker.

15. Author interview with Ben Holman, March 6, 1998.

16. Ibid.

17. "Profile: Robert Maynard," *Washington Journalism Review*, April 1981, 44.

18. Author interview with Ben Holman, April 27, 1998.

19. Clint C. Wilson II, *Black Journalists in Paradox: Historical Perspectives and Current Dilemmas* (New York: Greenwood Press, 1991).

20. Bradlee, *A Good Life*, 279–280.

21. Ibid., 280.

22. Opening remarks, "Kerner Plus Ten: Conference on Minorities and the Media," Howard R. Marsh Center for the Study, University of Michigan.

Notes to Chapter 3

Portions of several author interviews conducted for this chapter were originally published in the *Media Studies Journal.*

1. "Report of the National Advisory Commission on Civil Disorders," 210.

2. Ibid., 210.

3. Ibid., 211.

4. Ibid., 211.

5. Ibid., 213.

6. Author interview with Acel Moore, August 7, 1998.

7. Letter dated May 21, 1968, reprinted in "Memorandum Opinion and Order and Notice of Proposed Rulemaking," in *Petition for Rulemaking to Require Broadcast Licensees to Show Nondiscrimination in their Rulemaking Practices*, 13 F.C.C. 2d, 767, 775–777.

8. Ibid., 431–432.

9. Author interview with John Johnson, October 23, 1998.

10. Ibid.

11. Leigh Hermance, "Constitutionality of Affirmative Action Regulations Imposed Under the Cable Communications Policy Act of 1984," *Catholic University Law Review*, Spring 1986.

12. American Society of Newspaper Editors, annual survey.

13. "Problems of Journalism: Proceedings of the American Society of Newspaper Editors," 1970, 167.

14. Author interview with Joe Oglesby, June 1999.

15. Ibid.

16. "The Negro in Journalism: Surveys Show Low Ratios," *Journalism Quarterly* 46, no. 1 (Spring 1969).

17. "Journalism Schools Report Record 65,692 Enrollment," *Journalism Educator*, 32, no. 4 (January 1978).

18. Author interview with Karen Howze, 1995.

19. Author interview with Melba Tolliver, October 25, 1998.

20. Ibid.

21. Ibid.

22. Author interview with Dorothy Reed, October 22, 1998.

23. *Jet* magazine, February 19, 1981.

24. Reed interview.

25. *Springfield Morning News* (Springfield, Mass.), February 9, 1981, carried by United Press International.

26. "The Rise, and Dizzying Fall, of Max Robinson," *Washington Post*, May 26, 1988, E1.

27. Ibid.

28. "Packaged Homogeneity Produces a Skewed View," *Washington Post*, February 16, 1981.

29. "For Max Robinson, a Farewell," *Washington Post*, December 24, 1988, C1.

30. Wayne Dawkins, Black Journalists: The NABJ Story, (Sicklersville, N.J.: August Press, 1993, 34.

31. "Problems of Journalism: Proceedings of the American Society of Newspaper Editors, 1978," Report on Minority Hiring.

32. "Summary of Results of 1978 Journalism Graduate Survey Conducted by the Newspaper Fund."

33. "Problems of Journalism."

34. Ibid., 303.

35. Howze interview.

36. Ibid.

37. ASNE annual survey.

Notes to Chapter 4

1. Author interview with Steve Duncan, January 25, 1999.

2. "Ace Tyler's Patterson, Belknap; Can Nice Guys Finish First?" *American Lawyer*, July 1988.

3. Author interview with Dan Alterman, September 2, 1998.

4. Duncan interview.

5. Alterman interview.

6. Ibid.

7. Author interview with Les Payne, April 26, 1999.

8. "Bitter Fight Is Predicted in *Daily News* Discrimination Trial," *New York Times*, February 9, 1987, B2.

9. Alterman interview.

10. Author interview with David Hardy via e-mail, February 10, 1999.

11. "Bitter Clashes Resound in Daily News Bias Trial," *New York Times*, March 18, 1987, B3.

12. "Ex-editor Challenged: Changes Testimony," *New York Daily News*, April 1, 1987.

13. "Rule Pol Faked Deal," *Daily News*, December 4, 1981.

14. See *New York Times*, April 7, 1987.

15. "Loan with Pol Detailed at *News* Suit," *New York Daily News*, February 25, 1987.

16. "Ex-editor Says He Was Wrong," *New York Daily News*, April 7, 1987.

17. "*News* Ex-Editor Raps Plaintiffs," *New York Newsday*, April 8, 1987.

18. "The Trial of New York's *Daily News*," *Columbia Journalism Review*, July–August 1987.

19. Author interview with Leon Dash, February 25, 1999.

20. "Protest at the Post," *Time*, April 10, 1972, 50.

21. So aggressive was Alexander as IIOC chair that Senate Republican leader Everett Dirksen threatened to fire him if his "harassment" continued. See "D.C.'s 'High-Wire' Artist: How He Swung Stadium Deal; Strategy Included Secrecy," *Washington Post*, February 12, 1993.

22. Ibid.

23. Author interview with Hardy, February 10, 1999.

24. Author interview with Earl Caldwell.

25. Author interview with Janice Goodman.

26. Author interview with John Johnson, October 23, 1998.

27. Caldwell interview.

28. "Life in the Belly of the Beast," *City Sun*, March 11–17, 1987.

29. Letter to the editor, *Columbia Journalism Review*, November–December 1987.

30. United Press International, February 9, 1987.

31. "Lawyer Faults the *Daily News* for Racial Bias," *New York Times*, February 11, 1987, B3.

32. "Bettered Woodstein," *New York Daily News*, March 5, 1987.

33. "Editor Recounts Reporter's Work," *New York Daily News*, March 17, 1987.

34. "Reporter Assailed in Race-Bias Trial," *New York Times*, March 8, 1987, sec. 1, pt. 1, col. 1.

35. "Ex-News Executive Testifies," *New York Daily News*, March 31, 1987.

36. "Management Raises the Issue of Competence," *New York City Sun*, February 18–24, 1987, 4.

37. "News Ex-editor Recalls Work of Reporter," *New York Daily News*, March 26, 1987.

38. *New York City Sun*, March 11–17, 1987 4.

39. "Ex-editor Challenged: Changes Testimony," *New York Daily News*, April 1, 1987.

40. "Witness Describes Salaries at the *News*," *New York Daily News*, March 12, 1987.

41. Alterman interview.

42. "Suit charges *News* Firings Race Biased," *New York Newsday*, July 14, 1993, 28.

43. "Minorities Sue *N.Y. Daily News* over Firings," *Editor and Publisher*, July 17, 1993.

44. "Racial Rashomon," *American Lawyer*, March 1996.

45. Hardy interview.

46. *New York Daily News*, April 9, 1998, 87.

47. "Phone Home: An Opinionated View of the *Daily News* Trial," *New York City Sun*, March 11–17, 1987.

Notes to Chapter 5

1. Author interview with Dorothy Gaiter, 1995.

2. Ombudsman Report by Bill Green, *Washington Post* April 19, 1981.

3. "Rev. Lyons' Statement from News Conference," *St. Petersburg Times*, July 12, 1997, 14A.

4. "Lyons' Backers Successfully Use Race as Political Strategy," *St. Petersburg Times*, September 5, 1997, 8A.

5. "Tearful Baptist Leader Is Given 5-1/2-Year Term in Graft Case," *New York Times*, April 14, 1999, A19.

6. Author interview with Felicia Lee, 1995.

7. "Journalists Injured Covering Riot," *New York Newsday*, August 22, 1991, 35.

8. "Little Proof Inequity Persists," *New York Newsday*, September 3, 1991, 6.

9. Author interview with Michael Cottman, 1995.

10. Ibid.

11. Milton Coleman, "A Reporter's Story, 18 Words, 7 Weeks Later," *Washington Post*, April 8, 1984, C8.

12. "What Farrakhan Said," *Newsweek*, April 23, 1984, a transcript of Farrakhan's radio address.

13. "Jackson Deplores Threats against Washington Writer," *New York Times*, April 4, 1984, B7; "Meeting Urged with Reporter: Jackson Calls Farrakhan Threat 'Wrong,'" *Washington Post*, April 4, 1984, A8.

14. "Protesters Focus on Post's Coverage of Blacks," *Washington Post*, December 8, 1986, B1.

15. Ibid.

16. W. E. B. Du Bois, *The Souls of Black Folk: Essays and Sketches* (Chicago, 1903; New York: Fawcett, 1964).

17. "Black Journalists vs. Jackson: Racism Blasted," *San Diego Union-Tribune*, August 19, 1984, C1.

18. "Advisers Claim 'Vendetta,'" *New York Newsday*, April 28, 1989, 4.

19. Ibid.

20. Payne interview. Note that in 1998, C. Vernon Mason, Alton Maddox, and Al Sharpton were found guilty of defaming Steven Pagones, an assistant district attorney in Dutchess County, and ordered to pay $345,000 in damages.

21. Payne interview. Unless otherwise indicated, all of Payne's comments are based on author's interview.

22. Gaiter interview.

23. "Civil Unrest," *Wall Street Journal.* June 10, 1994, A1.

24. Author interview with Caroline Brewer, 1995.

25. "Hopher Shown Exceptional Kindness," *Dayton Daily News*, July 1, 1995, A10.

26. Brewer interview.

27. "Africa and the American Media," *Freedom Forum*, Occasional Paper no. 91, November 1991, 8.

28. "Preparing for Wednesday's TV Interview, BET's Reporter Says He Has 'Butterflies,'" *Atlanta Journal*, January 23, 1996.

29. Cornel West, *Race Matters* (New York: Vintage Books, 1993), 7.

Notes to Chapter 6

1. Ombudsman Report by Bill Green, *Washington Post*, April 19, 1981.

2. "Mayor Says City Ending Its Search for 'Jimmy,'" *Washington Post*, October 16, 1980, C1.

3. Ombudsman Report.

4. Ben Bradlee, *A Good Life* (New York: Simon and Schuster, 1995), 442.

5. Ombudsman Report.

6. Ibid.

7. Bradlee, *A Good Life*, 437.

8. Dan Collins, United Press International, June 12, 1981.

9. "The Stuart Case: Stereotypes of a Crime, Black and White," *Boston Globe*, January 5, 1990, 17.

10. This and the rest of the account is from Ombudsman Report.

11. "How *Washington Post* and the Pulitzer Board Were Duped by Writer," *Wall Street Journal*, April 17, 1981, 1.

12. James A. Michener, "On Integrity in Journalism," *U.S. News and World Report*, May 4, 1981, 80.

13. Ombudsman Report.

14. "Janet's World," *GQ*, June 1996.

15. Howard Kurtz, "As the *Globe* Turns," *Washington Post*, C1.

16. "Op Ed: *Globe* Still Plays Barnicle Enabler," *Boston Herald*, August 17, 1998.

17. Ibid.

18. Ibid.

19. Jack Thomas, the ombudsman, "Searching for Truth in the Patricia Smith Case," *Boston Globe*, July 20, 1998, A11.

20. "A Note of Apology," *Boston Globe*, June 19, 1998, B6.

21. Eileen McNamara, "A Matter of Integrity," June 27, 1998, B1.

22. Jack Thomas, "Patricia Smith's Betrayal of Trust," *Boston Globe*, June 22, 1998, A19.

23. Author interview with Burnham, September 1998.

24. "We Object to *Globe* Campaign against Ex-columnist," *Boston Globe*, July 19, 1998, A14.

25. "Editors: In Columnists We Trust," *Editor and Publisher*, June 27, 1998, 12.

26. Transcript, "Good Morning America," *ABC World News Tonight*," August 6, 1998.

27. Transcript, "Larry King Live," August 6, 1998.

28. Richard Cohen, "In Defense of Mike Barnicle," *Washington Post*, August 1, 1998, A21.

29. "What Was He Thinking?" *Newsweek*, August 17, 1998, 57.

30. Mike Barnicle, "Truths Learned on the Street," *Boston Globe*, June 23, 1998, B1.

31. "Standoff on Morrissey Boulevard; *Globe*'s Barnicle Refuses to Resign," *Boston Herald*, August 6, 1998, 1.

32. David Warsh, "The Lawyer and the Columnist; Economic Principals," *Boston Globe*, June 28, 1998, F1.

33. "Globe Advertiser Threatens to Walk over Barnicle Flap," *Boston Herald*, August 8, 1998, 9.

34. "Under Pressure, *Boston Globe* Keeps Barnicle," *Washington Post*, August 12, 1998.

35. Ibid.

36. "Protests Greet Decision Not to Oust Barnicle," *Boston Globe*, August 13, 1998, A1.

37. Transcript, "Crossfire," CNN, August 13, 1998.

38. "*Boston Globe* Reporter Mike Barnicle Keeps His Job," Transcript, "Crossfire," CNN, August 13, 1998.

39. Ibid.

40. Howell Raines, "Journalism Will Pay High Price for Reprieve of Mike Barnicle," *New York Times*, August 17, 1998, A9.

41. "No Double Standard At Boston Globe," Letter to the Editor, *NY Times*, August 14, 1998, A2.

42. "Under Pressure, *Boston Globe* Keeps Barnicle," *Washington Post*, August 12, 1998, D1.

43. "Globe Staffers Air Grievances—Many Call Handling of Barnicle Case an 'Outrage,'" *Boston Herald*, August 13, 1998, 7.

44. "All Columnists Use Brain Droppings," *Washington Post*, August 13, 1998, A20.

45. Mary McGrory, "No Joking Matter," *Washington Post*, August 13, 1998, A3.

46. "A Double Standard on Smith and Barnicle: Jack Thomas, the Ombudsman," *Boston Globe*, August 17, 1998, A11.

47. Kenneth Tomlinson, "Mike Barnicle's Demise," *Weekly Standard*, August 31, 1998, 16.

48. "Barnicle Resigns after News Questions on Reporting," *Boston Globe*, August 20, 1998, A1.

49. "*Boston Globe* Columnist Resigns over Authenticity of 1995 Story," *New York Times*, August 20, 1998, A1.

50. "*Daily News* to Feature Ex-Boston Columnist," *New York Times*, March 16, 1999, B3.

51. Author interview with Lamar Graham, September 1998.

52. Transcript, *Today Show*, May 13, 1996.

53. "Words of Wisdom from Unlikely Source," *Sacramento Bee*, May 20, 1996, E2.

54. "Why Her Lies Still Sting," *Washington Post*, May 31, 1996, F1.

Notes to Chapter 7

1. Author interview with Mark Whitaker.

2. Ibid.

3. "Race in the Newsroom," *New Republic*, October 1995.

4. *NABJ Journal*, June, 1993.

5. ASNE diversity survey, 1997.

6. "ASNE Pulls Back from Ethnic Diversity Goal," *Editor & Publisher*, April 18, 1998.

7. Lee Becker, "1997 Annual Survey of Journalism and Mass Communication Graduates," University of Georgia. See "Minority Prospects," *Presstime*, April 1999, 44.

8. David Shipler, *A Country of Strangers* (New York: Alfred A. Knopf, 1998), 304.

9. "Word for Word: The History Books," *New York Times*, November 8, 1998, sec. 4, p. 7.

10. Ibid.

11. Ibid.

12. "Monticello's Other Children," *New York Times*, November 8, 1998, sec. 4, p. 5.

13. "A Controversial 'Diary,'" *Los Angeles Times*, September 19, 1998, F1.

14. Unity 94 Report: "Fire Up Young People."

15. "1998 Media Usage Study," Newspaper Association of America and the American Society of Newspaper Editors.

INDEX

Index

ABOUT THE AUTHOR

Pamela Newkirk is Assistant Professor of Journalism at New York University. Her articles have appeared in numerous publications, including the *Nation*, the *New York Times*, the *Washington Post*, and *Artnews*.

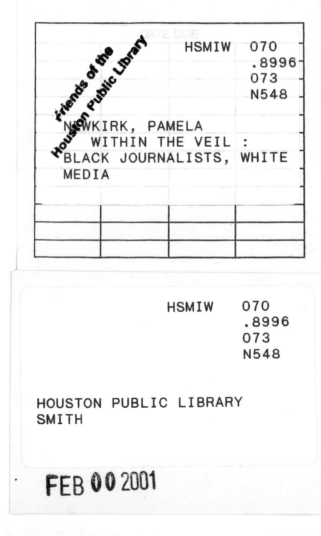